Reinventing
Chinese Tradition

INTERPRETATIONS OF CULTURE
IN THE NEW MILLENNIUM

Norman E. Whitten Jr.,
General Editor

*A list of books in the series appears
at the end of the book.*

Reinventing Chinese Tradition

The Cultural Politics of Late Socialism

KA-MING WU

UNIVERSITY OF ILLINOIS PRESS
Urbana, Chicago, and Springfield

© 2015 by the Board of Trustees
of the University of Illinois
All rights reserved

1 2 3 4 5 C P 5 4 3 2 1
♾ This book is printed on acid-free paper.

Cloth ISBN: 978-0-252-03988-1
Paper ISBN: 978-0-252-08140-8
Ebook ISBN: 978-0-252-09799-7

The Cataloging-in-Publication Data is available
on the Library of Congress Web site.

I dedicate this book to my parents.

Contents

Preface   ix

Acknowledgments   xiii

Introduction   1

CHAPTER 1. Paper-Cuts in Modern China: The Search for Modernity, Cultural Tradition, and Women's Liberation   31

CHAPTER 2. Narrative Battle: Fabricating Folk Paper-Cutting as an Intangible Heritage   64

CHAPTER 3. Traditional Revival with Socialist Characteristics: Propaganda Storytelling Turned into Spiritual Service   88

CHAPTER 4. Folk Cultural Production with Danwei Characteristics: Folk Storytelling and Public Relations Activities   105

CHAPTER 5. Spirit Cults in Yan'an: Surrogate Rural Subjectivity in the Urbanizing Rural   122

Conclusion   147

Notes   149

Glossary   159

References   161

Index   179

Preface

This book is about *minjian*, the Chinese term for folk culture. Minjian encompasses the intertwined meanings of folk knowledge and practices; rural and peasant society and native soil and their entanglements with nationalist politics; intellectual interventions; socialist propaganda; religious services and commodities; and rural communal changes. It is about how folk cultural discourse and practices figure in the cultural politics of post-Mao China. The project took place in contemporary Yan'an, headquarters of the Chinese Communist Party (CCP) from 1937–1947. Until today, Yan'an still figures as the revolutionary mecca in the national imagination and acquires its significance from being associated with the CCP vision of a united China against the Fascist invasion and the party's socioeconomic and cultural reforms in the rural area. This book chooses Yan'an as the analytical category of Chinese cultural politics because it is where national yearnings, socialist modern pursuits, and intellectual imaginations of a cultural China at different historical periods have been complexly embedded and intertwined with local traditional knowledge, rituals, and beliefs.

I was not a native anthropologist in Yan'an. Raised in Hong Kong, with Cantonese (a vernacular language in the Guangdong province of south China) as my mother tongue and English as my high school language, I never learned or spoke the national language of Mandarin (or *Putonghua*) before making friends with mainland Chinese students at graduate school in the United States in 2000. Growing up in colonial Hong Kong, my life experience, however, has never really been separated from mainland China. My father escaped to Hong Kong as a refugee after fleeing from rural Guangdong during the "sent-down" movement in 1970. In 1966, Mao Zedong called for the start of the Cultural Revolution in order to preserve "true" communist ideology by purging remnants of capitalists and traditional elements from society. The movement resulted in the government sending "educated youths" including high school and college students in urban areas to the countryside in order for them to learn manual agrarian labor and rid them of urban elitist thoughts. My father, separated from his parents, spent a couple of years laboring in the countryside and eventually fled to Hong Kong. He started anew as an unskilled laborer by delivering liquefied petroleum gas cylinders, and he subsequently met my mother, a textile factory worker, in an evening English class. I remember that in my childhood, we spent every Chinese New Year carrying electric fans, televisions, radios, and bags of used clothes across the Hong Kong–China border to see my father's family in Guangzhou in south China. It was 1980 when he was first allowed a reunion with his parents under Deng Xiaoping's regime. My father's sent-down experience, China's underdevelopment, and the June Fourth Massacre in 1989 inscribed a poignant impression of the country on me. But I also grew up learning about other facets of China that did not exactly fit with the dominant Western portrait of Mao's China as merely totalitarian, inefficient, and poor. Compared with my mother who grew up starved and uneducated in colonial Hong Kong and who started work as a child laborer in Hong Kong factories at the age of eleven, my father had a junior high school education and adequate food before he was sent down to rural Guangdong. Even though my father made his way to capitalist and wealthier Hong Kong, he was only a lower-class laborer, living from hand to mouth. In contrast, my father's younger brother, who failed three times to flee to Hong Kong during Mao's era, became a midlevel manager at a big state-owned enterprise. He has enjoyed a good social status, a decent living standard throughout the 1980s and 1990s, and now a retirement life with a pension. In the early 1990s, when manufacturing capital in Hong Kong started to move production lines across the border to cut costs, my mother, a veteran textile worker, lost her job. After thirty years of sweating in one textile factory, she has since led a retired life with no pension because the British instituted a very patchy welfare and security system in Hong Kong. Ironically, the hand-over of Hong Kong to China in 1997 anticipated the fall of Hong Kong as an economically vibrant Asian dragon and China's ascent to a world factory, and later to a global power.

When I was pursuing graduate studies in the United States, I kept going to mainland China because my husband moved to Beijing to work for an environmental nongovernmental organization. In Beijing, I met with socially concerned government officials, outstanding students, professors well-versed in Western theories, writers translating postcolonial literature, and middle-class migrants living comfortably with cars and summer houses. China has become surprisingly strong and rich, supporting an emerging narrative about a "China model" (*zhongguo moshi*) that is about strong government, controlled market, and limited democracy (Ramo 2004).

Yan'an in Shaanxi province nonetheless seems to defy everything about a thriving and globalized China. A year of intensive fieldwork in 2004 Yan'an was mind-blowing. I witnessed the grave rural-urban divides in the revolutionary birthplace and attempted to make sense of it. I also found that common people did not bother to talk much about the Maoist past. Instead, folk discourse and practices were omnipresent. The flourishing of a popular cultural and religious revival seemed to speak about an apolitical, ancient, and cultural China and about the place of tradition in the future of Chinese development. Later, I found that the reality is more complicated than it seems. Folk discourse and practice are indeed meeting grounds of contemporary state interests, rural society initiatives, new capitalist values, and local government propaganda. In the sphere of folk representations and practices, I found it possible to examine the political, economic, and cultural authoritarianism at the local level, exercised in the name of growth and stability on the one hand, and the diffused power, state, and society integration on the other. Eventually, I found it fascinating to think about folk cultural discourses and practices as actively manufactured by, and corresponding to, the late socialist governing ideology, state campaigns, and various grassroots initiatives from the rural society.

Studies explicating the changing politics and power dynamics of post-Mao China abound. One of the most important works is Andrew Walder's *Communist Neo-traditionalism* (1986), in which he argues that the party-state authority does not operate through a totalitarian control of atomized individuals but through the work-unit organization (*danwei*), in which workers were enmeshed in a situation of "organized dependence" on the cadre superior for jobs, security, housing, and all kinds of material benefits. While appreciating Walder's analysis of the subtle power dynamics, I am aware of his underlying assumption, which sees China's nonmarket structure of work and the associated provision of services and benefits to workers as merely a kind of entrapment (Womack 1991). His work might easily be conflated with a Western-centric view, which bashes the Chinese socialist modern experience as either a deviance from the market individualism ideal or the opposite of a capitalist modernity. Walder's work might also negate the liberating visions, progressive policies, and individual empowerment the socialist state has brought to many women, workers, and peasants (Rofel 1999) and easily overlook how the neoliberal market-oriented policies in Euro-American countries have also bred extraordinary financial greed, economic inequality, and social polarization.

Avoiding the dichotomized assumptions of a hegemonic party-state and subjugated people, my book highlights the integration of state and society, the construction of subjectivities by and through power, and everyday-life practices and resistance as key features of China society. At the same time, however, I try to avoid overemphasizing the concept of diffused power lest it might distract us from understanding the Chinese state power becoming ever more strengthened and controlling in the new era. In the end, I find it important to hold two poles of critiques at the same time while examining various late socialist sociocultural happenings in China. On the one hand, this book cautions against rendering the Chinese experience to a Western image of a totalitarian model and attends to the subtle ways the party-state socialist legacy, capitalist practices, and traditional cultural practices dance together. On the other hand, it cautions against simplifying the local, the social, and the rural as the opposite spheres of the state. Instead, *Reinventing Chinese Tradition* attends to various traditional cultural productions that ally with today's party-state campaigns and their simulations with capitalist, neoliberal values. With a lens of such a double critique, this ethnography aims to bring out a critical and nuanced analysis of the Chinese folk cultural productions in the late socialist era.

Acknowledgments

This research would not have been possible without the financial support of a number of organizations. These include the Department of Anthropology at Columbia University and the Wenner Gren Dissertation Fieldwork Grant, both of which funded research and writing stages of the project. Preliminary research trips were supported by the Weatherhead East Asian Institute at Columbia University.

In Yan'an, I am indebted for the support and hospitality of many people, but especially the two major hosts, the Fang family and the Fan family. In Mojiagou village, I am most thankful to Li Fengying, Zhang Chunsheng, Zhang Li, Zhang Jun, Zhang Jing, Zhang Yanqing, Li Hongwei, Li Tiantian and his family, Shi Guilian, Hou Jianqiang and his family, especially Hou Rongrong who transcribed many of my interviews, Hou Sheqiang, Hou Yuansheng and his family, and Xu Wenzhi and his family. In Yan'an city, tremendous thanks to Fan Zhenhua, Xu Xiaoping, Fan Xing, Zhang Yongge, Song Ruxin, and Ban Liang; in Ansai, thanks to Sun Shengli, Hou Xuezhao, Hao Guizhen; in Yanchuan, Jin Zhilin, Feng Sanyun, Feng Fen and his entire family, Liu Jieqiong, Feng Caiqin, Cao Peizhi, and Hei Jianguo. In Xi'an, I owe a tremendous debt to Ban Li. In Beijing, I thank Yang Shengmin for the most important reference letter, Qiao Shaoguang for the interview, Jin Zhilin for continuous support, and Guo Yuhua, Chen Guanzhong, and Yu Qi for intellectual inspirations.

Teachers and mentors at Columbia University provided critical intellectual support. Myron Cohen has given me all the support of the Department of Anthropology. Dorothy Ko not only read the entire manuscript and provided critical comments, she hosted my wedding party at her beautiful apartment. I cannot ask for a more supportive and inspiring mentor. Rosalind Morris read every chapter of the original manuscript with care and insight, but I only understood her critical intellectual effort years after I left Columbia. Michael Taussig has shared with me some of the most inspiring thoughts during his office hours. Eugeania Lean challenged me in the early version to rethink my arguments in key ways, for which I am grateful. I thank David Scott, Marilyn Ivy, Mahmood Mamdani, and Partha Chatterjee for their teaching and inspiring works, many of which I gradually picked up in my writing stage. I owe a tremendous debt to Lisa Rofel, who has given me guidance since my exchange years at the University of California, Santa Cruz, in 1996. I am extremely thankful to Pun Ngai who has always provided me with outstanding intellectual advice during and after my graduate study.

Earlier versions of some of the chapters have been published elsewhere. Major portions of Chapter 1 appear in "Modern Paper-cuts: The Search for Modernity, Cultural Tradition and Women's Liberation," *Modern China* 41 (1): 90–127, reproduced with permission from Sage Publications, Inc. Major portions of Chapter 3 appear in "Traditional Revival with Socialist Characteristics: Propaganda Storytelling Turned Spiritual Services in Rural Yan'an," *The China Journal* 66 (July 2011): 101–117, reproduced by permission of the University of Chicago Press. I am grateful for permission to include these materials.

This book has benefited from the generosity of many fellow students and friends in and out of Columbia University. At Columbia, many thanks to Pongphisoot Busbarat, Nigel Thompson, Poornima Paidipaty, Zhang Xiaodan, Shahla Talebi, Koga Yukiko, Jonathan Bach, Dattathreya Subbanarasimha, Min-Yen Kan, Pablo Dubio, and Maria K Chan for their support. I owe so much to Liu Yu and Zhang Enhua, my best girlfriends for numerous night talks and dinners that kept me going. Beyond Columbia, Irene Leung, Derek Lam, Michael Lok, and Alvin Lin provided the best friendship. Special thanks go to Michael Siu who has supported me continuously for the last two decades and who has become part of my family.

I am deeply grateful to Pang Laikwan, Angela Wong Wai Ching, Cheung Lik Kwan, Katrien Jacobs, Chung Peichi, Oscar Ho, Lai Chi Tim, Tam Wai Lun, and many other colleagues at the Department of Cultural and Religious Studies at the Chinese University of Hong Kong; they have provided me an excellent and engaging intellectual home. I thank my graduate students and staff members Wang Weiwei, Leung Po Shan, Li Danzhou, Li Siyi, Ray Lai Kwok Wai, Cheng Tung Yue, Cheung Chui Yu, and Leung Chun Kit for teaching and emotional support. Great thanks to Pun Ngai, Ben Ku, Yan Hairong, Anita Koo, Chen Juan, Helena Wong, Shae Wan-chaw, Chow Sung

Ming, Pauline Song, and Angelina Yuen at the Department of Applied Social Science, Hong Kong Polytechnic University, where I started my first teaching job. I am also thankful to Yip Hon Ming, Ching-kwan Lee, Gail Hershatter, and Eliza Lee for their teaching and years of support. Philip Leung, Kuan Hsin-chi, Jonathan Unger, Anita Chan, Rebecca Karl, Joseph Bosco, Gordon Matthews, Teresa Kuan, Wang Danning, SY Ma, and Cheung Siu Woo have supported my project in its different stages.

I am deeply grateful to the three reviewers for their productive suggestions. My sincere thanks to my Series and Acquisition editors, Norman Whitten and Danny Nasset, and to my managing editor and copy editor, for their meticulous readings.

Profound thanks to my parents and my in-laws, who have ardently supported my writing. Great thanks to my son Ruofei, who has given me so much love during the writing stage. Finally, I thank my husband Lo Sze Ping for the most incisive critiques, intellectual and activist inspiration, and love for the last twenty years.

Reinventing
Chinese Tradition

Introduction

On February 3, 2004, a photography contest was held on a hill north of Yan'an city. At eight o'clock sharp in the morning, two hundred photographers, professional and amateur, took several big coaches to the foothill to attend a waist-drum performance, an iconographic folk drum and dance believed to have originated from a festival dance dating back to the fourth century. By the time these cameramen reached the hilltop—having trekked the sandy slopes of the Loess for thirty minutes, and now hyperventilating in the thin air at thirty degrees Fahrenheit—one hundred waist-drummers in red costumes and Shaanxi peasant-style headdresses (*yangdujin*) had aligned into an impressive parade. When the sun shone above the surrounding ridges, the drummers raised their arms and beat the goatskin drums collectively. A solemn booming resonance overwhelmed the entire hill and echoed powerfully in the valleys like a reverberating thunder. Each with a drum obliquely tied to the left side of the stomach, the drummers twisted their bodies as they went about beating the drum while kicking the air and throwing red color runners high up, literally blending dancing with fighting and marching with drumming. No one, however, simply stood there to appreciate the remarkable performance and the atmosphere. We scrambled to capture every second of the spectacle on camera. Another three minutes of breathtaking dancing and shooting would pass, with no one noticing that the drummers were inching down the slope toward where the cameramen stood. Soon a huge layer of sand and ashes generated by the dancing gushed over those photographers in the front. In a split second, some cameramen fell on their backs and others ran away to cover their expensive lenses. Amid bouts of screams and shouts, the well-staged folk grandeur was brought to a halt as officers from the Hall of Culture came in between two groups and yelled, "Stop!"

This grandiose scene of folk drum and dance took place in contemporary Yan'an, the capital of the Chinese Communist Party (CCP) from 1937–1947 in Shaanxi province, China. The spectacle was organized by the Ansai county government in Yan'an—not for tourist consumption but for government promotion of Yan'an as a revolutionary mecca of modern China with colorful folk cultural traditions and scenic landscape. The photographers who attended the event came from state-owned newspaper and television enterprises all over the country.

Communist leaders would call this waist-drum performance a symbol of a liberated China (Figure 0.1). Traditionally practiced by villagers to celebrate the Chinese New Year, waist-drum dance was adapted by members of the CCP to promote social-economic programs, including land reforms, literacy programs, and grain production in the desolate Yan'an region in the 1930s. Ever since the CCP established the People's Republic of China (PRC) in 1949, the Yan'an waist-drum dance has been elevated to symbolize the party's promotion of folk peasant culture and its concern for rural cultural enrichment. It was, for instance, performed at the World Youth Festival in Budapest, Hungary, in 1950, and would later appear in all kinds of national and international events, including the handover ceremony of Hong Kong, a former British colony, to mainland China in 1997.

Folk Culture in Yan'an: Politics of Culture in Late Socialist China

Yan'an and folk culture are no coincidental juxtaposition of words. They are keywords that develop important meanings at different periods of modern and contemporary China (Williams 1976). After 1949, "Yan'an and folk culture" became an official model of appropriating and adapting local traditions for party-state policy promotion and has since shaped several decades of CCP's cultural policy nationwide. This model highlights the unique historical, social, and political relations between the Communist party-state and rural society, between revolutionary politics and folk traditions, and between urban intellectuals and rural villagers in modern China. Today, these keywords further articulate a peculiar relation between the government and local communities for heritage preservation and cultural tourism in the age of runaway urbanization.

Reinventing Chinese Tradition analyzes this relationship by looking at the moments of mobilizing and representing folk traditions in both socialist and late socialist Yan'an. This book reviews Yan'an as an indispensable ana-

FIGURE 0.1. The waist-drum performance organized by the Ansai county government for a photographic contest on the hilltop of Ansai county, Yan'an.

lytical category and therefore a crucial ethnographic site in understanding the politics of culture in contemporary China. Much has been written on Yan'an from the historical perspective because it is where the CCP experimented with soviet governance and land reforms as an oppositional party and fought against the ruling Nationalist party before coming to power (Snow 1968; Selden 1995; Apter and Saich 1994). Yan'an is also where forces of nationalist pursuits, socialist ideals, intellectual antielitism, and party appropriation encountered rural cultural traditions. Existing research predominantly understands folk cultural tradition in Yan'an as a tool of revolution, a medium of state propaganda, or an object of Mao's cultural reform (Holm 1991; Hung 1985, 1994).

One of the main objectives of this book is to provide new interpretations of the meanings of folk culture outside of such dominant narrative. It sorts out those folk logics and local initiatives that have been suppressed or evaded by nationalist or party-state reforms. However, this book does not claim to seek out an original and archaic folk cultural realm unmediated by political process and capital forces. It takes seriously the historical processes of socialist politicization and national mobilization as constituting the forms and contents of folk cultural productions as they continue to exist and effect emergence today. In other words, instead of seeing folk cultural discourse and practices as a nativist transcendental existence repressed, this book turns the questions around and examines how folk cultural tradition becomes the site of complex struggles where socialist legacy, state propaganda, local initiatives and, lately, market forces, heritage campaigns, and communal participation play out with each other.[1]

Reinventing Chinese Tradition focuses on three rural cultural practices in Yan'an: folk storytelling (*Shaanbei Shuoshu*), folk paper-cuts (*jianzhi*), and spirit cult practices (*wushen*), and their entanglement with political, capital, and local forces. Yan'an provides the best vantage point to examine these entanglements because it is the iconic place where Chinese national revolutionary politics and folk traditions, historical representations, and contemporary practices, have come into contact and collaboration. I choose these three cultural forms also because they are as traditional and widely practiced in rural Yan'an as they have been politicized, reformulated, or banned.

First, folk storytelling in Yan'an region was among the first few folk cultural forms that the CCP picked to reform traditional contents into modern socialist ones. Many folk storytellers went through socialist propaganda training during Mao's era and their job became that of promoting national policies and state campaigns in remote rural corners. Today, these storytellers continue to stage folk performance with propaganda content that contributes to a complex understanding of folk cultural production in post-Mao Yan'an. Alternatively, folk paper-cuts were a major peasant art form that attracted early Communists because of their bold graphic designs, auspicious motifs, and local popularity. The Chinese state, in the Mao and post-Mao periods, extensively deployed and continues to deploy folk paper-cuts in print media such as poster-designs, book covers, greeting cards, and so forth to promote the nation's development. Lately, the effort of making folk paper-cuts into international and national heritage listings again invoked some of the Chinese intellectuals' historical and nationalist complex of projecting the rural folk as that solution of Chinese modernity. Finally, spirit cults in Yan'an are popular religious practices in rural communities. Though illegal and banned, they engage a diverse range of deities, gods, and goddesses and involve medium possession in activities of worshipping, divination, and healing. The popular practices of spirit cults are significant sites of folk concerns and desires beyond state discourse and control and lately are a new form of rural identity-making in an era of rapid urbanization.

Reinventing Chinese Tradition has found that folk culture in Yan'an has shifted from a site of state control in Mao's period to a site of contest in the late socialist period. Today various levels of governments, urban intellectuals, and local communities compete to mobilize traditions for campaign promotions, public relations activities, communal development, and economic benefits. So, in contrast to a popular view that folk tradition is now free from state intervention with blossoming local revivals, my principle arguments about folk traditions are 1) they have become ever more well-integrated to the party-state campaigns and propaganda; 2) they have blended together with tourist spectacles, commodities, and consumption experience; and 3) they have been actively reconstructed and reenacted by rural villagers for the making of a new rural identity and communal sociality.

I articulate the cultural logic of the late socialist Chinese society that corresponds to a new form of political economy, which is yet to be fully theorized. By *late socialist*, I refer to a complicated condition of Chinese society in which a strong Communist party-state adopting both authoritarian rule and neoliberal-informed strategies is confluent with social, economic, and cultural transformations engendered by a new mass consumer culture and an increasingly commodified society (Ramo 2004; Zhang and Ong 2008; Hoffman 2010; Zhang 2001, 2012). In this late socialist political economy, the Chinese Communist party-state bureaucracy, institutions (*tizhi*), and practices remain resilient. Its spectacular economic growth goes hand in hand with powerful, global, and national state-owned enterprises (SOEs). China has ascended to become one of the major global capitalist power centers, made large-scale layoffs of its urban workers, urged its rural migrants to serve the world factories, and made revolutionary politics of the proletariat or the peasant superfluous. Scholars have called the China model a "flexible post-socialism" (Zhang 2012: 659–667) or a "fracture society" (Sun 2007, 2009). They highlight the "destatization of many social domains" (Wang 2003) and the "marketization of political power" of the Chinese governance at the expense of public welfare, equality, and the interests of the lower class (Lin 2006).

In the cultural realm, however, the production of culture is not entirely commodified in the process of marketization; nor is it exactly manipulated by the strong state. Folk tradition, in particular, witnesses the continuing party-state influence, increasing profit orientation, and civil and communal interventions in its production all at the same time. This book, therefore, examines the dynamic interpenetration among the party-state, cultural practitioners, rural villagers, urban consumers, and the uneasy politics of appropriation and engagements involved. I observe that the cultural logic in late socialist China as one that works to juxtapose the highly conflicting logic and interests of the state, the capital, and that of the local rural society.

This book joins critical anthropological analyses of national tradition, the modern state, and capitalist modernity. It traces the entangled linkages between the enchantments of ritual performances and modern state politics (Taussig 1997; Comaroff 1994; Comaroff and Comaroff 2000). Marilyn Ivy argues that it is in the "vanishing" of traditional marginalized culture and the ways it is recuperated by cultural industries and institutions that a national cultural imaginary Japan exists (1995). Looking into recent phenomena of ethnocultural theme parks in South Africa or "casino capitalism" by Native Americans, John and Jean Comaroff argue for a concept of "ethnopreneurialism" in which ethnic groups self-commodify and reify their traditions for heritage property, self-determination, and exclusive rights, as well as economic development (2009). These works argue against an orientalist othering of non-Western national culture or ethnic populations as exotic traditions or distinctive identities. They show the ways in which national culture or ethnic populations are constantly remaking themselves in the image of the corporation or cultural industries—while the corporations appropriate those cultural practices and representations to open up new regimes of consumption. Indeed, modern nations or ethnic groups in late capitalist societies increasingly articulate national essence, traditional identity, and ethnic authenticity with and through commodification and consumption.

In China, however, rural villagers and ethnic minorities have yet to assert local traditions for claims of intellectual property and land rights. Folk tradition has also been a major site of intense party-state control during Mao's era to promote national policies and interest. At the same time, China's rural area is much less developed than its urban centers, and folk cultural forms—though some of them are linked to the market—are far from the late capitalist process of commodification. China's severe rural-urban divide, nonetheless, epitomizes urban intellectuals' anxiety over the disappearance of national cultural traditions, and, lately, over the disappearing rural landscape, rituals, and forms of lives. These urban yearnings ironically spurred folk cultural productions, which also become the means for economically impoverished villagers to respond to emergent opportunities. The result is that production of folk tradition is, on the one hand, increasingly linked to rural economic developments catering to urban nostalgic desires; yet on the other hand, it is continually intertwined, and contesting with, the party-state agendas and various governments' campaigns.

Chinese folk traditional discourse and practices therefore uniquely situate in a late socialist condition where the strong party-state control, burgeoning market forces, and uneven rural-urban development get caught up with the late capitalist anxiety over the vanishing of national identity and associated consumption of folk authenticity. The situation is further complicated by in-

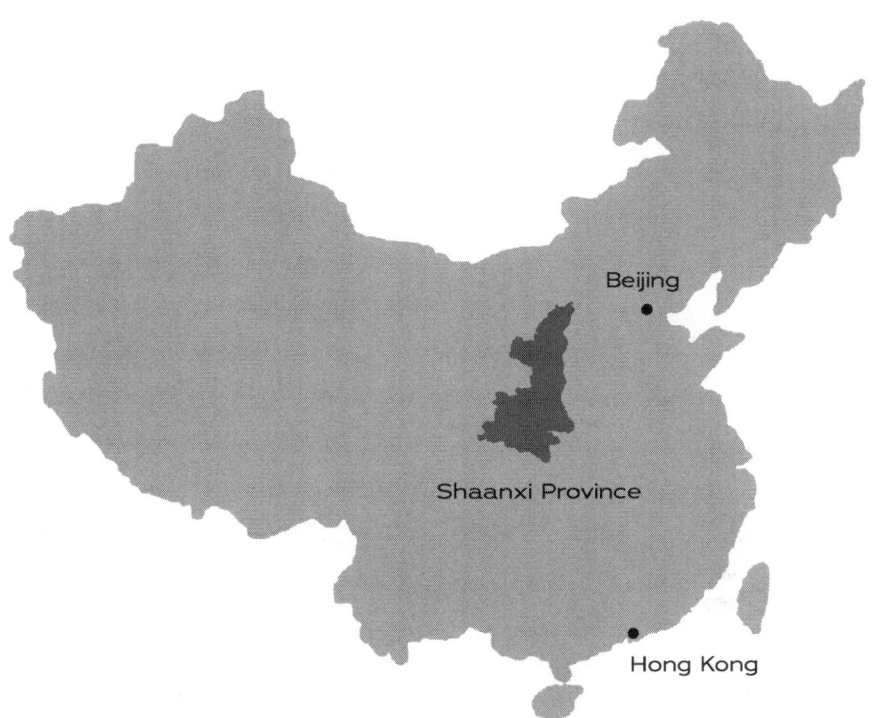

MAP 1. Map of China.

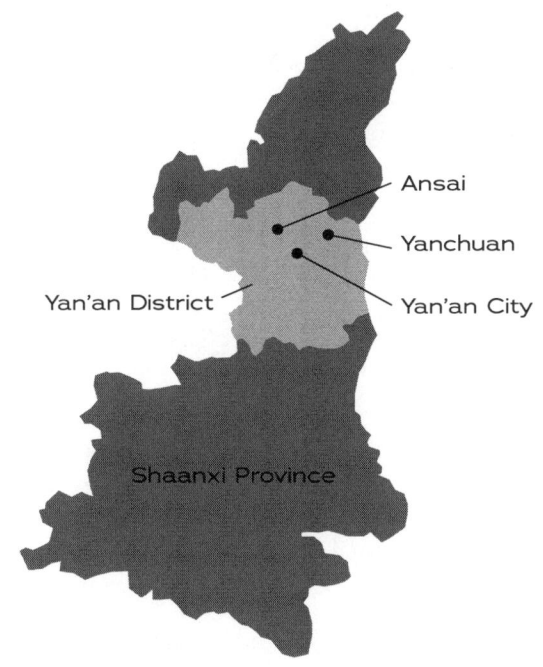

MAP 2. Map of Yan'an.

FIGURE 0.2. The hilly Loess landscape of rural Yan'an.

tense urbanization within and outside of the rural area. This book traces the production of Chinese tradition to such unexpected juxtaposition of various forces. While much has been written on Chinese urban cultural productions such as cinema, literature, and theater in post-Mao China, this book looks at the ways folk rural traditions intertwine with the economic boom, a new consumer culture, political intervention, and greater inequalities.

The two keywords of the book—*folk culture* and *Yan'an*—are loaded with complicated, historical, and political meanings in the history of modern China and in the history of the anti-Fascist effort and leftist movement. In the following section, I give a brief revisit to those historical events and narratives that contribute to the development and modern meanings of folk culture and Yan'an.

The Complex Layered History of Yan'an in Modern China

Yan'an certainly owes its national significance to having served as the capital of the CCP, but its physical landscape is one of the roughest in the country

(Maps 1 and 2 and Figure 0.2). Covered by the Loess Plateau of northern central China, Shaanxi province, Yan'an's natural environment is defined by a severely rugged topography of gullies, deep gorges, and rocky highlands; windy and droughty climate; barren terrain; and little vegetation. Local residents live in *cavehouses* (*yaodong*), earthy shelter dwellings dug out from the hillside that keeps the living space warm in the cold seasons and cool in the hot seasons. An arid climate and mountainous landscape demand that farmers hike for hours to work on thin strips of hilltop terraced fields to grow the region's main staples: millet, maize, wheat, buckwheat, potatoes, and different kinds of beans. At the turn of the twentieth century, drought, sparse population, low-level food production, acute poverty, and a bandit subculture characterized Yan'an. No wonder the CCP members once described it as one of the darkest places on earth. But the ruggedness of the highly eroded and hostile landscape eventually evolved to become a sanctuary of revolutionary ideals.

Yan'an was where the Communist Long March (1934–1936) ended and where the CCP reestablished its central base during its struggle against the Nationalist government led by Jiang Jieshi (Chiang Kai-shek).[2] When the Communist leaders arrived at the hilly and almost inaccessible Loess region bordered by Shaanxi, Gansu, and Ningxia provinces (later known as "the border region"), they found it best suited for guerilla defense. In the center of the region, Yan'an, they established a new soviet base and slowly recuperated military power. The Japanese invasion in 1937 gave the Communists a most needed chance to thrive, because the war threat created a popular aspiration to push the Nationalist government to cooperate with the CCP to form a United Front Government. With this agreement, the Nationalist government diverted less energy to attack the Communist forces. During the period of 1937–1947, the CCP opened up wasteland, distributed lands to poor farmers, increased grain production, rebuilt rural economy, and allied with local political powers in Yan'an. The CCP's pragmatic governance and its rural reforms on reducing poverty worked powerfully in a time when the rest of China, governed by the Nationalists, suffered from social polarization and serious inflation.

In the official narrative within China, Yan'an from 1937–1947 has been celebrated as a utopian community and a model of socialist vision, which held out a promise of a peaceful united China. Soviet Yan'an had attracted support from thousands of young intellectuals and professionals nationwide.[3] The positive official appraisal of Yan'an is understandable as it justifies the Communist seizing of power and its subsequent ruling legitimacy. But such evaluation is not limited to China. In the Western world, Edgar Snow's *Red*

Star over China (1968), first published in 1937 in England, also offers a favorable account of the Yan'an soviet, with overtly positive evaluations, such as, "Chinese Communism as I found it in the Northwest might more accurately be called rural equalitarianism than anything Marx would have found acceptable as a model child of his own" (1968: 219–226). Similarly, William Hinton's *Fanshen* (1966) glorifies the Communist land reform in the border region during 1937 as having "completely turned around" peasants' lives. Together, these accounts enthusiastically paint Yan'an as that moral center of the world revolution and a sanctuary of socialist ideals. Nonetheless, as much as they cover parts of reality, they also participate in the "discourse community," which celebrates Yan'an as that special time and space capable of enabling individuals to realize higher moral truths (Apter and Saich 1994; Epstein 2003). In the world historical context, such accounts can be better understood as part of the anti-Fascist effort against the rise of Nazism in Europe and the international left's later effort against the Euro-American capitalist hegemony.

A more grounded research on Yan'an comes later from Mark Selden's *China in Revolution* (1995), which argues that the "Yan'an way" was a unique combination of CCP's administrative and social reforms, including the rent and interest rates reduction campaigns, the "to-the-village" campaign, and the cooperative production and popular education movements. Selden argues that it was such socioeconomic programs that made "revolutionary processes as developmental processes," thus winning the people's hearts and minds (1995: 220–230). A more critical evaluation of the Yan'an soviet only comes later from Chinese Historian Gao Hua's *Hong Tai Yang Shi Zen Yang Sheng Qilai De* (*How Did the Red Sun Rise*) (2000). Gao found that many young intellectuals' well-intended criticism against the Communist governance brought them only unjust accusations as counterrevolutionaries in the Party Rectification Movement in 1942–1943 led by Mao Zedong. Gao thus uncovered a reality of tight party control, repression over different political views, and intense factional struggles behind the rosy image of the Yan'an soviet utopia.[4]

Fairly speaking, the Yan'an soviet would at once feature a utopia of a new China and the harsh condition of such possibility in the complicated historical context of the Japanese invasion, the Nationalist purge, the rise of Fascism, and the socialist resistance movement in the world context of the 1930s. Against all odds, Yan'an did stand out as a space where a more equitable economic redistribution took place and a faith of equality and peace held out. Politically, the CCP in Yan'an deployed moderate strategies to make alliance with various parties and class interests, including middle-class peasants and even landlords to achieve social reforms. The CCP's balancing of ideals and practical politics, advocating political moderation instead of a one-party dictatorship, and "social-leveling" instead of radical class struggles are keys to countrywide support for the CCP and its final defeat of the Nationalist government in 1949 (Huang 1995).[5]

Yan'an became a prominent symbol of a "land of bitterness turned into revolutionary ideal" in the early half of the twentieth century. The official narrative of Yan'an remains one of the most powerful origin narratives, which lends legitimacy to the existing governance. The CCP in particular likes to uphold it for its early vision to engineer for change in the most austere world war context. No wonder the party-state frequently hails Yan'an as the model "spirit," especially in a time when power corrupts and revolutionary passion fades.

Folk Cultural Traditions: Vehicle for the Nation

Folk culture, one of the two keywords of this book, as mentioned earlier, has distinctive meanings associated with the changing meanings of the rural areas, peasantry, and agriculture before the Maoist era, during it, and in the post-Mao period.

The staging of traditional folk culture and peasants as authentic, archaic, and elemental is not limited to modern China. Turning to the primitive, the traditional and the folk peasantry as objects of nostalgic desire have been recurring themes in the history of cultural representation of Western modernity, as in Enlightenment thoughts and modern social theory (Felski 1995). For European modernity and its lost spirituality and excessive materialism, the mysterious and exotic East, the Orient, became the intimate Other against which the progress-oriented and materialist West defined itself.[6] Edward Said used the term *orientalism* to refer to a post-Enlightenment European tradition of writing about the Islamic world in the nineteenth and twentieth century, which presumed not only the European moral and intellectual superiority but also the differences between Western and non-Western civilizations as ontological and fundamental (Said 1978). But orientalism is not only a Western production of the non-West. It is closely connected to the making of a national image and culture among non-Western countries. Analyzing the history of the idea of nationalism in postcolonial worlds, Partha Chatterjee found that although nationalist thoughts seek to refute the colonial claim that the colonized people are backward and culturally incapable of ruling themselves; it asserts that an economically backward nation could modernize itself while retaining its cultural identity. Nationalist thought thus inevitably produces a discourse that accepts the very intellectual premise of European modernity on which colonial domination is based: that the difference between the West and the East is fundamental and essential (Chatterjee 1993: 30). National struggle is therefore simultaneously resistant to and complicit in the project of orientalism.

Early Chinese nationalist thoughts operated similarly to such contradiction. May Fourth Chinese intellectuals, faced with Western imperial threats in the beginning of the twentieth century, unanimously attributed European scientific progress and military might to its cultural superiority, while lamenting the lack of such cultural attributes in China. While the more radical wing of the May Fourth intellectuals championed "Westernization all out," other nationalists worried of obliterating its national cultural distinctions. The characteristic solution for generations of Chinese nationalists was therefore to assert Western superiority in the materiality of its culture, while upholding Eastern superiority in the spiritual aspect of the culture.

This principal solution had since emerged in the form of numerous attempts to search for and locate "national essence" in order to achieve true modernity for China. The "Self Strengthening" movement by Chinese ruling elites during the late Qing dynasty, for instance, maintained the importance of upholding Chinese classics learning (*zhongxue weiti, xixue weiyong*) while adopting military and industrial technology from the West.

The "Folk Custom Study Movement" in the early 1920s advocated learning from, as well as educating, the peasantry. The movement led by intellectuals such as Li Dazhao, Gu Jiegang, and Zhou Zuoren called for collecting folklore and folksongs from the rural peasantry in order to find the convergence of the national and the popular (Hung 1985).

The inception of the Chinese national search for traditional cultural essence has therefore been dominated by the twin desires to modernize, to follow Western-defined scientific and military progress, and to conserve the cultural essence and moral purity of the nation. The woman, the child, the rustic, even the Confucius ethics were identified as locations of such eternal tradition in different periods of time as they were associated with timelessness and naturalness. Prasenjit Duara calls such ranges of figures symbolic of the alleged authenticity of the nation as a "regime of authenticity." (1988: 299). He posits that although the regime of authenticity celebrates the folk, the maternal, the minority, or the natural as the "soul of tradition-within-modernity," it selectively endorses certain images or elements of these categories. He argues that such a regime is inevitably cultural essentialist and "nationalist patriarchal" as it often rejects knowledge and practices seen as transgressing the prescribed social order and morality.

Folk Culture in Yan'an: Vehicle for the Revolution

Culture, specifically literature and art, was a prime site of the Communist struggle against the Japanese and the Nationalist government in Yan'an. It was where Mao Zedong delivered one of his most famous speeches, "Talks at the Yenan Forum on Literature and Art" (hereafter referred to as "Mao's Talk"). It is widely known that Mao's seminal talk highlights that "culture" is not an independent entity but part of the revolutionary cause, class politics, and the mass line (Mao 1965: 86). Mao's Talk defined the direction of the CCP's cultural policy: art and literature production should speak to the broadest mass and not just to a few elite; its message should enable and not criticize the CCP's revolution efforts. Mao's Talk was conceived just before the Rectification Campaign, which persecuted hundreds of dissidents. Indeed, the talk served to end the fervent debates and heterogeneous views from those among the Yan'an intellectual circle, with some yearning for raising artistic qualities through learning more Western or sophisticated art forms, while some insisting the use of national art forms in order to make it more understandable among common people (Holm 1991). Clearly, Mao Zedong favored "popularization of art" (*puji*) over "elevating artistic quality" (*tigao*).

As a result, intellectuals and artists went down to the countryside to locate, learn, and understand how "national art forms" might possibly serve interests of "the broadest masses." In the decades that followed, urban intellectuals took pains to rework traditional ritual contents of many rural traditional practices and reorganized them into simpler forms around the socialist, anti-imperialist rhetoric to mobilize social support. Many cultural forms have since become linked to the anti-Japanese war resistance and a broad range of social reforms, such as the promotion of gender equality, the cracking down of superstitious beliefs, and campaigns to raise literacy levels. A classic example is *yangge* (literally "rice-sprout song"). The traditional folk dance was originally associated with the Chinese New Year's ritual celebration, when villagers used dance and loud music for communal fun and good harvest wishes. Urban intellectuals redesigned this folk song and dance into a major cultural form in Yan'an by combining it with drama programs to expose social evils and to propagate virtues of the new society (Holm 1991).

The Ruralization of Chinese Culture since the 1940s

Mao's Talk has had two effects on folk tradition in and beyond Yan'an. On the one hand, it stands for the sole icon of the CCP political censorship and appropriation of art and literature for political purpose in the rest of the century. As late as in 2012, the Nobel laureate in literature, Mo Yan from China, was subjected to severe national and international criticisms because he willingly transcribed Mao's Talk at the request of the party-state in celebration of the sixtieth anniversary of its original presentation.

On the other hand, folk cultural traditions have since undergone a significant makeover to signify a forward-looking and socialist modern China against the previous image of a crumbling, poverty-stricken, rural countryside. This new understanding of Chinese rural culture is significant. Chinese culture was conventionally defined by male, literary—if not imperial—knowledge and practices. Chinese calligraphy, for instance, involves years of reciting and copying Chinese classics, poems, songs, and dynastic historical details. Chinese culture is a literati cultivation and privilege, as opposed to a mundane labor or means of survival in rural villages. Mao's Talk changed radically the ways Chinese culture would be defined and practiced.

Indeed, facing the Japanese invasion, concerned intellectuals of the time were actively reconsidering the target audience of their literary and artistic productions and their relationship with the peasants (Han 2005). Knowing that the countryside might have more resistance potential, not only in terms of the size of the peasantry but also in terms of the propaganda potential of folk cultural forms, urban intellectuals eventually came to terms with reassessing traditional folk cultural forms and genres and their artistic values. Such intellectual awakening is what Hung Chang-Tai called the critical shift in Chinese intellectual consciousness: the "ruralization of Chinese culture" (1994: 279). It is a paradigmatic shift that oriented Chinese culture toward the rural interior, knowledge, and practices, and which eventually gave birth to a "new village culture" (Hung 1994: 280).

Rural folk cultural forms were elevated to a new national status, linked to a new form of cultural consciousness and transformed in aesthetic forms, contents, and meanings. They were used to serve the war and later the party-state and its national policies. Urban intellectuals also tended to attach different images and characteristics to the peasants and their cultures for distinctive sociopolitical programs (Han 2005). First, under the discourse of ruralization of Chinese culture, the rural area became a politically active and promising space. Second, the peasants became agents of national and historical transformation. Third, various rural cultural forms connoted not only symbols of a joyful life and a united China but powerful weapons of words and images recreating a new national future. Last but not the least, though urban intellectuals continued to view themselves as superior in status and literacy, they reassessed their privilege and knowledge as they started to mingle with, learn from, and be inspired by the latter. As later chapters demonstrate, the historically ambivalent relationship between urban intellectuals and rural villagers recurs in the market reform eras and continues to be relevant in the contemporary debate of heritage listing.

In summation, the meanings of folk cultural forms in China, ever since the turn of the twentieth century, has been enmeshed with at least these forces: the Chinese nationalist conception of Western progress and reason, its contradictory search and projection for Chinese cultural origins and traditions, the urban intellectuals coming to terms with rural culture for resistance purposes, and the Communist party appropriation of it for the revolutionary cause. Folk culture has therefore always already been narrativized in and overdetermined by the processes and causes mentioned earlier (Duara 1995; Anagnost 1997). Never a nativist field of knowledge and practice, folk culture has been a major site of various sociopolitical experiments, truth regimes, new representation of the rural area, and nationalist discourse and practices before and after the establishment of the Communist party-state in 1949.

The Marginalization of Rurality: Yan'an as the Moribund Rural Other

In the 1980s, Deng Xiaoping embarked on the market reform. Yan'an's significance as a symbol of the Communist revolution retreated in the national imagination. But Yan'an, along with the folk traditions of the northwestern culture and region, has since entered into a new narrative, which shifts from one of rural culture linked to national future politics to that of rural culture as a spatial proof of a stagnant civilization, backward and impoverished.

The reconceptualization of folk culture in Yan'an can be traced to the cultural reflexivity movement of the 1980s when urban intellectuals targeted rural China and its traditional practices, symbolized by the isolated geography of the Yellow River, as molding a defensive, earthbound national character. In the nationwide broadcast of *River Elegy* (*Heshang*)—the most influential television program at its time—and in many of the fifth-generation movies during the 1980s, rural folk cultures are represented as the moribund Other of the enlightened urban self (Wang 1991: 28).[7] Images of ritual worship of deities in Yan'an, for instance, were used by urban intellectuals as visual criticism of a national cultural tendency to subjugate to a "collectivized authority," which was then related to the "non-development or ultrastability of the Chinese civilization" (Wang 1991: 28–29). I will not address the debates surrounding the cultural reflexivity movement here.[8] The main point is that cultural practices in most of the northwest rural regions have since become the cultural metaphor for China's stasis, closeness, and inertia.

Such a negative evaluation of the rural area and folk culture is related to the ways urban intellectuals try to come to terms with the material poverty of the rural area after decades of Mao's governance and development policy.[9] The new Communist state led by Mao Zedong from 1949–1979, even though it persistently constructed the rural area as a promising socialist future, had to exploit the rural peasantry for a primitive accumulation of capital for the purpose of quick industrialization and national-defense building. The Maoist state encouraged the peasants to think of themselves as "equal partners" with urban comrades, glorified agricultural labor, and enriched the rural area into a lively collectivist public sphere. In the process of making agriculture subsidize industrialization and urbanization, however, the state inevitably deprived rural villagers the rights to consume, process, and sell products of their own labor through the collectivization plan. The Maoist state also set up the household registration system (*hukou*), which prevented villagers from moving, marrying, and/or finding jobs in places other than their place of birth. Hukou especially kept villagers from moving to cities, where urban workers were given better provisions of infrastructure, welfare, and educational and career opportunities. The system has turned rural residents into the de jure second-class citizens with a hereditary rural identity and fate, and restricted mobility and opportunities (Chan 1994). After decades of supplying for the nation's needs, rural residents in some regions also became so economically impoverished that they barely had enough food and clothing for survival (Chen and Chun Tao 2004: 142).

Accordingly, what urban intellectuals of the 1980s revealed was part of a reality previously unarticulated: the rural area and the peasants had been overtaxed and unreasonably constrained. Intended as a critique of the Maoist ideology and governance, urban intellectuals, however, never imagined how the ensuing market reform would fail to alleviate the rural poverty and rural-urban divide. Such negative evaluation of the rural, nevertheless, had a sweeping discursive effect of making then predominantly rural and economically less developed Yan'an go from being a symbol of a holy revolutionary land to one of a moribund rural China.

China's rural-urban divide in the 1990s became ever more complicated after Deng Xiaoping's economic reform, which allowed rural residents to own their harvest, let them move out of rural hometowns to find jobs, and yet subjected them to various market challenges.[10] On the one hand, the decreasing state investment in agricultural infrastructures; the inflated prices of fertilizers, seeds, water, and electricity; and the general low market prices for agricultural products have gradually made grain production no longer profitable. Large-scale abandonment of farmland by rural residents started in the 1990s. On the other hand, millions of rural able-bodied residents rushed out of their hometowns to seek employment in cities, only to find the lowest paying and dirtiest jobs, together with all kinds of institutional barriers that blocked their access to basic urban welfare (Dutton 1998; Solinger 1999; Pun 2005). At the same time, growing administrative bureaucracy in rural villages without checks and balances, outrageous taxes and fees (Chen and Chun Tao 2004), and land-grabs of villagers' farms with no transparent systems and standards of compensation prevailed in the countryside (Lora-Wainright 2012). Many peasant protests broke out in the late 1990s and early 2000 as a result.

Scholars actively sought to explain the problems of rurality. Yan Hairong, for instance, attributes the "emaciation of the rural" to the neoliberal ideology inherent in the economic reform, which has discursively and in practice endorsed the city as the only legitimate space of capital investment, development, and modernity while rendering the rural as a material and ideological wasteland of "backwardness" and "tradition" (2008). Wen Tiejun (2005) sees the agrarian crisis to be a result of complicated historical development in which China, a country with a high population and a small amount of arable land, was first squeezed by the "state capitalist primitive accumulation" during the Mao era and, later, made to supply the global capitalist market in the post-Mao era.[11]

The problems of rurality are further complicated by the multiple processes of urbanization in today's China. Urbanization engages not only movement of the rural population into preexisting cities but also multiple levels of urbanization occurring all along the rural-urban continuum. "Townization," for instance, is a process in which existing rural villages and their surrounding areas are rapidly transforming by increasing flows of information, goods, capital, and people (Guldin 2001; Day 2008: 69–73).

My ethnographic field research was precisely situated in such complicated processes of rural-urban changes and divides, where some villages along the main road started to urbanize rapidly while those without the proximity to roads continued to face survival issues. I elaborate on the latest situation of rural Yan'an in a later section.

The Romantic Reappraisal of the Rural in the 1990s: Rural Yan'an as a Container of Living Civilization

Starting around the late 1990s, there was a new construction and representation of the rural area and folk traditions as idyllic, spiritually wealthy, and powerful. This new representation happened in both the countryside and the city. Rural Yan'an's Loess landscape, traditional art, cavehouse architecture, and religious ritual practices are becoming new attractions of cultural purity and origin. Books surrounding the themes boomed with titles such as *Fourteen Walks along the Yellow River* (Yang and Yang 2003), *Goodbye Tradition* (Lü 2003, 2004), *Rescue Folk Culture and Art* (Pan 2006), and *The Spirit of Rural Soil* (Feng 2010). The new representations of and interest in rural culture barely reflect the ongoing agrarian decline and underdevelopment. Yet they draw increasing attention among intellectuals, painters, writers, photographers, and collectors—and, lately, urban families and tourists—to go on trips to "experience and understand the disappearing rural elements and essence" (*caifeng*). They also arouse nostalgic pleasure in the experience of the mountain setting, organic vegetables and grain consumption, and farmers' homestays (*nongjiale*).

Griffiths, Chapman, and Christiansen have argued that the shift in values of the rural life reflects a "romantic reappraisal" of consumer values among middle-class citizens. Urbanites now find their desire to rediscover the familiar, the naive, and the innocent for their own self-cultivation, moral training, and even social cultural distinctions (Griffiths et al. 2010). But the renewed interest among urbanites in rural folk culture is related not only to a new urban middle-class consumption pattern but also a result of a prominent state effort. Wang Jing shows that the Chinese state actively initiated the cultural discourse of consumption as leisure culture (*xiuxian wenhua*) and institutionally boosted consumption practices through national policies throughout the 1990s. The result is a new realm of "cultural economy" where local government becomes an active player of staging culture for economic activities' rewards and business opportunities. Folk traditions and practices thrive in such a burgeoning cultural economy, too, and quickly have become linked to brand making of places and regional reputations (Oakes 2006; Goodman 2006). The rural countryside and rural residents are now depicted as nice, exotic, and traditional in many cultural tourism narratives, especially among the regions of ethnic minorities (Schein 2000).

In the countryside, there is also a large-scale resurgence of folk cultural and religious practices at the rural community level. Scholars have noted the "dilution" of folk tradition in such a revival and that the traditional practices being revived today are "cultural fragments recycled under new circumstances" (Siu 1989: 139). But most studies continue to see popular religion or folk tradition revival as the repressed rural society struggling with the symbolic order of the hegemonic state (Anagnost 1994) or a restoration of family and lineage role in a local power vacuum caused by the weakening of the party (Perry 1985). Recent research, however, has shown that the folk tradition revival does not denote simply "people's power" reclaiming power from a previously hegemonic Maoist state. Liu Xin argues that even everyday cultural practices in the rural area are modern inventions that "incorporate a particular combination of traditional, revolutionary, and modern elements" (Liu 2000: 81). Adam Chau ardently argues that the revival of folk popular religion and institutions is linked to the permissive and entrepreneurial attitudes of the local states in turning folk religious practices into useful "resources" to boost the local economy of rural China (2006).

Indeed, folk revival discourses in both cities and countryside invoke similar images of a pastoral and idyllic past, authentic homeland, and mythologized origin narratives. Both contribute to a broader trend of commodification of rural ritual practices and nostalgic consumption of folk tradition. The situation of folk cultural revival is therefore quite complex as "the romantic images of idyllic rural people have often mixed with the agony and anxiety of a displaced community in bringing about new forms of political association, economic enterprises, and a renewed sense of cultural identity" (Tapp 2000: 89). Nicholas Tapp observes that folk cultural revival, especially as coming from rural villagers and the rural society, might be related to a construction of a "real rather than imagined past." This further explains why villagers now strive to become "willing performers of folk knowledge" or "natural inheritors" of ancient heritage, not just to improve material livelihood (Oakes 1998) but also to control the power of representing one's own self in the process of consumption and urbanization.

In short, folk tradition revival by both urbanites and rural residents contributes to "the formation of a new power field" (Chau 2005). In this new field, "the local state interacts with local society in new ways and with new rules" as folk cultural practices are now entangled with new urban consumption desires, local state building projects, government regional branding, and a range of corporate, nongovernmental, and rural communal initiatives. Revival of folk traditions is especially related to villagers reconstructing rural communities against the broader trend of agrarian decline, rural underdevelopment, and rapid urbanization. In all these cases, contemporary folk revival has become a complex site of interest negotiations, narrative conflicts, new values, and identity making.

Hyper-Folk as a Cultural Logic of Late Socialism

Inspired by Jean Baudrillard's concept of "hyperreality" (1988), I use the term "hyper-folk" to understand the late socialist cultural condition in which the practice and representation of folk culture is no longer associated with any ritual reality, rural environment, or cultural origin in today's Yan'an. Hyper-folk is a mechanism of representation and experience making that replaces and resignifies rural reality. It constitutes rurality without origins.[12]

Contemporary folk cultural production involves creating historical symbols, primordial discourses, or folk performance, which represent traditional beliefs and ritual references that either no longer exist when rural communities rapidly urbanize or have never actually existed. In the context of this complex layered historical interconnections between Yan'an and folk cultural discourse and practices, I use the concept of hyper-folk to further articulate complex traditional phenomena and productions that blend together folk cultural knowledge and practices, state propaganda, intellectual interventions, mediated tourist spectacles, and rural religious service and commodity. With the concept of hyper-folk, I argue that the signs, discourses, and practices of folk traditions now ubiquitously and extensively appear in government events, tourist settings, intellectual narratives, and communal rituals. Not only do they pervade everyday life, public and private settings, and urban and rural spaces, their appearance also makes it difficult to distinguish a media representation from an original authentic ritual, or a state propaganda from a market or religious commodity. One very obvious example is the Yan'an waist-drum performance staged by the Yan'an government for the photographic contest I describe at the beginning of this chapter. The Yan'an waist-drum dance is now rarely performed at villages because the majority of young villagers, who could be drummers, now work as migrant workers in cities. But perhaps every Yan'an villager would appreciate the waist-drum performance in "The New Year Gala," a must-watch national television program for the Chinese Lunar Eve, produced and broadcast by the Chinese Central Television Channel. Moreover, on the seventh day of the New Year, thousands of villagers crowd at the main boulevard of Yan'an city center to watch the Yan'an government-organized New Year's festival, in which professional troupes stage waist-drum performances in the form of a street parade. In other words, the sign of a Yan'an waist-drum performance is now constantly mass-mediated, performed, and consumed out of its original and spatial contexts, and its live performance now engages rural performers and urban photographers, tourists, and government officials much more than rural neighbors. At the same time, the Yan'an waist-drum dance was a recent target of national heritage listing and conservation. Urban intellectuals rushed to investigate its historical meanings and performative forms and spoke of it as an unchanging tradition.

Folk tradition today therefore exceeds those narratives, beliefs, and practices in "real" or "original" rural communal ritual settings. In late socialist China, I argue that folk tradition has become an omnipresent sign reworked by the party-state for policy purposes, simulated and packaged by companies for consumption, fabricated and represented by urban intellectuals for heritage listing purposes, and still actively reenacted by rural villagers for identity construction and communal remaking. The prefix *hyper* captures that phenomenon of simulacra in which the sign of folk has not only detached from the original, but its meanings and circulation have exceeded the real and it has become something else.

In *Reinventing Chinese Tradition*, I argue that hyper-folk is a dominant mode of cultural production in late socialist China in which folk origin discourses, tradition reenactment, folk performance events, and heritage sites interpenetrate to an extent that one can no longer distinguish the simulated from the real or the original. Hyper-folk resonates with Hobsbawm and Ranger's "invention of tradition," a modern and nationalist effort to link certain ritual practices of a symbolic nature to a historic and mythical origin for the purpose of establishing social cohesion or collective identities (1983). Hyper-folk nonetheless complicates the invention of tradition thesis in which the state deployment of peasant art forms is intertwined with the communal initiatives of reenacting rural customs for the remaking of a public agrarian sphere (Chau 2006). Hyper-folk tradition also sees a changing role of the local state, which no longer suppresses "superstitious cultural contents" but rather turns them into useful resources for the creation of a local economy and temple-related religious business.

Finally, hyper-folk complicates Louisa Schein's concept of internal orientalism (2000: 100–131) by putting the production of cultural difference no longer between just Han urbanites and ethnic minorities, urban middle-class and rural peasants, but also between villagers who pursue urban careers and lifestyles and those who continue to stay in the remote and impoverished rural inland. Hyper-folk still involves the production of discourse and practice of urban cosmopolitan subjects fascinated with exotic rural cultures. But in the latest call for preserving the endangered rural tradition of folk paper-cuts, hyper-folk not only triggers the anxiety-ridden urban elite in their reimagining and displaying of the most authentic cultural rural China, it also heightens an awareness among villagers to represent their traditions for foreign and national visitors' understanding. Hyper-folk therefore resignifies, as much as it normalizes, existing gender, class, and rural-urban asymmetries within and outside of Chinese society.

Hyper-folk points to a complex site of late socialist cultural politics. It blends together tradition and politics, history and fiction, reality and representation, commodity and self-representation, government propaganda and folk initiatives. Hyper-folk simultaneously accommodates the party-state's logic of appropriation, the urban intellectual logic of imagining a cultural China, the capital logic of profit making, and the rural logic of making a public agrarian sphere. The convergence and negotiation of these often conflicting logics in the representations and practices of today's folk tradition, I argue, is one major feature of the cultural logic of late socialism. The juxtaposition of conflicting interests and strategies in the production of culture has much insight to offer in terms of understanding the similarly vigorous contests and negotiations among these forces in the political and economic realms in contemporary China.

Yan'an in the Twenty-First Century

If poverty, starvation, banditry threats, soil infertility, and social disintegration plagued Yan'an and the northern China region in the middle of the last century, a very different set of concerns has come to occupy contemporary Yan'an. Today's Yan'an is a prefecture-level city administering twelve counties, with a population of about two million people.[13] From a present-day point of view, Yan'an is far from any exciting center of China's prosperous growth. Located in central China, the Yan'an region has been largely insulated from the urban and industrial growth that swept along coastal China since 1980. It has therefore lagged behind in terms of levels of commercialization, urbanization, marketization, foreign investment, infrastructure, and GDP, as compared to national coastal counterparts.[14] In 2004, urban Yan'an was still defined by its extensive SOEs and government bureaucracies and the many memorial sites of former residences of Communist leaders. These SOEs continued to feed the majority of the urban residents with much "socialist happiness,"—a relatively more relaxed work culture, stable paychecks, and decent welfare associated with the work-unit structure or *danwei* (a place of employment, particularly during the socialist era, when the Chinese economy was still planned and most of the enterprises were state-owned). Social change is more or less located at the increasing number of visitors to the city memorial sites for tourist purposes. On top of its blossoming "red tourism," the revolutionary mecca has also seen the emergence of a class of super-wealthy businessmen and government officials, who have derived their fortunes since 2000 from the development of the regional oil and coal resources.

Unlike the city, where wealth, welfare, and a strong sense of collectivity prevailed, rural Yan'an was the opposite of the utopian land. But perhaps what was happening in rural Yan'an was representative of the larger rural China of the time mentioned earlier. This included split households with children away as migrant workers to support family income; middle- to old-age parents guarding the fields growing wheat, millet, and potatoes for basic consumption and apples, pears, and apricots for limited cash income; many more working as temporary construction workers as the cost of farming increased; bankrupt village schools; little village infrastructure such as paved roads, gas, and tap water; and a rural quality of life and styles astoundingly segregated from that of the urban area. The majority of households led a frugal life and had modest desires of improving their living standard. Those with small children and the elderly often struggled hard to make ends meet.

The years of 2003 and 2004 were particular years of anxiety and turmoil for rural Yan'an. The policy of "Restoring Farmland to Forest" (*tuigeng huanlin*) banned grain cultivation on terraced fields to alleviate serious soil weathering and desertification. While villagers were compensated for the initial few years, they worried the ban would eventually make them more vulnerable to soaring market prices in grain. Around the same time of the year, the Severe Acute Respiratory Syndrome (SARS), a fierce epidemic, broke out in China and triggered the World Health Organization to issue a global alert. Villagers in rural Yan'an, with little medical facilities, scarce water resources, and a different regime of sanitary practice, could respond to the epidemic only by guarding their village entrance physically and surrendering their household-raised poultry, initially but falsely regarded to have linkages to the disease, to the *xiang* level government (an administrative unit between the village government and the county government).

In Mojiagou village where my first phase fieldwork was based, life was so much more stressful than I imagined. Underlying a peaceful and idyllic community were murky money politics, cadre-villager conflicts, and interest-driven household calculations and anxiety. First, a small bridge construction in 2003 over a river finally connected the villagers' residences and their farmlands. The well-intentioned bridge project had the most melodramatic endings: a shockingly expensive price tag, collision between the village party leadership and the construction company, and the imprisonment of relevant village leaders (Wu 2007). Right after the fiasco, as the village was still digesting a huge debt attached to the corrupted bridge project, it received the news that the Yan'an city government would be appropriating the village's farmland for constructing a new campus for the Communist party cadres' political education. Worst still, there were no negotiations and no potential dispute in the process. Grievances prevailed and discontent proliferated. How would villagers be compensated? Would building good relations (*guanxi*) with local officials help bring up the remuneration of lost crops? What would villagers do without land?

"*Meirenguan* (no one cares)," villagers grumbled. But there was no time to complain. Everyone went ahead with planting more grapevines, digging up more wells to "increase the value" of land and maximize potential compensation. To quicken the cycle of crop turnover, my host, the Fang couple, worked until midnight in the summer of 2004. Some households planned marriages ahead to bring in daughters-in-law just in case compensation would be based on head count. Others tried different methods. No collective action plan was discussed as that was proven suicidal in other parts of China. Everyone panicked about the disappearance of farmland but no one dared to oppose it.

Facing the powerful state and lack of market information, rural residents I encountered were the opposite of the moralized, politicized, and heroic subjects exemplified in the official narrative of Yan'an. Instead, they demonstrated passive attitudes to state policy imposition even though they strategized to maximize interests in the process. The strategy they used—seeking acquaintance with individual government officers (bargain and rely on the network of personal relations)—was emblematic of social conditions in rural communities then, where the lack of a unified, standard, and proper procedure for the state deploying rural resources and compensating villagers created opportunities for grassroots bribery and intense injustice (Lora-Wainwright 2012).

For villagers in Mojiagou in particular, the challenge was not just about an imperfect market system and urban encroachment. Their loss of farmland was directly connected to a form of state violence in the name of upholding revolutionary legacy. Indeed, the more Yan'an was raised as that symbol of the Communist revolutionary success and legacy, the more alienation villagers often experienced as the norm of everyday life.

Folk tradition revival is part and parcel of the marginalization of rural life as land grabs and urbanization loom large. As I will show in subsequent chapters, villagers constantly seek folk discourse and practices to come to terms with the rapid rural change. At the same time, the local governments have seen folk cultural forms as valuable resources for political, economic, and governance purposes. Folk tradition, as a new form of commodity and heritage, has drawn intellectuals, artists, local entrepreneurs, government, and even rural villagers to ponder on the changing meanings of Chinese culture and tradition in the era of massive urbanization. In all these cases,

FIGURE 0.3. A cavehouse for a family in Mojiagou village.

folk tradition is a major site of mediating, contesting, and reflecting Chinese late socialist modernity and its problems.

Fieldwork, Methodology, and Chapters

Unlike many anthropologists who have ties to the field through family or kin network, my ability to do research in Yan'an hinged on my capacity to engage with different groups and different local agendas. My Hong Kong identity often provided the Yan'an residents with a strange sense of "exotic familiarity" (Liu 2000). Hong Kong and its turnover to China in 1997 rang a bell for everyone. But since no one—except for a few officials—I talked to had been there, not to mention understood what it was like living under the British colonial rule, my Hong Kong–ness became a curious, sometimes a nationalist, subject to start a conversation.

I first went to Yan'an in the summer of 2003 for an initial visit through a referral from an acquaintance, Lily, an officer at the Xi'an City All China Women Federation, who was a sent-down youth in Mojiagou village in 1973 (Figure 0.3). She recommended me to the Fang family because she had assisted the family's fifth child to go to high school through a poverty aid program. Initially, the Fang family accommodated me for a couple days as a gesture of gratitude to Lily and as a way of keeping a relationship with someone in the city. Mojiagou's village leaders, former party cadres, and women who had been party cadres came to see me and recalled for me the political meetings and production brigade experiences in the Maoist era as a courtesy. In the beginning, my colonial-turned-Chinese national identity and my relation with a former sent-down youth helped identify me as an interesting and trustworthy visitor. But after a while, when villagers felt that they had done enough talking, the response I increasingly got was "that is all!" Those who initially took me as a reporter and hoped that I could expose for them the government appropriation of farmland, eventually found that I was not useful after all and turned their back on me. In the end, my ability to probe into the various folk cultural discourses and practices in Yan'an came down to a pertinent question that confronts all fieldworkers: an observable and describable reality, such as objects, theaters, or texts simply does not exist (Clifford and Marcus 1986: 10–12). The field is always a site of multiple, divergent stories and positioned utterances (Rosaldo 1985) beyond the "knowing" of a set of prescribed research questions. Fieldwork, instead of being a process of confirming one's hypothesis, is a process where the anthropologists and the informants develop a set of shared symbols and intersubjective relationships (Rabinow 1977).

My fieldwork comprised a twelve-month residence covering Yan'an city, Mojiagou village north of Yan'an city, Caozhuang village in Ansai county, and the township and Xiaocheng village of Yanchuan county. I returned for a visit in 2008 and completed ongoing follow-up work with artist-intellectuals traveling between Yan'an and Beijing in 2008, 2010, and 2012. I constantly had to negotiate my ethnographic identity and interventions with various communities, concerns, and new situations.

In the beginning, members of the Fang family in Mojiagou village were the kindest. They let me "help" with agricultural labors: I trimmed apricot, apple, and peach trees at the hilltop for many days in the winter; I chopped hundreds of cornstalks for cow feeds and also went with Aunt Fang to sell vegetable seeds in neighboring villages. In the springtime, I spent much time planting grapevines, digging up wells, and harvesting in the cultivation field; I chatted extensively with fellow villagers about their landless future. I watched Uncle Fang selling vegetables in various city spots for many hours. All these projects helped me substantially in surveying the Loess ravine landscape; getting into villagers' cavehouses with a legitimate reason; understanding their dialects; sharing everyday schedules, jobs, and household practices; and tasting the stark difference between urban and rural life.

And just as I was exhausted and clueless as to how to continue fieldwork, the Mojiagou village leader trusted me and let me accompany a group of villagers seeking legal advice about the village's huge bridge debt. We made numerous trips to many different government departments to no avail. The event helped me further understand villagers' conundrums: the hegemonic state was absent when people most needed its intervention. Chapter 3 looks at how northern Shaanxi folk storytelling fits in isolated rural communities where villagers actively seek folk storytelling to reflect on new desires and problems. The peculiarity of folk storytelling performance in Yan'an lies in the fact that most storytellers helped promote party policies during the Mao era. Today, they continue to "go down to the village" (*xiaxiang*), but neither doing much propaganda for the state nor giving extensive storytelling performances. Rather, they have turned their performances into various forms of religious services. Chapter 3 shows how both state propaganda and folk cultural tradition continue to intertwine in their contemporary forms and contents, and yet both have been subjected to radical reinterpretations.

Meanwhile, Aunt Fang trusted me enough to take me to a secretive healing ritual and told me the local worship of spirit mediums. Then Aunt Fang's sister-in-law revealed to me a secret cult community within Mojiagou village, a sphere of "public secrecy" (Taussig 1999). Chapter 5 examines the public secrecy and popularity of spirit cults in the context of such rural change. It explores how deity worship figures as a powerful form of unspoken yet widely circulated knowledge, communal bonds, and spiritual services in rural Yan'an. My analysis does not view the spirit medium as a form of protest against the state or some repressed traditions. Instead I understand spirit cults in Yan'an as a crucial folk cultural discourse with specific systems of localized knowledge, symbols, and technical know-how, which produce what I call a "surrogate rural subjectivity." In the context of rapid urbanization, I argue that spirit cults provide occasions for the expression of disappearing rural communal relations, folk values, and ritual memories.

In urban and rural Yan'an, I got around by showing to local government departments and state-owned enterprises a letter of recommendation generously offered by Professor Yang Shengmin at the Central University of Ethnicity in Beijing. It indicated that I was a student from Hong Kong wanting to do "social studies" (*shehui diaocha*) in the region. Upon entering each village, I was always asked to show that letter, sometimes together with my Hong Kong identity card. Cadres at village levels always accommodated my needs after reading the letter: the Cultural Hall in Ansai county permitted me to stay with paper-cutting artists and the Caozhuang village leaders allowed me to participate in their communal rain ritual.

What this letter proved was not so much my researcher identity, but my danwei identity. It helped everyone to locate me as someone belonging to a certain work danwei or work unit. *Danwei* not only defines a worker's career, but also the worker's economic, social, and political lives. Today a government-related work unit continues to link workers to some housing rights, children's education, medical welfare, and better benefits (Xie, Lai, and Wu 2009). Government danwei are also major spaces and structures where workers are linked to the party-state policies and ideology.

This makes folk storytelling even more interesting in contemporary Yan'an because it is constantly performed in danwei-related occasions. In Yanchuan county, I gained the trust of a group of storytellers who allowed me to follow them to performances at various work units. Chapter 4 examines folk cultural performances staged in and by various government work units or state-owned enterprises for public relations purposes. I argue that the production of folk tradition is now closely tied to danwei business promotion, but little has been investigated on the subject.

While the Fang family gave me the best hospitality and support in and out of surrounding villages, from the spring of 2004 my fieldwork shifted to an urban residence in Yan'an. Aunt Fan became my new host. She was sent down to labor in Mojiagou village in 1973. When we met, she was in her half-retirement status from a state-owned enterprise, with a grown-up daughter. She was very curious about me, a young Hong Kong woman studying in the United States, who had lived in Mojiagou village and knew all the villagers she had worked with thirty years before. She passionately shared about her sent-down experience and eventually offered me a place to stay at her work-unit apartment. With Aunt Gao and her husband, who was a state official, I got to meet with many work-unit workers, writers, painters, calligraphers, historians, and musicians in various government-sponsored troupes, literary associations, and the city Hall of Culture.

The "literary circle" in the city was vital to my understanding of folk cultural production in Yan'an. Cao Peizhi, for instance, is a renowned musician, scholar, and educator in Yan'an, who had served at the Hall of Culture in Yanchuan county. In 2004, he ran a school, wrote books and scripts, composed music, and even managed a new resort ranch modeled on cavehouse architecture with ancient northern Shaanxi décor. Talking extensively with a group of urban intellectuals and "cultural entrepreneurs," I acquired a good understanding of how they become plugged into the narrative of cultural tourism capital and a new discursive production about the history and culture of Yan'an.

By the summer of 2004, I became acquainted with Prof. Jin Zhilin and Feng Sanyun, the two main architects of Xiaocheng Folk Art Village, which was the village base for the listing of folk paper-cutting as an intangible cultural heritage at the UNESCO from 2003 through 2005. I went to Xiaocheng as a translator for two tour groups from Japan and Spain searching for traditional China. There I was shocked to find a rural community where poverty alleviation, tradition revival, tourist development, and community organizing collided. Chapter 2 documents the process of making Xiaocheng rural village into a container of tradition and the practice of paper-cutting into an intangible cultural heritage. I argue that heritage making in China is a process of "narrative battle" in which various actors construct differentiated meanings of history and tradition against the official party-state narrative.

After leaving Yan'an, I reread and analyzed urban intellectuals' writings of Yan'an cultural traditions carefully in different periods of modern China. I seek to tease out how folk traditional cultural logic allies with, and conflicts and diverges from, the nationalist or intellectual interventions, as well as how it intertwines with communal and capital forces. Using paper-cuts as a case study, Chapter 1 delineates how folk paper-cuts have always served as a site of intellectual expressions and debates about the nation's future, the meanings of the rural, even women's liberation. Combining the analysis of historical and contemporary intellectual representations of folk paper-cuts and the ethnographic field research of women artists in Yan'an, the chapter shows that folk paper-cuts have become that "site of awkward engagement" where the agenda of the state, global capital regimes of values, and local tradition forces interacted with each other (Tsing 2004).

I went back to Yan'an in 2008, 2009, and 2012 to update field data, follow new changes and reconnect with informants, with whom I have become friends and even part of the family since. As I have shown, I have relied on informal interviews and day-to-day conversations and my research process was a multisited one. I did not focus on one group of people in one locale, but have shifted across places and groups, events and projects. Following anthropological conventions, I have used pseudonyms for individuals discussed, except for well-known public figures. The book chapters are organized in a way that put chapters with more historical information first and those with more recent changes later.

CHAPTER 1

Paper-Cuts in Modern China

The Search for Modernity, Cultural Tradition, and Women's Liberation

During the summer of 2004, I visited the seventy-year-old Gao Fenglian, one of the most renowned paper-cutting masters in China. A capable woman villager who had served as a civilian militia leader, head of the women's association at the rural administration level, and village party secretary, Gao began making paper-cuts in the late 1980s. She quickly stood out as a talented artist able to integrate folk knowledge, legends, and local stories into her designs. Since the mid-1990s, she has often appeared on Chinese television programs and has been recognized as Art Master by UNESCO. Her works are featured in museums around the world, and there are monographs, memoirs, and a Web site devoted to her life and art (Hei 1999; Liu 2003; Zhou 2005; http://gaofenglian.com, last accessed on March 5, 2015).

At the time of my visit, Gao Fenglian lived on a hilltop of Baijiayuan village, about an hour's motorcycle ride on a small trail along terraced cliffs from Yanchuan county, east of Yan'an city in Shaanxi province. Outside of Gao's cavehouse were acres of apple and apricot trees, grapevines, tomato fields, and the northern Shaanxi staple—millet. Gao's eighty-year-old husband was tending his beloved mule—a beast of burden that has all but disappeared in the Yan'an region because of improvements in transportation. Inside her cavehouse, Gao Fenglian spread out her paper-cuts on the *kang* bed and explained the symbolism of each piece: images of snakes or scorpions are hung on children during the Dragonboat festival to ward off noxious influences; "Sweeper of the Skies" brings an end to excessive rain; lotus (*lian*) is a homonym of the word to bear sons to continue the family line (*lianshengguizi*), as well as to fulfill wishes for wealth and honor (Wachs 2004). Every time I marveled at the use of visual puns, rebuses, and symbols, paper-cutting artists explained the ways the images were connected to language, lives, and longings of the people in rural China. Each of my subsequent visits to the homes of paper-cutting artists became a step in a larger process of understanding layers upon layers of the historical meanings of—and the entangled relationships between—culture, gender, history, and the state in modern China.

The Question of Tradition, Gender, and Modernity

The question of folk traditions, gender, and modernity has long been the subject of scholarly discussion (Chatterjee 1993; Mani 1987; Schein 2000). Rita Felski demonstrates that the equation of tradition, peasant culture, and woman with "Mother Nature" and an enduring tradition outside of historical development is a significant element in nineteenth-century modern Western thought and social theory, and a similar theme has been reiterated in a wide array of scientific (Darwinian model of evolutionary development), anthropological (the notion of savages), and historical texts as well as literature. Eastern philosophy, religion, and culture, for instance, have been imagined as an atemporal space of eternal truth and sacred authority in these writings. The major reason for making the traditional and the feminine as emblematic of a nonfragmented modern identity, Felski argues, is because they provide "alternatives or a source of authentic spirituality against which the progress-oriented, rational and materialist impulse of the West could be judged" (1995: 136). Similarly, in *Minority Rules* (2000), Louisa Schein has found that the ethnic minority Miao women, their outfits, and their songs and dance have been represented in the dominant public culture within China as simultaneously indigenous, promiscuous, close to nature, and infantile. She argues that the domains of the peasant, the folk tradition, and non-Han minorities have come to be regarded as the feminine keepers of Chinese tradition and the exotic Other against which the Han urbanites assert their urban modernity. In short, tradition, nostalgia, the feminine are no entities of primordial and transcendental meanings. Their meanings have been central to the nationalist constructions and the ongoing quest for modernization in different periods of time as they become equated with "authentic points of origin," "mythic referents untouched by the constraints of social and symbolic mediation," or a "symbol of the atemporal and asocial" (Felski 1995: 37–38).

Accordingly, Lata Mani and other theorists of gender and nationalism have shown that it is often in such discourses of tradition, gender, and modernity that a woman's experience and practices are associated with the gatekeeping or demise of national traditions or sexual morality while men are always supposedly the subject pursuing national progress and modernity (Ong 1990; Mani 1987; Yuval-Davis and Anthias 1989; Chow 1991; McClintock 1995: 355; Meng 1993). As I show in the following section, gender figures prominently in the narrative of the folk cultural form of paper-cuts in Yan'an and its later deployment by urban intellectuals in various nationalist campaigns.

Yan'an Paper-Cutting

Paper-cutting (*jianzhi*) has been practiced in China for centuries, not always by women only and not exclusively in rural areas. Archeological evidence suggests that it dates to as early as the Northern Dynasties (386 to 581 C.E.) (Zhang 1980: 7). Approximately the size of one's palm, paper-cuts are commonly called "window flowers" (*chuanghua*) in Yan'an. The designs are cut out from red-colored paper with scissors, and pasted as decoration on wood-framed windows made of rice paper (Figure 1.1). Popular during special celebrations such as weddings or the Chinese New Year, paper-cut designs are well-known for symbolizing good harvest and auspiciousness. Today, they also exist as stand-alone works of art, larger and more varied in size. Paper-cutting of Quanzhou in Fujian province, Foshan in Guangdong, Nanjing in Jiangsu, Weixian in Hebei, Gaomi in Shandong, and Lüliang in Shanxi are well-known examples of such.[1] In these places, paper-cuts are produced in large-scale workshops, some being made with knives rather than scissors by professional male craftsmen. In this book, I use the term *paper-cuts* to refer to the art form and *paper-cutting* to refer to the practice.

Yan'an paper-cuts, sometimes also called Shaanxi paper-cuts, have a special place in the People's Republic of China (PRC) because it was in Yan'an where the CCP leaders started to write about, reform, and re-create the traditional cultural form of paper-cuts for the purpose of resisting the Japanese, winning people's support, and spreading revolutionary ideas. After 1949, paper-cuts were mass-produced in large workshops; used for illustrations in newspapers, stories, greeting cards, and children's movies and also exhibited abroad—all of them professing the happiness of the peasantry under the new government (Wachs 2004: 16–17).[2] In and outside of Yan'an, paper-cuts are a symbol of prosperity, modernity, and the better lives of the masses under CCP rule.

Yan'an paper-cuts also have a special place within the debates about tradition and modernization. Since the 1980s, Yan'an paper-cuts have become the subject of folk cultural studies (Chaowen Wang 1993; Fu 2000; Pan 1992a, 1999; Zhang 1980, 1999) but most importantly of historical (Ansaix-

FIGURE 1.1. Traditional small paper-cuts on the wood-framed windows of a cavehouse.

ian Wenhua Wenwuguan 1999; Jin 2001, 2002), social, and anthropological inquiries (Chen 1992; Li 2003; Fang 2003; Qiao 2005). Today, Yan'an paper-cuts continue to remain a powerful cultural form and have made recurrent appearances in the nation's major events and diplomatic exchanges, such as the Fourth World Conference on Women in Beijing in 1995, and recently the Beijing Olympic Games in 2008.

However, both in and outside of China, paper-cutting is almost exclusively treated as or reduced to a simple time-honored traditional practice, a domestic craft, and a folk art form. Considered a rural and feminine practice, paper-cutting has often been included in what is thought to be authentic Chinese culture. In 2006, it was elevated to a national intangible cultural heritage and became a marker of the Yellow River civilization. The relationship of paper-cuts with the socialist political power, Chinese intellectual concerns, and modern cultural governance has not been systematically investigated.

This chapter challenges the assumption that paper-cutting is a quintessential feminized traditional cultural form. It examines the practice as operating in Duara's notion of regime of authenticity (1998), in which paper-cuts become intimately affiliated with the domestic sphere, the nonindustrial Loess, the nostalgic mourning for both an unchanging folk tradition and an idealized past. It also treats paper-cutting as a medium of articulation in which the Chinese male intellectuals discussed the meanings of the modern progress, cultural origins and traditions, and their projection of a cultural China in different periods of time.

My objective in this chapter is to investigate the changes in paper-cutting as it was transformed from a rural practice to a national heritage. It seeks to trace the various actors, debates, and themes through which paper-cuts were discussed in relation to the questions of traditional culture, the modern state, and their relationship with each other. In each of the periods under discussion here, paper-cutting has come to share a number of newly created discursive spaces: on the use of old forms in promoting modern new lives in the Yan'an period, as the site of recovering the lost Chinese civilization in the 1980s, as an urban nostalgia for vanishing ritual practices in the 1990s, and as the emphasis on capital, profit, and personal success in the 2000s. In other words, paper-cuts are more than just a symbol of Chinese tradition; they serve as a signifier of the different desires and visions in modern China.

This chapter, however, does not intend to read paper-cuts as just products of modern political appropriation or a state propaganda tool. Through a limited reconstruction of the cultural history of Yan'an paper-cuts, it reveals several logics that are not always consistent with the modern political history of the state: paper-cuts as part of folk indigenous knowledge and ritual power in rural society, the urban intellectual recovering and articulation of such folk knowledge; and the contemporary practice and market values of paper-cuts. Presenting these several logics shows how the modern Chinese state, urban intellectuals, and rural practitioners are in constant tension and negotiation with each other. Finally, by analyzing the shifting meanings assigned to the practice, I explore rural culture, political appropriation, and Chinese tradition not as taken-for-granted concepts, but as being actively manufactured and contested in various historical contexts.

The following sections present three portraits of paper-cuts in the respective periods of early (1949) and early reform era (1981), mid-1980s, and 2000s in Yan'an, based on published writings and my ethnographic fieldwork with various artists and intellectuals involved in the production of paper-cuts. I present my own ethnographic encounters of paper-cuts in 2004 and in 2008, during which I stayed with and interviewed paper-cutting artists in Ansai and Yanchuan counties in Yan'an. I have also conducted in-depth interviews with major urban artists in Yan'an and in Beijing, who have for the last few decades taught and written about Yan'an paper-cuts. Combining historical sources, ethnographic experience, and interview data, this chapter explores paper-cutting as a lived experience of villagers and as a site through which modernity and tradition in China have been imagined.

Paper-Cutting in the
Yan'an Period (1937–1947)

At the "Talks at the Yan'an Forum on Literature and Art" in 1942, Mao Zedong asked the urban intellectuals to go to the countryside "to observe, experience, and study" the masses and to "sinicize" Western art forms. Art and literature, he expounded, should identify with the lives of commoners and promote the ideals and policies of the CCP government in the border region rather than serve for the enjoyment of highbrow elites. This was the context in which urban intellectuals first set out to learn about paper-cuts in the region. This section focuses on the first CCP-sponsored collection of paper-cuts, *Northwestern Paper-Cuts* (*Xibei Jianzhi Ji*) (1949), edited by Ai Qing[3] and Jiang Feng.[4] It provides significant insights on how the early Communist urban intellectuals understood this folk cultural form in the Yan'an period, an understanding that extended throughout the Maoist era and beyond.

Ai Qing, the renowned poet, and Jiang Feng, a leading woodcut artist were among the most authoritative figures in the field of art in the People's Republic of China. Both Ai and Jiang went to Yan'an to participate in leftist revolutionary activities, and both held top bureaucratic positions in the Communist party-state–affiliated art academies after 1949. During the Yan'an period, Ai was the vice director of the Literature and Arts College at the Shanxi, Chahar, Hebei North China United Revolutionary University (*Jin-Cha-Ji Huabei Lianda*) between today's Shanxi and Hebei provinces, and Jiang Feng was an instructor at the Lu Xun Academy of Literature and Arts (*Luyi*) in Yan'an.

In response to Mao's call, Ai Qing and Jiang Feng, along with other urban writers and artists such as Gu Yuan and Li Qun, set out from their academic institutions to learn about popular cultural forms such as paper-cuts, New Year prints (*nianhua*), and various folk literature and songs in the area (Holm 1991). Their task was to create a socialist art form that would absorb local cultural resources, yet reject elements considered as superstitious and feudal, and at the same time appeal to the broad illiterate masses in the border region. Paper-cut designs, with their bold lines and bright colors, convey a sense of optimism, fitted well with these intellectuals' desire to depict peace, joy, and abundance of life under CCP rule in the area (Hung 1994: 244).

In 1944, the artists put together an exhibit of the paper-cuts they had collected during their travels (Xu 2005: 96) and put together the volume, *Northwestern Paper-Cuts* (1949) (Figure 1.2).[5] The collection could therefore be considered a crucial text by Communist urban intellectuals when they first interpreted paper-cuts' meanings within a socialist, modern, and realist framework.

FIGURE 1.2. The book cover of *Northwest China Paper-Cuts* (1949). The featured paper-cut is entitled "Feeding Chickens."

In the preface to the volume, Ai Qing describes "going down to the village" with woodcuts artist Gu Yuan and a cooperative member Liu Jianzhang to the townships of Yanchi, Dingbian, and Jingbian in the border region. There, they met with herdsmen, Mongolians, and a few well-off families living in villas. Ai saw paper-cuts displayed in their homes and obtained a number of pieces. He described paper-cuts as "a product of the rural households" (*nongcun jiating chanwu*), "an art form without print condition (*meyou yinshuatiaojian de chusuo de yishupin*)" created out of the hands of the common folks, mostly household women (*jiating funü*)."[6] He described paper-cuts as pure and beautiful, just like folk songs in their vivid portrayal of people's feelings, flavors, and aspirations (*renmin de ganqing, quwei he xiwang*). To be sure, Ai allowed, some paper-cuts did contain feudal and superstitious elements, such as the dragon, the phoenix, and the Eight Immortals, and some designs, such as "Deer Holding *lingzhi*" or "Monkey

Tasting Peaches," did not relate to common folks' lives but reflected the tastes of wealthy families. But, overall, it is "the healthiest and the most genuine art form." He especially praised horse designs from Mongolia and camel designs from Jingbian as they reflected the peasantry's benevolent, healthy, and delightful ways of thinking as well as their love for animals.

Northwestern Paper-Cuts features one hundred designs, eighty of which came from the border region. Included are quite a few traditional designs of heroes, gods, and good-luck charms. The remaining twenty paper-cut designs were created by urban artists (including Gu Yuan, Xia Feng, Li Qun, and Zhang Ding), combining both woodcut and paper-cut methods. Urban artists first designed the motif using the woodcutting method—making a woodcut print on a piece of paper and then turning it into a paper-cut. The fusion art form, known as a "woodcut paper-cut" (*muke chuanghua*) has motifs including "The Militia," "Sowing Seeds," "Weeding," and "Learn Culture" (Figure 1.3). In particular, two images, "An Eighth Route Soldier Riding on a Horse" and "Weaving," were drafted by Li Quan on a piece of paper but were cut by a young woman, Niu Guiying from the rural northwest region. These new paper-cut designs signal the intellectual response to Mao's theory on art and literature and the CCP cultural policy to portray a modern life in Yan'an. As a concluding remark to his preface, Ai Qing (1949) wrote that "we artists should closely examine 'folk window flowers' (*minjian chuang hua*), their features and the ways people see and treat objects. From these very truthful lines and shapes, we should better understand their flavors. . . . Accordingly we could reform the art and utilize it to describe new lives. These new window flowers will eventually replace the old designs. The people's lives have been changed. New life will anticipate new art."

To conclude this section briefly, Yan'an urban intellectuals viewed paper-cuts as reflections of "the thoughts and feelings of the wider laboring people" as it "shows the peasants' direct impression of an object but is able to retain the object's major features." Ai Qing's concept of simple realism and his high regard for rural aesthetics need to be understood in the larger context of the CCP's drive to create a "village literature and art" (*xiangcun wenyi*) in the 1940s. These urban intellectuals wanted to view village literature and art with a vision of the countryside as the future and the hope, in contrast to the May Fourth intellectual understanding of it as gloomy, poverty-stricken, and backward (Hung 1994: 266). Communist intellectual valorization of rural folk culture was therefore not at all about finding the essence of Chinese tradition—an approach they inevitably would have to consider with folk practices they regarded as backward and full of superstitions and hence they rejected altogether—but, instead, about the pos-

FIGURE 1.3. The woodcut paper-cut design, "Sowing Seeds," by Gu Yuan, 1949.

sibilities to offer a future-oriented socialist culture. This explains the reasons why they must leave out some of the more "traditional" iconography and symbolism in folk paper-cuts. A major paradox therefore emerged: the more the urban intellectuals looked to rural folk culture for the creation of a new socialist art form, the more they become suspicious of the contexts, forms, and contents of these folk cultural practices. This paradox was one that urban intellectuals had to grapple with as they tried to develop a new socialist art form out of rural culture. More importantly, this paradox set the stage for analogous paradoxes that have reappeared in more recent decades as urban intellectuals have appropriated folk cultural practices for very different purposes.

Paper-Cuts in the Late 1970s

In 1976, Jin Zhilin observed:[7]

> A girl holds a pair of small scissors,
> cutting window flowers under an oil lamp;
> We have already occupied all the window fronts,
> sweeping capitalism out of homes;
> A girl holds a pair of small scissors,
> cutting window flowers under an oil lamp;
> The Old World shattered by a pair of small scissors,
> capturing Asia, Africa and Latin American in her heart.
> (quoted from Zhang 2009: 38)

Throughout the Maoist era, paper-cut designs with motifs of floral, fauna, and agricultural production appeared in many different types of policy-promoting media. In the Yan'an region, for instance, paper-cut designs were utilized in various state social and political campaigns. In Yichuan county, they were used for campaigns boosting agricultural outputs in the 1960s and promoting birth control policy in the 1970s (Fu 2002: 242–244). In Huanglong county, the government edited a paper-cuts volume on expanding agriculture (*daban nongye jianzhi xuan*). Famous motifs from the 1950s to the 1960s included "Ten Types of Fruits," "Loading Fertilizers," "Fowls and Cattles" (Wang and Yang 2002: 249–250). Although certain traditional motifs such as the Twelve Zodiac Animals or legendary figures like the Monkey King were downplayed, there is a great resemblance between the new socialist motifs and the traditional ones, both of which stress themes of abundance and happiness. Both use the method of caricature to highlight certain features in an exaggerated manner.

During the Great Leap Forward in 1958, the policy of art serving politics was reinforced in the national "peasant mural painting movement" with thousands of art teachers and professional painters going into factories and down to the countryside to instruct workers and peasants on mural painting. The aim of the movement was to encourage commoners to learn art in order to glorify the collectivization movement. It also aimed to reeducate the professional artists by urging them out of their comfortable studios and by mingling with workers and peasants. With slogans such as "paint what you labor" (*gan shenme, hua shenme*) or "wherever you labor you find art" (*shengchan dao nali, meishu huodong dao nali*), the campaign made art a crucial element in increasing production for the nation.[8]

The peasant mural painting movement subsided after the Great Leap Forward, but it left behind the mass art centers (*qunzhong yishuguan*) at the provincial and county levels, at which party-affiliated artists or art cadres (*meishu ganbu*) continued to instruct villagers in training classes (*xuexiban*) on painting. Even during the Cultural Revolution (1966–1976), painting classes were held and organized at the county whenever resources were available. In 1974, in Wuqi county of Yan'an, for instance, there were art training groups at the county machinery factory, the county Chinese People's armed police force, and villages of the Jinfo commune, Zhangguanmiao commune, Zhouwan commune, and the Luzuigou area in 1974. In these art training groups, workers or villagers received basic art skills in sketching, perspective, anatomy, and shading (Zhang 2009: 33–34). Villagers who went through art training would be responsible for decorating village walls or the walls of newly built dams. Although the training classes aimed to put art at the service of politics, they also created a unique space at the village level for commoners to access art training for free and to work with professional artists. As I will explain further in this section, it was ironic that through these training classes, urban intellectuals in the 1970s became exposed to indigenous themes, ritualistic meanings of paper-cut designs, and other folk knowledge not endorsed by the party-state.

Despite some attention paid to paper-cuts by intellectuals in the 1940s and that paper-cuts often appeared in state propaganda materials, traditional paper-cutting motifs were continually associated with the feudal tradition and therefore not allowed during the Cultural Revolution. Jin Zhilin, an artist from the Central Academy of Fine Arts in Beijing (CAFA) who served as an art cadre at the Yan'an Hall of Culture in 1973, however, gained a new understanding of the traditional art form after getting to know women villagers in the training classes.[9] The more Jin learned about paper-cutting, the more interested he became in its forms of representation and its meanings. He began to ask the women villagers questions that were seldom asked before:

> Why put a spider in between two dragons for the motif of "two dragon play ball (*erlong xizhu*)?" He asked a student in the training class.
>
> "To take the pun of spider. (The regional pronunciation of spider, *xizhu*, sounds like 'playing ball')" She answered.
>
> "Why put a peony flower on the back of a rooster?"

Villagers told him that the motif is a representation of the Chinese proverb *Jinshang tianhua*, which means "to gild the lily," because the Chinese words, *jin* (meaning "perfection" in this proverb) and *ji* (meaning "rooster") share very similar pronunciation. But because the flower the woman villager cut was a peony (*mudan*), she actually developed another motif out of the first one, making it into "A Phoenix Plays with Peony (*fenghuang xi mudan*)," a euphemistic expression for sexual pleasure between male and female. Through replacing the original fauna prototype, the rooster, with a legendary and more powerful figure, the phoenix, the paper-cut design carries two auspicious motifs that gives perfect appraisal to someone and to wish a couple the best fertility and happiness (Jin 1989: 179–190).

Jin Zhilin and his fellow Yan'an art cadres figured that a folk paper-cut design is not a direct representation of the reality, as urban intellectuals claimed in the 1940s. Its designs are full of local metaphors, ritual knowledge, and hidden folk meanings. They began to actively seek out paper-cut designs. What they uncovered surprised them. Chen Shanqiao, an art cadre in the Ansai Hall of Culture, walked twenty miles of mud road into the deep valleys of rural Ansai in 1978 and came upon Yan Xifang, a talented woman who showed him many paper-cuts left behind by her mother-in-law. He remembered the encounter, "I was dumbfounded to see the designs. I had heard of the motifs 'Snakes Encircling Rabbits' (*she pan tu*) or 'Mouse Eating Melon' (*laoshu ken gua*) but had never seen them. Both motifs are euphemist expressions of marriage, sex, and fertility with the snake and mouse as metaphors of male and the phallus, while rabbit and melon as metaphors of female and the womb) (Figure 1.4). I asked her to give the designs to the Hall of Culture and I would double the payment. But she refused and said she wanted to keep them for the later generations in her family" (Tongdao Zhang 2009: 82). Jin Zhilin was similarly impressed when he first saw the motifs of "Fish Playing with Lotus (*yu xi lian*)" (Figure 1.5) and "Mouse Marrying Daughters (*laoshu jia nü*). "I have never seen these designs all these years in Yan'an," he said. "What are their stories? What do they mean?" (Zhang 2009: 91). Zhang Yongge, art cadre in the Zhidan Hall of Culture, collected about 100 pieces of paper-cut designs and explained, "this (folk paper-cuts) was something entirely new for those of us in the circle (artists and art cadres). We were relatively more sensitive to the issue but we had no theory or substantial support for it" (Zhang 2009: 78). What Zhang meant by "the issue" is not exactly clear, but I think it refers to the complex ritual meanings, metaphors, and symbolism and their representations in folk rural society (Wang and Dang 1988), all so foreign to the urban art cadres. Trained to see paper-cuts as either unsophisticated rural culture or feudal tradition, these art cadres found themselves amazed by the richness and depth of this cultural form.

The reason that even local Yan'an art cadres had become disconnected from the meanings of traditional designs certainly had much to do with

FIGURE 1.4. The paper-cut design, "Snakes Encircling Rabbits" (*she pan tu*) by Hao Guizhen, 2004.

FIGURE 1.5. The paper-cut design, "Fish Playing with Lotus" (*yu xi lian*) by Hao Guizhen, 2004.

the Communist appropriation of this cultural form, which had erased its traditional symbolism since the Yan'an period. It also had much to do with the Cultural Revolution, during which old culture and ideas were under severe criticism. To avoid unnecessary trouble, villagers decorated their windows with pieces of red paper instead of traditional paper-cuts, and many women villagers even stopped making paper-cuts altogether (Jiang 1981: preface; Feng 1989: 231). One peasant woman, Bai Fenglian, refused to cut a traditional design in an art training class as late as 1979 because she had once been put on stage and publicly criticized for making traditional paper-cuts. It was only after the Director of the Ansai Hall of Culture stepped in to confirm that old designs no longer had any political consequences that she was eventually persuaded to resume her craft (Zhang 2009: 90).

With an initial understanding of the creative use of folk metaphors, legends, puns, and styles of representation in paper-cutting, Jin Zhilin and the art cadres in the fourteen counties in the Yan'an region started a regionwide survey. Among these results, those for Ansai county stand out (or stood out?). The Ansai survey revealed that out of a total population of 50,000 people, 20,000 women could make paper-cuts, 1,000 were "more talented," 200 could be considered artistic, and 40 had reached "master" level (Jin 2005: 36). At the same time, the Ansai Hall of Culture supported the renewed interest in paper-cuts by holding more training classes in order to put talented people together and enable them to create more designs. Between 1977 and 1980, four large-scale surveys and twelve training classes on folk paper-cutting were held across the Yan'an region, resulting in a collection of about 8,000 pieces of traditional paper-cutting designs (An 2002: 237).

In April 1980, the National Museum of Art in Beijing held an exhibition on folk paper-cuts, gathering together some of the best designs collected in the surveys and in the training classes. This national-level exhibit marked a milestone for paper-cuts as a folk cultural form. Out of this exhibit, a picture collection, entitled *Yan'an Paper-Cuts* (*Yan'an Jianzhi*) (1981) was published. In it, twenty paper-cuts designed by early Communist intellectuals and included in *Northwestern Paper-Cuts* (1949) were reprinted under a section entitled "Yan'an Paper-Cutting during the Anti-Japanese Period." But, as the editor emphasized, the heart of this collection was the "traditional" motifs created in the art training classes or collected in the regionwide surveys from 1977–1980.

Two motifs from *Yan'an Paper-Cuts* received the most attention and discussion and continue to be the two most representative images of Yan'an paper-cuts. The first is *zhuaji wawa* (Figure 1.6), which is featured on the book's cover. Literally and pictorially, *zhuajiwawa* represents a human figure with braided hair buns. The word *zhuaji* is translated as "holding hair buns,"

FIGURE 1.6. The paper-cut design "Zhuajiwawa" by Chen Shenglan. It was featured as the book cover of *Yan'an Paper-Cuts* (1981).

and *wawa* refers to a baby or a small child. In Yan'an, a paper-cutting design similar to the shape of *zhuajiwawa* is often used in a spirit-summoning ritual to calm colicky babies or to treat minor illnesses. Such a mundane figurative design had not been singled out before. But the unique *zhuajiwawa* design of a woman villager, Chen Shenglan, had caught the eye of Yan'an art cadres in 1977. In place of two hair buns were a pair of roosters. Scholars saw that the image bore a surprising resemblance to that of a female head jade ornament dating back to the Shang Dynasty (1700–1100 B.C.E.), then kept in the Forbidden City Museum in Beijing. On both the *zhuajiwawa* paper-cuts and the jade ornament, a pair of roosters, symbolizing life and vitality, replaced the hair buns. Both representations made use of the metonymic pun of rooster, hair bun, and auspiciousness, all of which share the homonym *ji* in Chinese. The resemblance between a paper-cut design by a peasant woman and an archaeological object more than three thousand years old was astonishing, to say the least (Chen Ruilin 1991: 1; Hu 1989: 193).

FIGURE 1.7. The paper-cut design "Picture of Ox Plowing" (*niu geng tu*) by Bai Fenglan from *Yan'an Paper-Cuts* (1981: 33).

Another motif that brought nationwide attention to Yan'an paper-cuts was "Picture of Ox Plowing (*niu geng tu*)," designed by a peasant woman named Bai Fenglan (Figure 1.7). This design depicts a large tree growing out of an ox's body, with the tree shaped in the face of a deer with branching antlers. No one, including Bai herself, could explain why the pattern had anything to do with "ox plowing," her assigned task at a training class at the Ansai Hall of Culture. This unusual representation was later found to closely resemble a tomb engraving dating to the Han Dynasty (25–220 C.E.). Also entitled "Ox Plowing," the stone carving contains similar representation of an ox with the branching antlers of a deer. Chinese historian and archaeologist Teng Fengqian explains that the two images share the same theme. He suggests that the image of new antlers on male deer signals the arrival of spring and hence the beginning of the agricultural calendar—an archaic calendar based on the seasonal changes of animal behavior and the life cycles of plants (Teng 1988: 1; Jin 1989).

Yan'an Paper-Cuts is a groundbreaking publication that helped to redefine the meanings of folk culture and rural art forms in the PRC. At the back of the book is Jin Zhilin's essay "Introduction to Folk Paper-Cutting in the Yan'an Area." He starts by describing Yan'an as the cradle of Chinese civilization in the Yellow River region. He narrates Yan'an as geographically located where the Yangshao civilization (5000–3000 B.C.E.), the Longshan civilization (2900–2100 B.C.E.), and, then much later, the Qin and Han dynasties thrived.

Jin believes that "an abrupt cessation of economic and social development in the Ming Dynasty, followed by a sealing off of cultural exchanges with the rest of the continent, led to a situation in which a large array of ancient cultural traditions, folk habits, and artistic practices, mostly extinguished in other regions, were preserved here (Jin 1981: 193).

To say that the paper-cut designs of *zhuaji wawa* or "Ox Plowing" preserve an aesthetic tradition many thousand years old is certainly a stretch because its assumes people of the region were not exposed or connected to any modern ideas and practices, including those introduced by the modern Communist revolution and reforms, after those ancient civilizations. Yet what is significant is that Jin and other urban intellectuals and artists struggled to put paper-cuts in what they thought were their rightful place in the folk canon by establishing their relationship with ancient art forms and civilization framework. For instance, Chen Shanqiao, who later became the director of the Ansai Hall of Culture, expressed a similar view in his publications on paper-cuts. The style of paper-cuts, he wrote, "possesses an inherent power and preserves many artistic features of the Han Dynasty" and therefore "provides important historical materials for the study of the northern culture and our nation's customs" (Chen Shanqiao 1989: 220).

These intellectuals' endeavors were not wasted. In 1982, the Yan'an government sent Li Xiufang, a woman villager from rural Yan'an, to stage a paper-cutting performance at the International Labor Day Exhibition in France. In 1985, four elderly women from rural Yan'an—Bai Fenglan, Cao Dianxiang, Hu Fenglian, and Gao Jinai—were invited to teach paper-cutting at the Central Academy of Fine Arts (CAFA) in Beijing (An 2002: 237–238). Hu Bo, a lecturer from CAFA who attended the women's class, explicitly linked paper-cutting with Chinese national culture. As he reflected, "some people looked to the West for our national cultural development. Considering that cultural exchange is crucial to prosperous growth, that is understandable. But one is not going to help with our nation's culture without understanding our cultural essence. . . . Aren't there many nutrients for us to tap into if we can situate ourselves in our own national folk culture?" (Hu 1989: 192–199).

In sum, the *Yan'an Paper-Cuts* charted a radically different intellectual orientation toward understanding tradition and the past. Highlighting the value of the folk, intellectuals of the early 1980s demonstrate that paper-cuts not only reflect villagers' disposition and flavors but reveal forgotten cultural traditions from ancient dynasties (Dang 1989; Hu 1989; Lü 2003a, b).

Before ending this section, three points need to be underscored. First, the renewed appreciation of paper-cuts actually emerged in the late Maoist period, before Deng's market reform. The ability of the art cadres to go into the countryside to conduct surveys and to collect materials was supported by the systems of Halls of Culture and People's Communes, whereby villagers could be called upon to assist in the surveys and to otherwise accommodate the visiting art cadres. Moreover, the success of the training classes was based on the flexible arrangement of the People's Communes that gave work points to villagers who attended the class. That enabled participants to be exempted from their commune labor and allowed the classes to be held at a low cost (Zhang 2009: 86).

Second, perhaps the most crucial factor behind the creative success was the extraordinary respect given to the villagers by the urban professionals and artists. Putting aside their socialist modernist framework, the art cadres saw the traditional motifs in a new light and dared to ask new questions about the images. For their part, the villagers, relieved of possible accusation and criticism, were more than willing to explain how the images were related to shamanic rituals of healing, religious festivals, and even local sexual metaphors.

Images of sexual unions are indeed abundant in folk art forms as well as crucial to the ritual, household arrangement, and cosmological mapping of the peasant world (Bourdieu 1990: 272–280). Bakhtin (1993) uses the term "grotesque realism" to describe a folk style and principle that put much emphasis on the bodily organs and functions related to growth, pregnancy, childbirth, and rebirth. Similar motifs of sexual reunion, excess consumption, and fertility of the people, of the animals, and of the earth abound in Chinese folk paper-cuts, through which northwestern Chinese peasants celebrate and aspire to the sensory pleasure of reproduction and regeneration. Interestingly, both capitalist and socialist aesthetics put forward principles of severance, asceticism, and privacy in order to expunge the symbolic degradation of moral authority inherent in folk cultural forms (Bakhtin 1993: 18–20). The training classes, in this sense, provided an exceptional and relatively open space for exchanges between urban socialist intellectuals and villagers, with the intellectuals attempting to articulate a new language to speak of the unexplored meanings and metaphors of the folk rural society on the one hand, and the villagers given more respect to share their local knowledge, values, and worldviews on the other.

Third, although *Yan'an Paper-Cuts* was compiled by the Yan'an art cadres, it was edited by Jiang Feng, the reason being that Renmin Publishing House would publish it only if Jiang Feng served as the editor.[10] After twenty-one years of political marginalization, Jiang Feng reemerged as the director of CAFA, special advisor of the Ministry of Culture, and a member of the Political Consultative Council (Andrews 1994: 386–389). Once again exercising a great deal of power in the art world, Jiang Feng reaffirmed the paper-cut art form as a "product after labor, not yet aesthetically perfect ... [but which] would gradually mature through continuous exploration" (Jiang 1981: preface).[11]

Jiang Feng's support represented an official party-state endorsement of folk paper-cuts as a legitimate art form in the PRC. This in turn was part and parcel of the party-state's reconsideration of the place of China's traditional culture and history in the new China. The early Communist urban intellectual in the 1940s attempted to foster "a new village culture" in the border region, hoped to answer the pressing problems of rural decline, and envisioned a Communist perspective of the countryside: enthusiastic and empowered (Hung 1994: 266). They refashioned paper-cuts into a modern socialist art form by discounting their imagery and narrative themes connecting to a traditional past, thus highlighting the CCP's role in breaking away from the past and charting a new course for the country.

The Yan'an intellectual artists in the late 1970s were quite different. Jin and others were much more inclined to emphasize the linkage of Yan'an paper-cuts with ancient cultural and historical elements and to speak of a consistent national culture, uninterrupted by the socialist period. By stressing "going among the people" (*shenru minjian*), they conflated the concepts of "folk traditions" (*minjian*) and "the masses" (*dazhong*). This conflation enabled them to explore folk art forms without being labeled as "feudal," thus successfully aligning the CCP's cultural policy with understanding, instead of refuting, traditional knowledge.

Since the 1980s, Yan'an paper-cutting has become a brand in and of itself. It was described as "relics on the ground" (*dishang wenwu*) in both official and commercial narratives of Yan'an folk culture, seen as revealing ancient aesthetics, archaic philosophy, and historical knowledge. It has since prompted much discussion on the relationship between paper-cuts and ancient civilizations (Dang 1989; Ansaixian Weiyuanhui Wenshi Ziliao Yanjiu Weiyuanhui 1989). The significance of this new understanding of paper-cuts is that the CCP as a radical political power ready to turn culture into politics was transformed. Instead, the Chinese state has allowed the logic of the folk rural society to coexist with that of political appropriation, albeit uneasily.

The Folk Culture Paradigm: Making Civilization and Recording History

The socialist realist understanding of paper-cuts was eventually transformed to a more cultural-oriented interpretation throughout the 1980s. After *Yan'an Paper-Cuts* (1981) came out, Lü Shengzhong, a leading folk scholar and artist, reworked the relationship between paper-cutting and folk culture in his book *Chinese Folk Paper-Cuttings* (*Zhongguo Minjian Jianzhi*) (1987).[12] The author of more than ten monographs on traditional New Year prints, paper-cuts, and, more recently, four volumes on Chinese folk traditions (Lü 2003a, b, 2004a, b), Lü maintains that it is important not to study paper-cuts through their "superficial forms" (1987: 3). He argues that paper-cutting designs are *not* direct representations of the real world, and their meanings should be allegorically or metaphorically interpreted. His classic example concerns a design in which two men are sitting down and smoking pipes, and between them is a child who is also smoking. At first, Lü thought that the design was a direct record of daily rural life because it was common for children in North China to smoke. But he was later told that the design was named "Passing the Fire" (*chuanhuo*) which means "to carry on one's ancestral line" (*chuanzong jiedai*) (Lü 2004b: 96). The paper-cuts therefore conveyed the auspicious meaning of a blessed family in which the father and son would continue the family line.

Lü might be the first scholar to understand fully the extensive use of paper-cuts in various rural spiritual, even shamanic rituals, including soul-calling (*zhaohun*), rain-asking (*qiuyu*), and sun-asking (*qiuqing*), in north China rural society. Paper-cuts in these contexts in particular contain multiple layers of meanings implicated through the metonymic or metaphoric use of language in relation to the power of a talisman and/or local deities. A paper-cut design of "Fish Playing with Lotus" (*yu xi lian*), commonly displayed at weddings, for instance, not only mimics the shapes of fish and lotus to suggest male and female sexual union, but taps the power of fertility from fish to suggest the unspoken desire for human reproduction. Similarly, when villagers displayed a paper-cut design of an ox on the door during the SARS epidemic in 2003 in Yan'an, it was because they believed the protective power of the ox could be released by the mimetic capacity of paper-cuts. This might be what anthropologist James Frazer calls "the sympathetic magic of contact" (on the door) in which the paper-cut became a magical shield against external attacks (Frazer 1911: 52).

Anthropological inquiry into the phenomenon of mimesis is useful here (Benjamin 1968; Caillois 1984; Taussig 1993). In these discussions, the word "mimesis" designates not only a production of an imitation or copy but also "a behavior in which a subject actively engages in making oneself similar to an Other, assumes the character and power of the original, and even affects the original" (Taussig 1993: 45–46). Similarly, what is stored in paper-cutting is not its imitating quality. Instead, it enables an abstract connection between the matter and its visual image, concept and sign, the original and a copy, human and spiritual. Its power lies beyond replicating the phenomenological world, but it mediates between the sensuous particularity of the reality and its interaction with our perceptibility. It works simultaneously as an image, a copy, and a kind of spiritual power in rural China. Such aspects and power of paper-cutting, nevertheless, were taboo throughout the Maoist period and were deliberately avoided.[13]

This renewed understanding of paper-cutting as folk magic and ritual power also brought forth a different view of the practitioners. In *Goodbye Tradition (Zaijian chuantong)* (Lü 2004b), Lü spoke of rural women as "the talented mothers who are the last successor of traditional folk culture and who passed the time-honored civilization to modern times" (2004b: 8). They are not the illiterate, oppressed daughters-in-law as represented in the Communist narrative of salvation, but the knowledgeable spiritual facilitators and composers of daily ritual celebrations in rural society. His view that the countryside and in particular women villagers are capable of retaining ancient cultural motifs and historical knowledge has become influential in understanding paper-cutting in the economic reform era. Throughout the 1990s and 2000s, the view of the rural as an authentic realm of tradition and a redemptive refuge from the constraints of modern development has become a new paradigm of understanding or rediscovering traditional culture in China (Jin 2001, 2002; Li 2003; Qiao 2004, 2005).

For the Chinese intellectuals, folk paper-cuts in the late 1980s became increasingly a new topic of reflecting a concept of Chinese culture and tradition as ancient and unchanging. Paper-cuts have also become a key traditional cultural symbol just when China is determined to become more like the West economically. As Lü Shengzhong wrote in *Chinese Folk Paper-Cuttings* (1987), "Our highest national culture is being shaken by foreign culture. Now we can know about the world better but at the same time understand that a national culture can gain world respect only if it does not follow the others. Re-understanding our own national culture has therefore become an urgent topic. . . . Many have laid eyes on the folk. People are surprised to know that hidden in the bottom level of our country is a big new world" (Lü 1987: 25; my translation).

Yan'an paper-cuts were particularly well-suited for the intellectual quest to narrate a time-honored Chinese national culture precisely because the Yan'an region remained relatively underdeveloped throughout the 1980s and 1990s compared to the coastal urban areas of the country. Ironically, therefore, Yan'an paper-cuts have come to signify an authentic space capable of retaining traditional cultural elements rather than, as it had, a socialist rupture from traditional Confucian culture. As a result of heightened intellectual concern and coverage, Yan'an paper-cuts have drawn hundreds and thousands of collectors, art connoisseurs, fine art students, photographers, journalists, folklorists, and historians from all over the country and even from overseas to Yan'an, all hoping to collect, document, learn, or simply see paper-cutting designs.

Paper-Cutting Artists in Contemporary Ansai County, Yan'an

The notion that historical motifs and ancient beliefs can be preserved through paper-cuts captivated not only tourists but the anthropologist as well. Although my informants frequently mentioned popular jokes about Ansai's distance from modernity, I went to Ansai on a newly constructed highway. But once we were away from the town center, we traveled on muddy trails alongside hilly cliffs dotted by cavehouses. Ansai county was considered an underdeveloped region within the Yan'an region with its rural villagers earning about 2,399 RMB annually in 2005 while the national figure for rural villagers that year was 3,255 RMB.[14] In addition to its economic marginalization, Ansai was also divided between the haves and the have-nots. From the 1990s, private oil developers began to operate there, and associated industries such as transportation proliferated. Individuals engaged with these new industries started to accumulate wealth quickly, but the majority of rural residents still had no electricity, phone connections, or tap water supply, and most remained impoverished even into the early 2000s (Gu 2003).

In 2004, I had the opportunity to live for two months with the fifty-three-year-old Hao Guizhen, a paper-cutting artist who was recommended to me by the Ansai County Hall of Culture and whose designs have been published in *Fine Selections of Ansai Folk Paper-Cuts* (*Ansai minjian jianpin jianzhi*) (Ansaixian Wenhua Wenwuguan 1999). Hao had a round face, short hair, and smiling eyes. Sun exposure had inscribed deep lines on her forehead, and she had lost all her teeth during her fifties. Her plastic dentures did not fit well and moved whenever she talked, giving the illusion that a second mouth was trying to speak, but with a muted voice. On the first day of my visit in 2004, Hao showed me her beautiful embroidered beddings and many paper-cutting designs. However, my naive expectation of finding the source of the Yellow River civilization as personified in a rural feminine figure was quickly shattered as I became familiar with Hao during the two months that followed.

Hao, along with some twenty other women villagers, belonged to the 1990s generation of trainees in the Ansai Hall of Culture training classes. In 1993, art cadres went to Hao's village inquiring after women with nimble

FIGURE 1.8. The paper-cutting artist Hao in her paper-cuts–decorated cavehouse.

fingers (*shouqiao di poyi*), and the villagers unanimously nominated her. In return for going to the class, she received a "salary" for leaving farm work and housework behind. In fact, when Hao told me about her experience of training, she used the word *shangban* (working for a salary) at the Hall of Culture. Hao said she was the in-house "worker" employed to create cutouts modeled on famous motifs of the 1980s, such as Bai Fenglan's "Ox Plowing" design. She used the term *fuzhi*, meaning to duplicate, to refer to her work. Her reproductions of popular motifs were sold at the Hall of Culture to tourists. In response to increasing demand for this folk art, the Hall of Culture had transformed itself into a minifactory to reproduce paper-cut designs. After serving in the Hall of Culture, Hao returned home and started to make and sell her own designs. But because she lived quite far away from the town center, she did not have many customers (Figure 1.8).

Hao's experience at the Hall of Culture was precisely what Wang Jing describes about cultural transformation and production in the post-1990s China (2001). Wang argues that culture was reconstructed in the 1990s as the site where capital can be accumulated and profits can be guaranteed. At

Paper-Cuts in Modern China   53

the same time, the state became increasingly interested in expanding and promoting culture specifically linked to a region's reputation, branding, and associated industries. Folk paper-cuts in the 1990s, claimed by the Yan'an government to symbolize an ancient civilization, became closely related to the region's tourist, business, and investment opportunities.

Hao Guizhen might be a talented artist in this expanding folk paper-cutting industry where the interests of government legitimacy, business profit, and regional branding became intertwined. But she remained an impoverished villager, only remotely connected to a developing urban Yan'an and the new world of capital and cultural tourism. The paper-cutting designs hanging on her walls might be what scholars consider to be living traces of a glorious civilization. But even though she recited the symbolic meanings of the motifs to me, I found that they had little place or meaning in her rural daily life. During the months I stayed with her, it was apparent that she felt socially and economically stressed. We ate modestly, usually plain noodles and potatoes. Hao also felt unsafe, fearing someone would break into her home. I eventually found out that her anxiety was related to the loss of her husband a few years earlier, and the financial stress of supporting her son to attend a cooking school in the city. Bearing much stigmatization as a financially stressed widow in a rural village, Hao is not living out the prosperity and auspiciousness expressed in her paper-cuts.

Since the 1990s, official government narratives have attempted to present paper-cuts as primitive fossils. Implicit is the assumption that rural folk culture contains traces or "remnants" of earlier stages of cultural development. But if urban intellectuals in the 1990s still attempted to project—through paper-cuts as an art form—the possibility of locating the "true" Chinese culture and envisioning a new cultural path for modernizing China, such attempts have failed to address two problems.

The first is the tendency of culture to become capital itself. This phenomenon, dubbed *wenhua datai, jingji changxi*, means that culture is merely the staging platform while economic interest is the real performance. Another problem is the vanishing of traditional cultural practices in the context of rapid urbanization and agrarian decline. During the Chinese New Year in Yan'an, I seldom saw anyone display "window flowers" since rice paper windows have been replaced by glass windows. With the exception of artists who make their living by selling paper-cuts and those living in very remote villages, no one else seemed to be making them anymore. In addition, many women in today's Yan'an no longer use scissors everyday because clothing, shoes, and bedding are all commercially ready-made. Paper-cuts have ceased to be sought after except by tourists.

Even Qiao Xiaoguang, professor and director of the Intangible Cultural Heritage Research Center in CAFA, Beijing, had to admit the fast disappearance of paper-cutting practices and various ritual celebrations in the Loess area during his survey in the early 2000s even though he calls them a living culture in his book *Living Culture* (2004). Qiao laments that "the cultural ecology in rural China was like the sea at low tide, rapidly disappearing every second" (2004: 25–26). Worse still, he finds that even the Spring Festival (the Chinese New Year), supposedly the most important ritual celebration in the country, was also vanishing and villagers celebrated it through watching the government-sponsored television program, the Chinese New Year Gala, which features various folk song-and-dance performances of the country.

The disparities between the official discourse on paper-cuts as associated with an unchanging Yellow River civilization—and my field observations of the practice—expose the "internal orientalist" discourse that shapes folk culture as the cultural carrier of ancient Chinese tradition. Such discourse, as suggested by Louisa Schein, not only fuels the fascination of the urban Chinese for the peasant and the folk, but it also detaches one from understanding the harsh material reality of villagers and the constructed relations between their contemporary practice and a certain time-honored national culture by the Chinese state (Schein 2000: 100–131).

In the new millennium, such internal orientalist imagination is almost always shattered when a rural area transforms into a modernizing/urbanizing one. As Yan'an increasingly urbanizes, Yan'an paper-cuts become the site through which intellectuals lament the loss of an idyllic landscape and call for the preservation of vanishing traditional cultures. In these discussions, however, scholars were inevitably drawn into technical discussions and strategic planning for staging paper-cutting demonstrations at international or global cultural platforms such as UNESCO (Qiao 2004). Ansai paper-cuts eventually were included in the first national list of intangible cultural heritage under the category of "folk art" by the Chinese State Council in 2006.[15] Yanchuan paper-cuts were entered into the third batch of the national list in 2009 but under the category of "traditional art."[16] The contradictory drives of retaining more national traditions yet linking with the world remained intertwined. But perhaps no one would deny that today's paper-cutting has entered the age of "culture as capital," in which its designs, sales, and ranking in the heritage lists are intimately connected to local governments' tourism revenue, scholar's research funding, and the market share of folk commodities.

Paper-Cutting in the New Millennium: Market Yearnings and the Neoliberal Form of Human

In July 2004, when I was in Yanchuan, a rustic township east of Yan'an city, I ran into a group of people in urban outfits with expensive photographic equipment. The group was from a New York–based art foundation called the Long March Foundation, which had just finished a survey on paper-cutting and had collected more than 10,000 pieces. The foundation director told me that the survey project was planning major exhibitions of these paper-cuts, including at the Shanghai Art Biennial in late 2004, the Taiwan Art Biennial of the same year, the Vancouver Art Gallery in 2005, and Sao Paulo in 2007 (Figure 1.9).[17]

In order to conduct this survey and persuade villagers to contribute paper-cuts, the foundation recruited volunteers who could speak local dialects. One of these volunteers was Liu Jieqiong, daughter of the aforementioned paper-cutting master Gao Fenglian. Liu was herself a famous paper-cutting artist in Yan'an (Ai Sheng 1998).[18] When I met her in 2004, she was married to a businessman and residing in Yanchuan town.

After three months of surveying in the rural area, the foundation survey committee asked the volunteer team members to write up their thoughts to be included in the exhibits and published in the foundation catalog: *The Great Survey of Paper-Cutting in Yanchuan County* (Lu and Tung 2004). The aim was to include in the exhibit the survey process and experiences, including its difficulty, frustration, and joy. Liu's writing was not published in the foundation catalog, but she shared it in the committee evaluation meeting. What follows is a combination of Liu's writing and other survey volunteers' writings together with Liu's verbal comments about the experience, which I gathered from several visits to her home.

In her personal writing of the paper-cutting survey, Liu wrote of the experience she had visiting 46 villages and 5 schools and surveying 1,408 people in Tugang *"xiang."* Xiang is the lowest rural administrative unit within a province in China. In those villages, Liu needed first to seek permission from the party cadres and then assemble the villagers together and try to persuade them to contribute paper-cutting designs and fill in the survey forms. The difficulty involved was enormous as villagers were suspicious of the outsiders' visit and mistakenly took the surveyors as government officials responsible for executing the one-child policy. Many villagers ran away from the surveyors and simply refused to talk. In addition, there were no monetary rewards for participating in the survey, which also reduced the number of willing subjects.

FIGURE 1.9. Paper-cutting artists, Yan'an intellectuals, and the author (far right) sitting on an oversized paper-cut design.

Apart from the difficulty of their survey work, what most troubled the team members was the utter poverty of the area. In her piece, Liu describes the typical villager in Tugang as "living in a backward primitive society." In Shadi village, she was shocked by the "ignorant and uneducated way of life" when she heard of a man who had died because he was poisoned by the insecticide which he had put on his own clothes to kill fleas. Other survey volunteers shared her dismay. One participant recalled how dumbfounded he was to discover that the villagers had nothing to cook but watermelon skin rinds. Another recalled that what made the deepest impression on her was seeing an old woman villager with bound feet (Lu and Tung 2004).

During the survey, Liu met with four teenage girls, two of whose mothers had left their poverty-stricken villages long ago. Taken with their beautiful paper-cuts, Liu wanted to bring the girls to Yanchuan town for further training, but their fathers and the other villagers resisted mightily. Liu wrote of one of the girls: "her father was a stubborn guy. It was painful to see the girl's eyes, full of the hope of leaving here. But the father was like the elderly Runtu in Lu Xun's story.[19] Any child growing up in a mountainous area like this, no matter how clever and spirited, would become someone who does not turn a hair anymore." Eventually, the four girls managed to leave their village and came to live with Liu in Yanchuan town. Liu now addressed them as "daughters" and instructed them in her style of paper-cuts. I did not ask how they adapted to their new lives but can speculate that the girls contributed to an increase in Liu's paper-cutting production and sales in return for Liu's teaching.

Instead of unearthing ritual practices and age-old customs, the survey seems rather to have been more of an exercise in cultural shock. Survey members were disoriented and emotionally disturbed by all the evidence of family breakdown and destitution at the margins of rural Yan'an. Liu, for instance, invoked Lu Xun to depict its economic backwardness and cultural stubbornness, reminiscent of the rural China before 1949. But perhaps the most significant aspect of the surveyors' reflections is the language they used to persuade villagers to contribute their paper-cuts. The following comes from Liu Jieqiong's writing, but she echoed the same sentiments in person when I visited her Yanchuan home. Liu wrote:

> I told them about the Yellow River tourism, economic prosperity, and the road to riches. I said folk paper-cutting had become a tourist attraction somewhere else where the villagers' income has improved as a result. Moreover, the women's social status has been raised, too. Before paper-cutting, women were inferior. They labored in the field, burnt their skin to the color of an eggplant, and still had to mill the grain at home! They tired themselves out like fools, but some still risked divorcing. Now some of their incomes can reach 10,000 RMB per year. Now they are completely liberated and their status is lifted like from the level of grandson to the granddad. With my own experience, I said I have grown to be famous and live like a human being (*ren mo ren yang*).

Assumptions of individual freedom and opportunities are readily discernible in Liu's trope of success. Paper-cutting became associated with the possibility of these assumptions. These assumptions might be understood as part of the prevailing neoliberal discourse of development and success in today's China, one that celebrates the self-engineering potential and capital accumulation capacity of the *homo economicus* under turbulent market conditions. In the rural areas, it is not uncommon that local government officials mobilize neoliberal narratives for their own political or economic agendas (Yan 2003). Officials often encourage rural residents to become self-enterprising citizen-subjects, competitive and efficient, yet ignoring the structural problems they face.

In rural Tugang, however, the situation is more complicated as Liu Jieqiong is neither an urban intellectual nor a government official. I think the instance instead reveals shocking socioeconomic polarizations even between town residents and more remote village residents within the same rural area of Yanchuan. It was the extreme rural poverty and underdevelopment that shocked Liu (who also grew up in a rural village) and made her ever more determined to share paper-cutting as an upward-mobile opportunity with her fellow county people. Her sympathetic narrative, however, only echoes prevailing urban neoliberal logic that endorses the dominant version of urban good life (getting out of the rural mountains), as well as a particular form of being human (an urbanite who can make a decent living without getting dirty and sunburned). In the end, Liu's narrative exposes the unresolvable contradiction inherent in the practice of folk tradition today: villagers have to leave their rural hometown and deploy their nimble fingers to sell folk art in order to get rid of poverty. Liu's linking of paper-cuts with women's liberation is reminiscent of one of the early Communist visions of promoting social equality. But her vision of gender equality is no longer attached to a revolutionary regime change that would redistribute material wealth and values between the city and the countryside. Instead, gender equality is imagined through encouraging rural villagers to participate in an emerging tourist economy that often thrives on the basis of such rural-urban divide.

Conclusion and Further Reflections

This chapter examines the multiplicity of practices, ideologies, and logics of Yan'an paper-cuts from the Yan'an period to the post-2000 era. The production of paper-cuts is no simple traditional practice, but rather engages heavily with and is constituted by different state-engineered discourses, political campaigns, economic motivations, modernization debates, and a plurality of actors. The tropes of gender and rural cultural tradition are juxtaposed in all these portraits. But their heterogeneous meanings and the different relations between them in specific historical moments need to be underscored. In this concluding section, I explicate these meanings and relations with three different logics: political appropriation, rural society, and capital.

During Mao's era, urban intellectuals understood paper-cuts as related to the economically and culturally marginalized rural areas, yet also as something that could become a modern socialist art form under Communist governance. The early socialist intellectual deployment of various "old forms," including paper-cuts, was to appeal to the illiterate rural masses and yet still communicate sociopolitical messages. Intellectuals, such as Jiang

Feng, were largely suspicious of the concepts, metaphors, and moral values embedded in the old forms and regarded them as inherently backward and ideologically suspect (Holm 1991). Ai Qing's and Gu Yuan's attempts to incorporate woodcut designs, new motifs, and modern styles into paper-cut design in turn demonstrate the difficulty of drawing a distinction between the "use of old forms" and "the development of a new literature and art." For these intellectuals, liberation of the impoverished peasants, including women, certainly did not come from practicing paper-cutting. Liberation could come only through the building of the Communist government and the subsequent, social, economic, and cultural reforms. But paper-cuts in the Yan'an period and later Mao's era clearly demonstrate a dominant logic of political appropriation in which the Communist intellectuals endeavored to pursue the challenging goals of communicating with the broader masses with acceptable cultural forms and still inventing a modern socialist art form without reference to traditional content.

The Communist state after 1949 did bring about a drastic gender transformation by incorporating women into various political, social, and economic activities and by reinterpreting the traditional meanings of femininities and masculinities in both the public and private spheres, especially through the state-owned enterprises in the urban areas (Rofel 1999). But, of course, many of the old customs, old institutions, and old attitudes persisted (Gao 1994), resulting in a double burden for rural women. This became especially vivid to me during my 2004 visit to Yan'an when many elderly women recalled a scene from the Maoist past: one needed to start needlework at night after a day of collective field labor, plus endless housework of cooking, cleaning, and putting the children to sleep. On the *kang* bed, they straightened their backs, crossed their legs, and started needlework. With dim lighting from a candle and later an oil lamp, they fixed torn outfits by patchwork (*budin*); made new clothes from old fabric; sewed shoes; made pillowcases, bedsheets and blanket covers for a family of six; and stitched their shoe soles tight enough for work in the fields. When asked why needlework was related to paper-cutting, all of them smiled. They said a night of needlework often ended with lots of paper scraps and cloth fragments, and the creative minds among them would sometimes make paper-cuts out of the scraps to decorate their modest cavehouses.

Paper-cutting and needlework, as gendered survival skills, were therefore well integrated into the gender division of domestic labor in the rural context. While telling women to engage in production outside of the home in order to be emancipated from domestic bondage, the Communist party-state nevertheless withheld drastic change within the family in order to win loyalty from its main base of support—the male peasantry (Johnson

1983). The Communist state could not entirely tackle the issue of the double burden that had since been imposed on women. In between the suffering associated with double burden and food scarcity on the one hand, and the "vision of liberation" associated with collective labor and literacy class on the other, rural women were indeed empowered, broke away from some traditional roles, and yet also became subjected to a new form of gender inequality (Guo 2003).

The connections between paper-cuts, rural cultural traditions, and an ideal femininity become only more conspicuous and articulated in the post-Mao period. Numerous paper-cutting monographs published in the 1990s cited the proverb "If you give birth to a girl, have a nimble-fingered one, she will improvise paper-cuts of pomegranates and peony" (*sheng nvzi, yaoqiao de, shiliu mudan maojiao de*) to affirm the connection between ideal domestic womanhood and the practice of paper-cutting. It expresses the aspiration for a newborn baby girl to possess skillful hands capable of making paper-cuts. But because pomegranate and peony are symbols of fertility and sexual love, the proverb carries a hidden meaning as well: hope for a skillful daughter who is also a fertile daughter-in-law. The practice of paper-cutting thus becomes associated with womanly virtue, defined by her fertility and domestic labor in reproducing the family, associations that have been downplayed in the Maoist period.

The intellectual articulation of folk paper-cuts as a symbolic logic of rural society, outside of the previous socialist political logic, was pioneering at the time. But the most recent discourse of folk paper-cuts eventually remade a connection between folk tradition and a conservative understanding of femininity in the market era. The discourse contends that the countryside and, in particular, the women villagers become bearers of ancient cultural motifs and the ancient civilization. In this new representation of folk paper-cuts, there is an alignment of the feminine and the rural with an authentic realm of rural experience and traditions. This yearning for the rural and the feminine as emblematic of a nonfragmented identity and an uninterrupted tradition, I think, is related to not only what Felski called a "redemptive refuge" from the chaos and anxiety of modern development; it also is related to a new form of imagining femininity, masculinity, and the meaning of patriarchy in post-Mao China. Today folk paper-cuts and women villagers have ironically come together to stand for an idealized rural past and the nostalgia for traditional feminine virtue.

Precisely because the assumption in the recent discourse of folk paper-cuts is intrinsically urban and masculine, the discussions of it with broader cultural debates of Chinese modernity, Confucian traditions, and the implication of Western theories seldom treated the women practitioners as fully vested and legitimate participants. Jin Zhilin's description of Yan'an as a historical geopolitical hub might be valid. But it also risks dismissing the creative initiatives of the women villagers, valorizing instead the idea of folk-culture-as-fossil. It attributes the villagers' creativity to a certain notion of cultural stagnation and therefore elides the great sociopolitical upheavals that had drastically altered Yan'an's landscape during the last century. Jin's invitation of the four women villagers to teach at the Central Academy of Fine Arts in 1984 was salutary. But, in fact, these women, who had contributed so many designs to the Yan'an government and who had helped promote the region's tourism, lived in dire poverty during their old age (Gu 2003: 562). Moreover, although they were encouraged to create their own designs, they were also often told that "traditional designs" were what collectors and tourists wanted.

In the end, then, women villagers are seen as rather passive cultural bearers of the so-called Yellow River civilization rather than as autonomous creative agents. Their assigned task of preserving tradition and the idealized Chinese past reinforces the broader post-Mao understanding of the countryside as a place of unchanging tradition. The vigorous debates of the Maoist period on the rural area as the future of China, on the use of folk art forms, and on the perceived vulgarism in folk culture vanished altogether. What emerged in the 1990s was a wholesale acceptance of tradition as a virgin origin to be discovered and preserved.

Since the late 1990s, the narrative of paper-cutting has further articulated a new logic: the logic of capital in which the meanings of culture and tradition are again transformed. As shown in the *Great Survey of Paper-Cutting in Yanchuan County*, the economic, social, and cultural differences between the rural and the urban became even more polarized by the year 2000. If the early "going down to the village" movement envisioned a new future for the countryside under the guidance of the educated party-affiliated artists, and if the 1980s cultural fever debate viewed the rural as bearer of ancient Chinese culture, post-2000 is markedly different. In the new millennium, the rural area is recast as the place of lack, as economically static and culturally ever more backward (Yan 2008). This notion of the dark rural now justifies more than ever state-initiated development programs, such as Yellow River tourism, in hopes of improving livelihoods.

Today, Yan'an paper-cuts are almost exclusively a commodity. Their folk quality and bold designs are little more than a good sales pitch. They have little to do with the historical meanings of Chinese civilization, or at best only very superficially. Rural women's liberation is once again hailed, but this time it is an interpellation of a neoliberal version of urban freedom and human dignity. It is worth being reminded, however, of how neoliberalism often operates as an exception and regularly marks out the excludable subjects (Ong 2007: 5). The "nimble fingers" of the migrant women (*dagongmei*) in the industrial zones are often associated with efficiency. But the nimble fingers, instead of equipping women for urban success, have often been deployed as a technique of discipline and subjected them into flexible and disposable workers (Lee 1998a; Pun 2005). Much the same can be said of the nimble fingers of the village women paper-cutting artists.

Lastly and most ironically, the three contradictory logics of capital, folk rural society, and political appropriation operate comfortably together through paper-cuts in the new millennium. The contemporary Chinese state and the urban intellectuals draw on these various logics rather effectively for purposes of tourist development, regional branding, and simultaneously promoting the socialist legacy and heritage conservation. In the promotion of folk paper-cuts, the rural feminine functions persistently as a signifier for the native soil and a naturalized sense of continuity with history that the modern, urban Chinese no longer possesses. Gender and rural differences continue to be two fundamental references by which Chinese cultural and modern development has been conceived and legitimated. Through the representation of paper-cuts, the binary oppositions of gender and rural/urban relationship have become part of the meanings of Chinese modernity itself. In the end, paper-cuts seem to become that flexible cultural symbol of nostalgic desires, where the state and urban intellectuals seek legitimacy and profits and interpret the meanings of a cultural modernity for a rising China.

CHAPTER 2

Narrative Battle

Fabricating Folk Paper-Cutting as an Intangible Heritage

Paper-cutting has grown from a finger-size domestic craft to a painting-size exhibitive art today. But it is not just art. It is now an intangible heritage to be preserved and promoted. In Xiaocheng Folk Art Village (Xiaocheng *Minjian Yishu Cun*), Yan'an, paper-cutting was a main focus around which rural development, heritage preservation, and cultural tourism were vigorously debated. Xiaocheng Folk Art Village (hereafter Xiaocheng) was a place of no interest a decade ago. Since 2001, its name has become well-known because it was the rural base upon which the Central Academy of Fine Arts (CAFA), Beijing, wished to list paper-cutting as an intangible cultural heritage at the UNESCO.[1]

A search for Xiaocheng village in Yanchuan county on the internet produces over a hundred thousand results. The place is often described as a remote and ancient village by the Yellow River, sealed off from broader social change, where men have farmed and women have woven through time-honored history. It is said that Xiaocheng retains numerous ancient customs, such as folk religious rituals and paper-cutting. In Xiaocheng, one can view the spectacular Yellow River Meander called "Bay of Heaven and Earth" (*Qian Kun Wan*). *Qian Kun* means an origin, in which river and mountain, fluid and solid, twist and turn, and yin and yang are the cycles of lives. Tourist books say that the legendary figure *Fuxi*, ancestor of the human, might have been inspired by the Yellow River Meander at Xiaocheng, and that he later came out with the cosmological knowledge of life and death, female and male, yin and yang ("Quanjing Yan'an" Editorial Committee 2008: 19) (Figure 2.1).

FIGURE 2.1. The view of the "Bay of Heaven and Earth" (*Qian Kun Wan*) as seen from the Xiaocheng Folk Art Village.

Xiaocheng's best attraction is the living heritage of paper-cutting, and women villagers here hum a *xintianyou*, a regional folk song, as they turn the songs' themes into paper-cut designs. Xiaocheng also features a thousand-year-old cavehouse and a folk museum exhibiting peasants' agricultural and daily household tools. Visitors can stay at a cavehouse homestay, sample a local noodle specialty, buy tailor-made paper-cuts and embroideries, and watch a *yangge* song-and-dance performance. Xiaocheng regularly attracts thousands of visitors as urban middle-class travelers seek holiday refuge for scenic canyons and cultural tourism in the Loess. In 2011, its annual visitors reached 86,000, quite an impressive number considering its remoteness from major city centers and conventional historical sites.

This chapter explores the meanings of heritage making in contemporary rural Yan'an. It documents some major moments in the building of Xiaocheng as a container of tradition and the making of folk paper-cuts as an intangible cultural heritage. It asks how villagers, urban intellectuals, the local government, and the Chinese central government participated in the process. Specifically, it examines how differentiated meanings of heritage are constructed and understood by different actors. This chapter understands the concept of heritage authenticity as not only linked to the invention of tradition (Hobsbawm and Ranger 1983) or the "tourist gaze" (Urry 1990) but also to the notions of the "vernacular history" of the commoners and the rebuilding of a dislocated community (Dicks 2004). As I demonstrate, the establishment of Xiaocheng Folk Art Village is no simple invention of national tradition. My main argument is that heritage making in China is a critical process of what I call a "narrative battle." A narrative battle opens up a new condition of possibilities of producing and reinterpreting local history, knowledge, and tradition against the national state narrative. It is a site where new local knowledge contests dominant and official understanding of tradition. This chapter examines the new interpretations of folk culture in the process of authenticating folk paper-cuts as an intangible heritage in Yan'an.

Staging Authenticity in a Village Theme Park

The construction of a heritage site is not a unique Chinese experience but a major element of modern tourism where visitors search for authenticity and an experience of nostalgia (MacCannell 1973). All over the world, tourists flock to country houses and reconstructed historical sites to collect signs of the familiar and to express regret for the loss of an idealized rural or dynastic past (Lowenthal 1985). David Lowenthal said that the mass appeal of historical theme parks and museums has led to a worldwide "heritage explosion" (Lowenthal 1998b: 3).

In China since the 1990s, hundreds of folk museums and "ancient towns" (*guzhen*) reconstructed from existing rural villages have joined such heritage explosions, feeding popular quests for rural humble roots and pristine origins. Many reconstructed ancient towns highlight historical architecture, old alleys and workshops, a flowing river along residents' houses, local food and crafts, and "simple and harmonious" village lives and traditions (Pred and Watts 1992: 146–147). In general, the making of ancient towns is an attempt to fix the boundaries of an essential China, where the national past and essence is exoticized in a distant village space. In turn, urban tourists are the modern subjects who, in an effort to seek the authentic "national," find meanings and continuity in a world of rapid changes. Nostalgia for the nonmodern world is a major driving element behind what Urry (1990) refers to as the "tourist gaze" in such rural heritage seeking. Griffiths, Chapman, and Christiansen have called the recent commodification, proliferation, and consumption of idyllic representations and the experience of rurality in China a "romantic reappraisal" of urban consumer values over a rural landscape, people, and customs (2010).

Unsurprisingly, many reconstructed ancient villages and towns are made as replicas for display purposes, and most of their original residents have moved out. Some might condemn such ancient villages as "village theme parks," full of fake settings, "fabricated" heritage, and contrived scenes (Lowenthal 1998a). But recent discussion has shown that the binary opposite between authenticity and replica, history and heritage, is a constructed one. Labeling heritage as fake or fabricated owns an underlying assumption that authenticity and history are always associated with the original, a sense of genuine, or the real, while the replica of heritage is marked as a copy, simulated, and hence, unreal. Tim Oakes argues that such dichotomy prevents understanding authenticity as equally constituted by historical, social, and cultural processes (1998).

The Splendid China theme park in Shenzhen is a good case in point. A miniaturized landscape of "timeless China" set within the most modern and transient city, Shenzhen, Splendid China showcases village architectures from many regions of China (Anagnost 1993). While some of the village architectures are uprooted from their place of origin in their entirety, there are many more "replicas" juxtaposed alongside the "real" ones. Visitors can see northern Shaanxi mud cavehouses built from concrete carefully disguised as mud, on which plastic red peppers and ears of corn hang. But once visitors step in the "fake" cavehouse, their interest is immediately turned into the "nostalgic ideal" informed by the old furniture, black-and-white pictures, and a much more modest and simple version of rural life. In other words, the authenticity of a cavehouse is not so much judged by its replica materials but is partly constituted by those objects and decorations associated with the memory of the impoverished national past. Authenticity, instead of possessing any intrinsic or inherent values, is always relative, constructed (Wang 1999), contextually determined (Salamone 1997), and even ideological (Silver 1993). Authenticity works as a "regime of power" that authorizes certain subjects as the locus of the nation's core values and identity while excluding other possibilities (Duara 1998). It is always a social process in which competing interests argue for interpretations (Oakes 2006).

This chapter responds to the discussions of construction of cultural authenticity and the invention of tradition in the broader context of intense urbanization and agrarian crisis in China by focusing on Xiaocheng Folk Art Village, Yan'an. Many of Xiaocheng's rural features are reconstructed for the purpose of the tourist gaze and heritage performance, and there is much to say about the fabrication of heritage there. But to simply say that Xiaocheng and its paper-cutting are fabricated and thus are inauthentic prevents one from asking further how the heritage-making process proliferates contesting narratives, new local claims, and new meanings of the rural. These new meanings of local tradition and rural areas are previously evaded and unendorsed by the national state narrative and the dominant discourse of urban modernity.

My objective in this chapter is to discuss the politics of heritage authenticity by attending to the differentiated narratives that various actors construct. In the process of listing paper-cutting as a heritage in mid-2000 Yan'an, for instance, it was taken for granted that local villagers, urban intellectuals, and the local and the central governments collaborated in unison to promote the tradition. The fact is that these actors' interests converged and diverged in different periods of time. Their strategic alliance and differentiated interpretations of culture are often not noticed, if not completely neglected. In the end, I argue that the authenticity of Xiaocheng Folk Art Village and paper-cutting lies in the production of multiple narratives that contest dominant and official discourses on folk culture. I show that folk cultural revival is not necessarily a reconstruction of a backward-looking and conservative past catering to urban consumption but instead is a making of vernacular history, which focuses on the understanding of folk rural everyday life from the view of the ordinary people (Dicks 2004). I also show how folk cultural revival is intimately related to rural villagers' personal empowerment, autonomous governance, and democratic struggle.

The data in this chapter is based on fieldwork conducted in 2004 and 2008 in Xiaocheng Folk Art Village, Yanchuan county, Yan'an. I worked closely with Jin Zhilin, a CAFA professor, and Feng Sanyun, a Yan'an artist, two main architects of Xiaocheng Folk Art Village, to receive a group of visitors from Spain and Japan and to translate between local villagers and foreign visitors at Xiaocheng for a month. I revisited Xiaocheng in 2008 after an International Festival of Folk Art was held. I conducted interviews with major paper-cutting artists and organizers of the village and participated in their organizing committee meetings concerning planning of the cultural development project.

The Origin Narrative of Xiaocheng Folk Art Village

Xiaocheng village, with fifty-four households and a small population of 205 people, perches along the bank of the Yellow River and is known for producing dates. When dates ripen and turn red in September, the whole village looks burgundy red, giving the Loess landscape and the roaring Yellow River a rosy blush. Inside the Jinshan Great Valley, Xiaocheng village is about thirty-five kilometers from Yanchuan township by car. For years, villagers picked the dates, dried them under the sun, and sold them to other towns by carting produce on a narrow pebble trail that did not support vehicles. A good harvest earned a household about 2,000 RMB a year. If the rainy season came before harvest and wet the dates, villagers earned only a few hundred or even nothing. For years, villagers lived scantily without basic infrastructure such as electricity and tap water. Yet Xiaocheng is located right at the hilltop above the spectacular Yellow River Meander, in which the river bends into a loop, forming a magnificent canyon landscape.

When I first went to Xiaocheng in 2004, it took about four hours of rocky riding, passing numerous villages crouching along dangerously steep cliffs and crossing two tributaries of the Yellow River on stone bridges standing precariously in a roaring current. When Jin Zhilin, an art professor from the Central Academy of Fine Arts, and Feng Sanyun, a local woodcut artist who served in the Yanchuan Hall of Culture, gave me a ride in their "Red Flag" jeep, I learned the most popular origin narrative about Xiaocheng, one that is widely circulated in books and the internet and even among oral interviews with Xiaocheng villagers.

This is the narrative they shared with me: In 2001, Jin Zhilin was captivated by the Yellow River Meander and decided to paint landscapes in Xiacheng village because its hilltop allowed a spectacular view of the river. To proceed, he paid a local villager to provide accommodation, meals, and a daily donkey ride up the hill for two months. Curious, friendly villagers also started to deliver food for the artist. At the end of his painting trip, Jin gracefully asked to do something for the community. Villagers wanted him to put forward their demand for electric cable connection in the village at the county government, as they believed a Beijing intellectual would be more persuasive. Jin frowned at the request, but eventually he got an idea when he found out that quite a few women villagers could make paper-cuts and that there were a few interesting sites in the village. He spun out an ambitious cultural development plan: promote paper-cuts (both as an art form and a practice) as an intangible cultural heritage, establish a folk museum, and put together a *yangge* song-and-dance troupe. The plan was to attract visitors, turn Xiaocheng into a unique cultural tourism site, and in turn pressure the county government to equip the community with electricity connection. Today, not only is there electricity and tap water in Xiaocheng but also a paved road to the township!

This popular narrative on the birth of Xiaocheng Folk Art Village and the magic of paper-cuts is indeed a moving one. Upon careful examination, however, it works like a classic Communist story line of salvation with certain stereotypical characters, beginnings, and endings: the poverty-stricken and illiterate villagers eagerly wait in remote hills for enlightenment; the conscientious urban intellectuals go down to the villages and passionately serve people's welfare (*wei renmin fuwu*); the government gives a happy ending to everyone; Xiaocheng rises as a successful heritage site and villagers enjoy the prosperity of cultural tourism!

Such a narrative is problematic at least for the following few aspects. First, although Xiaocheng village was a remote village without much basic infrastructure, its villagers were not stuck in premodern darkness. The majority of its households had income earned by young men and women working away as migrant laborers in cities and relied on left-behind wives and elderly to tend the date trees and the terraced fields. Second, even though intellectuals from Beijing initiated the Folk Art Village project and brought in visitors and business opportunities, their initiatives were initially met with much suspicion and even resistance. Last, the county government did eventually connect Xiaocheng with cables, tap water, and a concrete road but its intervention was much more than infrastructural.

The next few sections complicate and enrich this origin narrative of Xiaocheng in order to contest the ways that local tradition and rural place are often seen as naturally existing, waiting to be discovered and promoted. Instead, I examine the complicated ways places and practices "become" traditional and heritage-relevant after processes of external engagements and locals' reflection and negotiations.

Beijing Intellectuals: Searching a Folk China and Living Culture

Urban intellectuals did not promote paper-cutting solely for villagers' welfare. The truth is that intellectuals, represented by Jin Zhilin and Qiao Shaoguang at the Beijing CAFA, were actively planning to list Chinese cultural practices at the UNESCO's intangible cultural heritage list after 2001. The first Chinese cultural practice that went into one of the Masterpieces of the Oral and Intangible Heritage of Humanity at the UNESCO list was *Kunqu*, an older form of Chinese opera in Jiangsu, south China. The successful listing of *Kunqu* in 2001 immediately put the opera art form and associated institutions under national and international spotlights. Relevant departments and academics have since been given unprecedented resources, legitimacy, and reputation to do research and offer training courses.

With the UNESCO recognizing the values of local languages, literature, music, dance, games, mythology, rituals, customs, handicrafts, and cultural spaces, Chinese intellectuals in the fields of folklore, religious studies, and anthropology all start to re-understand the meanings of their work in the broader national and international framework. Upon hearing the successful listing of *Kunqu*, the CAFA artists were ready to embark on the listing exercise. That said, however, the UNESCO definition of intangible heritage was not easy to meet. To be listed as an intangible heritage, the cultural form needs to be anchored in an existing, not past, cultural community and its transmission should be based on oral or imitation means. It also requires the practitioners to see the cultural form as part of their social and communal identity and values. In other words, the listing exercise recognizes those cultural practices that are continuously relevant to people's lives today.

The challenge for these Beijing intellectuals, therefore, was not about identifying a particular cultural form but locating a community that continues to practice it. They must have immediately thought of Ansai county in Yan'an, where the CAFA engaged with many women artists in the 1970s and 1980s (see Chapter 1). The problem of Ansai county, however, is that it has so rapidly urbanized since 1990 that it was impossible to identify a large group of practitioners by 2000. Moreover, in and outside of Ansai, traditional mud cavehouses with wooden window frames mounted with rice paper where paper-cuts used to be pasted have mostly disappeared and the majority of households have changed their homes to stone cavehouses with modern glass windows. Locals had long turned to shiny commercial posters with pop stars' faces as interior decoration and paper-cuts were seen limited to wedding occasions. In other words, if the CAFA intellectuals wanted to find a rural community that kept practicing the paper-cutting tradition, they would have to invent one.

Xiaocheng fitted well into the imagined rural community—remote and underdeveloped with the most beautiful river landscape. Most importantly, the place is full of interpretative potentials. First, it has a deserted cavehouse with exotic stone carving images on its facade. These include images of two men with long noses in non-Han outfits, a lotus, and "two lions rolling on balls" (*shizi gunxiuqiu*). How and why these stone carvings are there remains unknown. One possible explanation is that villagers used stones from broken temples as construction materials. But the urban intellectuals spun out a much more attractive story from it. Jin Zhilin interpreted that these stone carved images might be related to the presence of *Xiongnu* and *Jiang* ethnicities (ancient nomadic people residing in current Mongolia) in the region and the import of Buddhist religious symbols from India in the West Xia Dynasty (1038–1227 A.D.), during which the Mongols conquered northern China. Jin stretched so far as to speculate that Xiaocheng might be a major cultural crossroad where the non-Han ethnicities settled one thousand years ago. Jin's claims are now popularly reiterated in tourist books or Web sites about Xiaocheng as they obviously give the place a much more exotic history.

Second, right next to Xiaocheng is another village called Nianpan where about twenty old-style mud cavehouses had been deserted for years and the villagers had moved away to build new stone-structure cavehouses. The Beijing intellectuals thought it a perfect space to put together a folk museum exhibiting local agricultural and household tools.

Still, an old cavehouse with exotic stone images, twenty mud cavehouses and a magnificent river meander landscape were not enough. The best scenario would be that villagers still practice paper-cutting in their daily lives. After some initial surveying, the urban intellectuals found that three women villagers could make paper-cuts while others knew basic needlework and embroidery. Without much hesitation, the urban intellectuals immediately invited a few professional paper-cutting artists from outside of Xiaocheng and started training classes for all women villagers.

The urban intellectuals were absolutely aware of the ways they manipulated historical narratives and reinvented paper-cutting practices in order to qualify for the listing exercise. But it would be reductive to see their engagement as a utilitarian one. Some of them did genuinely believe in a cultural China rooted in village life and rural community.

Jin Zhilin, for instance, has ardently promoted the view that Chinese culture and philosophy is rooted in rural folk cultural practices (Jin 2001, 2002). He argues against the conventionally elitist view that Chinese culture is exclusively owned by imperial, literary, male cultural traditions. He believes that folk art and peasant cultural forms are major, but underevaluated, sites of cultural production. For instance, many would regard Chinese calligraphy, practiced by urban educated males, a major form of Chinese cultural representation. But few would regard it so for paper-cutting practiced by illiterate female villagers. Jin also understands paper-cut motifs of "bird," "fish," and "tree" as no simple representations of flora or fauna in nature but related to totemic patterns of fertility and life worship in ancient civilizations. In the essay "The Transmission and Development of Chinese Folk Paper-Cutting Culture," he argues:

> [T]he motifs of "phoenix facing sun" (*fenghuang chaoyang*), "water basin" (*shuipen*), "Rohdea plant" (*wannianqing*), and "tree of life" (*shengming zhi shu*) present in *Hemudu* civilization (7000 years ago in downstream region of the Yangze River) and *Dawenkou* civilization (5000 years ago in downstream region of the Yellow River) continue to appear through today's paper-cuts in these regions. At the same time the symbols of "frog," "dragon," "snake," and "human face with fish," prominent in *Yangshao* and *Majiayao* civilizations (5000 years ago in upstream region of the Yellow River), stay to be popular motifs of paper-cuts in today's Gansu and Qinghai areas. The paper-cut design of "people holding hands" for spiritual healing, excavated from

graves in Astana, Xinjiang, during the Tang Dynasty (618–907 C.E.), continues to be a major paper-cut motif used in ritual ceremony of warding off evil spirit in today's West China. From animals, plants, human figures, to everyday objects, paper-cut motifs correspond to cultural and philosophical representations of ancient Chinese culture, in which life, reproduction, fertility and the interconnection of yin and yang are vital. Paper-cutting practice is vital to the continuation of our nation's ancient culture, philosophy and art" (Jin 2005: 32–33).

Qiao Xiaoguang is another major CAFA professor writing about paper-cutting as a "living heritage" (Qiao 2004). He said that the majority of Chinese ritual ceremonies and festivals are organized and represented through paper-cutting: Spring Festival; Tomb Sweeping Festival (*qingming*); Dragon Boast Festival; Mid Autumn Festival and Ghost Festival; and wedding, funeral, spiritual healing, and ancestral worship. In all these occasions, paper-cutting mediates ceremonial forms and festival values, and it becomes the major aesthetics of ritual events and everyday rural life. Qiao wrote, "folk paper-cutting is a universal, multi-ethnic and living cultural form. It expresses features of a living heritage. It is a paradigm of living culture" (Qiao 2005: 385–396).

To sum up, for the Beijing intellectuals, Xiaocheng village was the perfect site to elaborate their polemics and politics of reinterpreting Chinese history and culture as transmitted through rural folk practices. Training paper-cutting artists was not about faking something for the listing exercise. Quite the other way around—they saw the listing exercise as a legitimate means and the best opportunity for both the state and society to attend to a long-neglected aspect of Chinese civilization: rural folk China.

Mobilization work started in 2001. The Beijing intellectuals persuaded women villagers to make and sell paper-cuts as a source of income and men villagers to organize a *yangge* song-and-dance team. They made sure that the women sought inspirations from folk legends, local stories, folk religions, and folk songs when making paper-cuts. When they asked villagers to donate traditional agricultural gears, oil lamps, pottery containers, embroideries, paper lanterns, handmade cloths, and shoes for museum exhibits, they insisted that these exhibits were not solely for tourists' visual consumption but about reconnecting rural ordinary tools with Chinese culture and philosophy (Figure 2.2). By the end of 2011, a preliminary plan was in place: Xiaocheng could become a site where visitors appreciate the spectacular Yellow River landscape, tour around the old cavehouses community, visit a folk museum, and still get in touch with a "traditional" community where women villagers continue the heritage of paper-cutting.

FIGURE 2.2. Jin Zhilin, the founder of Xiaocheng Folk Art Village, and the exhibits of traditional lanterns decorated with paper-cuts at the Folk Museum.

Yan'an Intellectuals: Reviving a Cavehouse Culture

Villagers' objectives and concerns were clearly different. They could not care less whether paper-cutting was a medium of transmitting ancient totemic values and philosophy to the present. All they wanted was electric cables and tap water facilities. Upon hearing Jin's counter proposal of building an art village first and requesting the government later, many were doubtful. One of them, Hao Xiuzhen said, "The teachers said that we could make money by selling paper-cuts. I don't know about that. I told them I don't want money but cables. I think they were cheating me. I don't think this piece of broken paper sells!" (quoted from Zhang 2009: 201). Many male villagers thought the plan of having their wives make paper-cuts for tourists simply crazy, if not outrageous, because that meant taking away a major labor power from heavy agricultural work and household chores.

Only three women made it to the first training class meeting. The urban intellectuals were still very encouraging and gave positive comments to their participation. Gradually, more women villagers started to go and some started to perform well. As days went by, more villagers—women and men, elderly and children—flocked to the class like going to a theater, all hoping to check out what the term "good paper-cuts" really means. Eventually, the class became the focal point around which the villagers got together after a day of hard work, listened to Jin Zhilin recounting the history of Ansai paper-cuts artists performing in France in the 1980s, and thought about his plan for the Xiaocheng makeover.

After a month of training, the two groups started to gain a better understanding of each other. When I was in Xiaocheng in 2004, I heard Jin Zhilin still patiently explaining to villagers various cultural meanings of tools and ritual practices in rural society. He hoped the latter would see the cultural development plan not exclusively in monetary gains but in terms of rediscovering local folk knowledge and rural worldview. Many villagers slowly came to terms with his intention. Most importantly, the process gave many new perspectives on their traditions, the rural environment, and the identity of peasants. They said the plan affirmed enormously their identity as villagers and their rural lifestyle, which was often considered low and worthless by both urban and rural residents.

This is particularly true for a group of local learned individuals who gained a high school education and continued a self-taught pursuit of knowledge, and who are now major writers, artists, and photographers of the Yanchuan county. I called them Yan'an intellectuals thereafter. Feng Sanyuan, who finished his high-school education in the late 1970s and has since worked as a professional woodcut artist at the Yanchuan county Hall of Culture, is one of them. Inspired by Jin's theory of rural folk culture, Feng and a group of Yan'an intellectuals thought it important to study local customs, rituals, and folk arts anew. Knowing the opportunity to build the Xiaocheng Folk Art Village, Feng immediately assisted in the mobilizing effort. He told me in an interview and also wrote in one of his essays:

> [W]hen I was setting up the marriage custom section for the folk museum, I got to finally understand the intriguing implications of our local customary practices: fertility and reproduction. In the wedding ritual, the bride and the groom each needs to hold four steam buns, in which hide some dates and walnuts. Walnut, with two shells, is a metaphor for sexual coupling; and date, sharing a pun with the word "early," is a wish for "giving birth to a son early." Before the bride goes into the couple's bedroom, the flute musician must break through a piece of paper on the window. All these small details and actions are important local metaphors for sexual union. (Feng 2005: 326–330)

Slowly, local Yan'an intellectuals became much more interested in what they call a "cavehouse culture" (*yaodong wenhua*), in which northern Shaanxi people form their unique sociality, customs, religion, and daily practices. They understood a cavehouse as no simple functional form of dwelling but saw instead its architectural design, which is a rectangle in the lower part connected to a semicircle in the upper part. This corresponds to the Chinese view of cosmology: round sky and square land (*tianyuan difang*). Local rituals, such as rain praying and worshipping river god and earth god, are usually arranged in and out of the cavehouse spaces for auspiciousness and effectiveness (Feng 2005: 328).

For the Yan'an intellectuals, the Xiaocheng project was a golden opportunity to explore this rarely studied local culture and ritual meanings, previously regarded as less sophisticated due to material impoverishment and the remoteness of the area. At the same time, they had an urgency to understand local culture before the area urbanized quickly and villagers massively turned cavehouses into modern, concrete, villa-looking, multistory buildings. As Feng made sense of his objective in participating in the Xiaocheng project, "our goal is not about putting together data on papercuts, folk songs, local religion and customary practices but about protecting and sustaining our culture on this soil" (Feng 2005: 327).

The Rise of Xiaocheng Folk Art Village

Seeing the villagers' effort, the county government eventually agreed to provide electric cables and tap water service to Xiaocheng to make the Yellow River cultural tourist spot work. Villagers were overjoyed and decided to hold a ceremony on December 13, 2001, to celebrate the setting up of Xiaocheng Folk Art Village and the electric cable connection. The rural administration leaders and county government leaders were the speakers of the night, and villagers, including those from the surrounding area, performed *yangge* song and dance. The ceremony also conferred "paper-cut artist" certificates to twenty-eight selected women villagers in Xiaocheng. Hao Guoqiang, the first elected leader of Xiaocheng Folk Art Village, remembered about this evening, "Everyone was excited. We were using oil lamps and all of a sudden, there is electricity! Everyone sang and danced together. Many could not fall asleep that night. We did not believe in Teacher Jin before. Now we respect him like we respect Mao Zedong!" (Zhang 2009: 205).

In April 2002, an academic conference on "Paper-Cuts and Intangible Cultural Heritage" was launched in Xiaocheng, bringing in over a hundred art experts and professionals from the CAFA and various state departments.

These visitors bought many paper-cuts and stayed in cavehouses for food and accommodations. Xiaocheng's name has blazed up since that time. In the same year, the Intangible Cultural Heritage Center at CAFA and the Chinese National Folk Paper-Cuts Association officially included Xiaocheng village in its project of listing paper-cutting as an intangible cultural heritage at the UNESCO (Qiao 2004).

Xiaocheng quickly became a site of interests—local, national, and international. In 2003, the Long March Foundation in New York and the CAFA collaborated on a survey of paper-cuts in Yanchuan county. They initiated the survey in Xiaocheng. The foundation later put together the 15,006 survey forms, containing villagers' basic information and individual statements and their paper-cut samples, in a large-scale art installation exhibit. Entitled "The Great Survey of Paper-Cutting in Yanchuan county," the exhibit toured in museums in Beijing, Taipei, Shanghai, San Francisco, and Sao Paulo from 2004–2010 (see Chapter 1).

In 2004, the Ford Foundation gave seed funding to support the Xiaocheng project, its paper-cutting training classes, the renovation of old cavehouses, and associated projects of "developing cultural resource into a sustainable cultural industry" (Qiao 2004: 221–248). With the foundation support, the old cavehouse with special stone carvings was cleaned up and given the title of "A Thousand Year Old Cave" (*qiannian guyao*). The twelve deserted cavehouses were turned into twelve exhibit spaces for the Folk Museum, covering themes of agriculture, transportation, daily life, weddings, local religion, folk art, ceremonies, and so forth. The first cavehouse is devoted to displaying agricultural tools, with a big wooden plough in the foreground of the center of the space and, on the two sides, several kinds of tilling tools leaning against the wall. The second cavehouse has a neat positioning of grain containers, drainers, and measuring boxes in different sizes. Next to each tool is a framed picture on the wall with a brief explanation of the tools' names and uses. In the cavehouse in which traditional oil lamps and gas lamps were placed, a special display platform is set up so that the lamps could be placed in several layering heights, according to the time of production and styles. A traditional loom is also set up in a cavehouse space entitled "Weaving," and a local tour guide can demonstrate the old method of that craft.

By 2003, the village had received visitors from Italy, France, Switzerland, and Japan. Many colleges and universities in China also made Xiaocheng into a "teaching base" (*jiaoyu jidi*) for their folk art curricula. As visitors increased sharply, the Yanchuan county government paved a concrete road from the Yanchuan town center direct to Xiaocheng and significantly improved the infrastructure surrounding the area.

The Birth of Creative Rural Subjects, Reconfigured Domestic Relations, and a New Public Village Life

Because of the influx of visitors, women villagers got busy making and selling paper-cuts, traditionally dyed fabric, handwoven cloths, handmade shoes, old-fashioned toys, and embroideries. Heritage tourism motivated many to revive folk indigenous knowledge and techniques. In 2004, many told me that they sought advice from the few elderly women on the weaving technique using homegrown cotton and dying with natural organic dyes. Some of the elderly women told me that they had not felt so much respect from the young people for a long time.

In general, women villagers who practiced the newly invented tradition were conscious of seeing tradition as a process of active engagement and reflection, instead of replicating some essentialized unchanging practices. Feng Meizhen, my host in Xiaocheng, for example, loved to make paper-cuts of baby's vests (*xiaoguagua*) that actually fit on a child's body. She decorated the paper-cut vests with popular fauna and flora images and motifs of good fortune and happiness. By making a paper-cut into a wearable vest, Feng creatively connected the visual satisfaction and talismanic quality of paper-cuts to a corporeal one. Feng Ruimei had a special style of making a whole piece of paper full of indistinctive cuts, urging viewers to find the hidden principal subjects. She learned modern cubism from Jin Zhilin's "training class" and has since made paper-cuts that merged the subject with the background, the cut with the uncut. Blurring the intended representational subjects, Feng Ruimei injected modern art elements into a traditional folk art form and experimented with different styles of paper-cut representations. One day, when Feng proudly showed me her Chinese calligraphy, I could see that she gained a great sense of achievement in the process of reenacting the paper-cutting tradition. Hu Meilian's paper-cuts unconventionally put themes of popular religion into her designs. In one of her paper-cuts, which I studied carefully, she told a story of the death of a woman, her son's pleading to a local deity, and, last, her rebirth, through four images on a piece of paper. Hu thus turned paper-cutting into a medium of local storytelling, demanding visitors to read the sequence of images and to understand local knowledge concerning the spirit medium, filial piety, and the boundaries between life and death.

Professional paper-cuts artist, Liu Jieqiong, also a Yanchuan local, best articulated her reflection and mission on reenacting the paper-cutting tradition. She wrote:

I love *xintianyou* (local folk song). *Xintianyou* is audio; paper-cuts [are] visual. I want to combine the two and create my unique paper-cuts style.]*Xintianyou* hums like this, "*caoji shangqiang gongji zhui, you chuai nainai you qinzui* (the hen runs up the wall and the rooster chases, fondle the breasts and kiss the lips). Its lyrics are sensational, arousing and sexually explicit. Full of love and emotion, *xintianyou* makes people blush. When I turn a *xintianyou* into paper-cuts, I can best express the characters and emotion of northern Shaanxi people. It is my duty to preserve, continue and develop local folk art like this. Tradition is a flowing river; folk art is its bedrock." (Liu 2005: 346; my own translation)

Reviving local knowledge and folk tradition was not limited to women villagers. Many middle-age male villagers actively helped to organize the Folk Museum and the team of *yangge* song and dance. I participated in one of their organizing meetings and observed how Jin Zhilin shared his experience of touring museums in France and the United States and his view of curatorship. It was true that those villagers had never been out to any museum visit. But it was in these occasions that they were hard-pressed to think how to present themselves, their traditions, and their communities to visitors. Hao, who gave up his urban career and went back to his Xiaocheng hometown in 2001 to start a cavehouse homestay business, told me firmly, "I need to come back to do this because I want to tell outsiders that we have good things (*haode dongxi*) in rural village!"

The villagers' remaking and reenactment of rural folk culture and art definitely fed into the "romantic reappraisal" of the rural landscape and lifestyle by the urban middle class, who wanted to escape tense urban life. But the Xiaocheng case shows that the process of folk cultural revival was equally important for local identity building and for a radical self-reevaluation of rural values and experience. The experience of everyday life in the post-Mao countryside has often been regarded as a site of inertness and meaninglessness, as opposed to the city where everything happens and where jobs and opportunities abound. Rural young women found their rural life particularly meaningless as they often have no personal development after marriage but "are trapped in the domestic sphere and activities surrounding the stove" (*weizhe guotai zhuan*). Yan Hairong argues that rural youth in the post-Mao countryside have been domesticated as they are often not required by their parents to work in the fields and simply help with household chores after high school graduation. Many also find no modern possibility and future development in their rural hometowns (Yan 2008: 44–52).

In this context, the Xiaocheng folk revival project provided once again a focal point for public life in the village and a communal participation long gone after decollectivization. The folk project opened up opportunities for villagers to explore, learn, and represent folk ritual knowledge and practices seriously and creatively. Villagers started to approach their own culture in a new light and understand anew the complex relations among their household arrangement, crops, and ritual customs and values. Schoolchildren also started to pick up the change as the Xiaocheng primary school officially included folk art into its teaching.

To most women villagers who were not very well educated, the folk project was a rare opportunity to get special skill training, interact with outsiders, and build a new social circle outside of the traditional gender spatial and social confinement. Selling paper-cuts did not bring in much income as tourists did not come in regularly. But almost all the women artists whom I talked to, married or not, said the practice had changed them and their dynamics with their husbands or family members. Some said "they could speak louder" in the household with the extra income they made. Hao Xiuzhen, who had conflicts with her husband over the paper-cut training class, said, "my husband said I did not do my job well and making paper-cuts is a waste of time. He broke my pencil and I got myself a new one at night. I thought if he breaks another pencil, I would get another one. I want to keep drawing" (quoted from Zhang 2009: 203). Through paper-cutting, Hao found a way to demarcate her private boundary, activity, and interest within the household. Another woman villager said, "my household finance was really stressed with two children going to school. I could not help but work as migrant worker [in the city]. Once I got my salary I feel better and I will start to make paper-cuts. When I got stressed in work, I hum some folk songs and I turned the songs into paper-cut designs" (Feng 2005: 327). She thus found the aesthetics and practice of paper-cutting useful to soothe the stressful rural life that is increasingly connected to urban consumption and cost. Paper-cutting did not bring in gender empowerment overnight in terms of raising women's income and status significantly. In Xiaocheng, paper-cutting has changed the ways many women villagers position and value themselves in rural households.

Democratic Struggles over Folk Art and Government Interventions

Xiaocheng Folk Art Village was not just a plan of rural creativity. It was a serious plan of local governance, endorsed by a charter, and operated along with existing village administration. The new charter stipulated that an art village head and an art group leader be democratically elected by its members and governed by a board of directors composed of a group of intellectuals. The charter ensured that the art village leadership would be responsible for attracting visitors and income, be accountable to the village members, and be autonomous from potential government intervention. In principle, the art village should actively motivate villagers to participate in cultural and community development affairs, but in some ways it conflicted with the role of the Communist Party–led village administration.

The relationship between the art village leadership and the party leadership was never smooth from the beginning. Feelings of unease and awkwardness arose when, for instance, the art village leader received incoming visitors and took the credit for hospitality without even meeting with the party village leaders. In turn, there were instances—such as a blackout, a frozen pipe, or visitors in accidents—when the art village leadership had to rely on the party administrative leadership to keep things going, but the latter would sometimes delay requests. Facing challenges of lineage interest and the official party administrative body, Xiaocheng Folk Art Village remains a vanguard democratic grassroots initiative. I show in the following the ways the county and central governments made their interventions at Xiaocheng and the ways the Folk Art Village became a site of ongoing and lively community building, self-governance, and even democratic struggle.

As the number of tourists increased, many of the villagers who previously migrated to cities came back home and renovated their old cavehouses into farmers' homestays or local food specialty businesses. "Bed and Breakfast cavehouses" have mushroomed along the main road. Tapping into the blooming local tourism profits, the county government opened a luxurious cavehouse-style hotel at the village entrance in 2005 and put up a kiosk on a hilltop for viewing the Yellow River Meander. But the Ming Qing style of the kiosk architecture, commonly seen in the Beijing palace or royal parks, seemed strange in the Loess environment. The government-run hotel also hurt the villagers' cavehouse B&Bs and the paper-cutting artist's business as visitors staying at the hotel no longer went into the women artists' households scattered in different corners of the village. Tourists today would roam around the Folk Museum and take pictures of the Yellow River meanderings without visiting the paper-cutting artists. The changing nature of tourism, from initially a more culture-oriented one to, later, a massive, leisure one, slowly marginalized those early creative initiatives.

Despite the failure of the CAFA to enter paper-cutting into the 2005 list of UNESCO Oral and Intangible Cultural Heritage of Humanities, it was eventually listed in the Chinese State Council Intangible Culture List in 2006. In order to reinvigorate the initiatives and spirits of the Folk Art Village among villagers, Jin Zhilin and the CAFA colleagues made a great effort to host the International Folk Art Festival at Xiaocheng and invited folk artists from Africa, France, Switzerland, and Bulgaria in 2007. The event had the intention of continuing to engage villagers in Xiaocheng in the cultural development initiatives, to gain exchange experiences with folk artists from different countries, and to raise more media attention to folk tradition preservation within China.

The new leader of the Yanchuan county government, unfortunately, did not consider heritage listing of paper-cuts as a relevant agenda to the county development and refused to approve the event. The fight between the Beijing CAFA intellectuals and the Yanchuan county government later turned into a fiasco. The former eventually sought approval directly from the Bureau of Culture in Beijing to host the festival, openly defying the county government authority. The county government took revenge by not sending representatives to the opening ceremony and, worse, not promising any hotel rooms for the international visitors. But Xiaocheng villagers and the Beijing intellectuals stood together as a group in solidarity. It was in a cold winter (under 30 degrees Fahrenheit) when the festival was held and the foreign visitors stayed at villagers' cavehouses with low internal heating and no toilets for four days. Villagers supported the event by preparing thick layers and heating up the *kang* beds in cavehouses as much as possible. The incident proved that villagers genuinely defended Xiaocheng's art village development.

Thereafter, the county government continued to promote Xiaocheng as one of its major tourist spots. Yet in its official tourism narrative, the county government no longer promotes paper-cutting as representing a living civilization but merely as one local art form among many others ("Quanjing Yan'an" Editorial Committee 2008: 126). There is also no mention of the unique regional cavehouse culture and local sexual culture.

Xiaocheng invited not only the county government's intervention, but also that of the central government. In 2006, the central government decided to build the Museum of the Yellow River Meander Geological Park (*Huanghe Shequ Dizhi Bowuguan*) right next to Xiaocheng. The grand museum building features a three-dimensional cinema and a multilevel exhibition hall. When I visited the museum in 2008, there was a spectacular mammoth fossil exhibit in the lobby to demonstrate the paleontological values of the area. In the main hall, the exhibit displayed different kinds of stones, rocks, and sands, with explanatory titles of "Triassic Age," "Cretaceous Age" or "Paleolithic Age." In graphics, words, and mineral materials, the exhibits traced the climate changes, geological and topographical histories, and natural evolution of the Yellow River over millions of years. Walking through the exhibits, I soon sensed that the central government intended the Geology Museum to present a museum of natural history of the region. Explaining in specialized terms how the river meanders and the canyon landscapes are formed through a long process of sedimentation, weathering, and flooding, the exhibits aim to establish a natural historical narrative to understand the Yellow River as the founding site of the Chinese civilization.

Most interestingly, the exhibit included the early historical presence of the Chinese Communist Party and its anti-Japanese invasion effort in this highly scientific narrative, implying that the authority of the CCP is just as natural, legitimate, and inevitable as the formation of river meanderings. Toward the end of the exhibit, there is a brief mention of a few local customs, including *yangge* song and dance and *zhuanjiuqu*, a local form of a Chinese New Year parade. Paper-cutting is introduced by a mere passing remark about a professional male paper-cutting artist whose masterpiece is entitled "The Yellow River Is Dragon's Home."

The building of the Geology Museum by the central government could be read as an official reclaiming of narrative authority over the region. Sitting right next to the Xiaocheng Folk Art Village in the form of a grand architecture, it dwarfs the villager-led folk cultural initiatives and makes folk paper-cutting and other local practices relatively insignificant in the long process of natural evolutionary changes. The Geology Museum thus resurrects the national, historical, and scientific grand discourse that sees the Yellow River, and associated with it the Chinese civilization, a natural and evolutionary product (Figure 2.3). In its scientific and authoritative tone, the central government–sponsored museum reconstructs an "official" understanding of the region, discounting the folk cultural one that the Xiaocheng initiative offers.

To sum up, the different levels of government of the Chinese state clearly saw themselves as major players in the process of heritage making even in a small village site like Xiaocheng. The luxury cavehouse hotel, the Ming Qing–style viewing kiosk, the National Museum of Geology, the evolutionary narrative of the Yellow River Civilization, the exhibit of the CCP revolutionary struggle in the region—all represent the multiple government interventions. These interventions carried the aims of establishing official and authoritative accounts of the place over the folk or intellectual accounts of local history, culture, and place making.

Seen in this light, the folk cultural project is no simple initiative catering to the romantic desires of urban consumers over the imagined rural. Instead,

FIGURE 2.3. The Museum of the Yellow River Meander Geological Park.

folk cultural revival is a major means for local villagers to assert their new identity and new aspiration over their desired rural lives. In Xiaocheng, folk revival initiatives are directly linked to the issues of autonomous governing implementation. It is also related to grassroots democratic struggles against not only the hegemonic urban discourse and practices, but also against local government suppression or appropriation of local initiatives.

Heritage Making as a Narrative Battle

This chapter has looked at the process of active invention and multiple interventions in the remaking of paper-cutting as a heritage in the Xiaocheng art village. I have shown how paper-cutting is fabricated as a communal cultural practice first by the urban intellectuals and later reenacted by villagers for modern development, creative training, and gender empowerment. I have argued against the rosy narrative of putting urban intellectuals in a moral position of serving the people and painting Xiaocheng villagers as victims of a backward society. I have shown that the process of heritage making was complexly layered with the Beijing intellectuals' ambition for a folk-cultural China, the local Yan'an intellectuals' awakening to significance of the cavehouse culture, and the villagers' coming to terms with their own place and tradition in a new light.

In *Tourism and Modernity in China*, Tim Oakes suggests the notion of "a web of linkages" to understand the various actors and the ways they connect and conflict with each other in a project of tourism (1998: 189–193). The web-of-linkages perspective refrains from an easy conceptualization of political, intellectual, or economic forces as imposing on a village community in a top-down fashion, but, instead, it sees the many actors as strategic agents in a dynamic system of connections. Similarly, the making of Xiaocheng into a heritage site is a process of collision and collaboration of many competing forces and interests.

But the web-of-linkage perspective is not adequate in capturing the subtle power contests among the actors and each of their contestations to the hegemonic discourse on tradition in contemporary China. Using the case of Xiaocheng in Yan'an, I propose to understand heritage making in China as a process of narrative battle. By *narrative battle*, I mean to highlight the process as opening up alternative readings of the official party-state discourse. In making the Xiaocheng art village, the Beijing intellectuals' narrative departs radically from the Communist Party's reductive view that peasants' culture is naturally modest and benign. Instead, they propose a new understanding of folk culture—rich, legendary, complex, and full of ritual totemic meanings. This folk culture traces its roots to ancient civilizations and is popularly represented and enacted in the everyday life of the rural society. This folk-centered narrative not only challenges the elitist convention of Chinese literary culture, it also contests the Communist party-state view of peasant folk culture as naturally receptive to revolutionary class struggle.

Analogously, the local Yan'an intellectuals' narrative of heritage preservation has its specific agenda. Their focus on a cavehouse culture departs from a dominant narrative of the Yellow River civilization often assumed to be homogenous and unitary across different regions of the north China plain. Instead, Yan'an intellectuals speak of a Yellow River folk culture that is spatially specific to the Loess Plateau, defined by the cavehouse architecture and ritually corresponding to distinctive forms of popular religious worship of the dragon king and other local deities. Individual women artists, in turn, have their own interpretations of the folk cultural initiatives, some attempting to counter the gender power imbalance in the household sphere, some finding themselves a new hobby, others hoping to explore local sexual and gender meanings in the region. In short, local Yan'an intellectuals' and women artists' differentiated understandings of paper-cutting heritage further complicate a grand narrative of a Yellow River civilization stretching across regional, ethnic, and linguistic differences. Both claiming a unique northern Shaanxi regional identity, their views differ from and contest the Beijing intellectual view of a Chinese folk culture assumed to be unitary, ontological (*benyuan*), and historically transcendent.

Conclusion

It is important to understand heritage making and its authenticity not simply by judging whether it is a replica or an original, historically existed or recently invented. All heritages are products of fabrication, weaving history and fables, legends and facts together. But that does not make a heritage inauthentic. Instead, part of the heritage's authenticity lies in the production of multiple meanings generated by contesting narratives. This is particularly true in China where the Communist party-state often holds a tight control on interpreting history and tradition of local places. Every heritage making thus becomes a crucial process of contesting the official party-state version of truth and therefore generating alternative historical facts and interpretations. I argue that it is these various alternative historical views and new claims of traditions that make heritage authentic and meaningful.

Xiaocheng may be evaluated critically for commodifying local traditions and making villagers perform for tourists and money. Yet what happened in Xiaocheng at the same time is also a radical re-understanding of the meanings of the rural community in the broader context of urbanization and agrarian demise in the 2000s. Like the majority of rural villages in northwestern China, Xiaocheng was "emptied out," its young labors drained to the city and its residents composed of abandoned wives, children, and the elderly. Xiaocheng folk cultural initiatives therefore meant resisting the omnipresent discourse of urban modernity and the fatalistic trend of villagers leaving hometowns for opportunities. The initiative attracted many migrants to return home to start local businesses and cultivated a renewed understanding of the rural community and the values of folk traditions.

Bella Dicks argues that heritage is not a *retreat* from the present but is *stimulated* by the present (2004: 13). She shows that heritage making is not necessarily a representation of looking backward to a conservative past but makes vernacular history or ordinary people or working-class lives visible (2004: 132). Similarly, the experience of Xiaocheng shows that villagers are picking up their own vernacular knowledge and coming to terms with representing local culture to outsiders in a new light. The process allows villagers to gain a new awareness concerning their own traditions, their own rural spaces, and even democratic governing initiatives. Indeed, Xiaocheng villagers become "reflexive performers of modernity," who re-understand local identity, link themselves to faraway places, and grab entrepreneur business opportunities (Oakes and Schein 2006). At the same time they become aware of the broader socioeconomic context that constructs their performance as boundary markers of modernity and tradition (Schein 2000).

Whether Xiaocheng villagers and local Yan'an intellectuals can keep such vernacular history and community renewal initiatives alive remains a genuine test. In an age of mass tourism during which the government is not very supportive of creative local initiatives, defending an alternative folk cultural narrative and space that seeks to empower local members becomes ever more needed.

CHAPTER 3

Traditional Revival with Socialist Characteristics

Propaganda Storytelling Turned into Spiritual Service

At around eight o'clock in the evening on July 13, 2004, residents of Heijiawa village, an impoverished rural community east of Yan'an City, gathered at their leader's cavehouse for a storytelling performance. Inside the cavehouse, the performer, Master Xu, was preparing for the evening show. When Master Xu was ready, he plucked his three-stringed instrument, the sanxian (a Chinese lute), and flapped the wooden clapper tied around his left leg. After about ten minutes of rhythmical plucking, Master Xu wrinkled his sightless eyes and sang:

> Sing along as the sanxian sings; comrades, please sit on the sides,
> Today at Heijiawa we have a new atmosphere,
> Tap water flows well, and a wide concrete road is paved all the way from Yan'an [city].
> We are so happy to see the lines of pear and poplar trees,
> Villagers' lives have improved as the sound of television buzzes and as a gas stove is installed in every household.
> We can make meals easily now that tap water flows directly to the household water pot.
> Good life will last for millions of years!
> Under the leadership of the Party and the village committee, we will build our new affluence in Yan'an.
> Lift our spirit! Believe that new life rests in the Chinese Communist Party!

This politically charged preamble to Master Xu's performance reveals the complicated relationship between the folk practice of northern Shaanxi storytelling (*Shaanbei shuoshu*), the Chinese party-state, and the rural community in Yan'an. At various historical junctures, the sphere of folk society (*minjian*), broadly understood as the various cultural discourses and popular practices in grassroots communities in China, has been shown to possess a powerful symbolic value in local societies. Prasenjit Duara has identified this sphere as a "cultural nexus of power" which, prior to the twentieth century, the imperial authority endeavored to appropriate in order to legitimate its power (1988).

Since the mid-1940s, the Chinese Communist Party (CCP) has actively reformed and appropriated this sphere to convey its revolutionary narrative and to galvanize mass support for its ruling power. After 1949, the new nation's cultural policy made sure that various local culture, art, and literature serve the nation's political, economic, and social campaigns. Existing literature therefore often understands the form and content of traditional cultural forms during the socialist era as broadly subjected to the Communist party-state deployment to promote the nation's campaigns (Holm 1991; Hung 1994), whereas folk cultural forms and contents in the post-Mao economic reform period are largely transformed into catering to urban or tourist desires and to generate capital (Wang 2001; Schein 2000: 169–202; Griffiths et al. 2010). Some of the literature focuses specifically on how traditional cultural forms are revived in the rural communities to rebuild local identity and retrieve destroyed memories of the communal past (Jing 1996; Siu 1989; Dean 1997: 172–194; Mueggler 2001). Yet little attention is paid to the ways in which the political content and networks, which informed these cultural forms during the socialist era, have persisted. This leaves an unexamined domain of cultural complexity, as the revival of tradition in rural communities today is a process in which the villagers negotiate actively not only with market forces but also with early socialist resources.

Using the case of northern Shaanxi storytelling, a musical drama prevalent in the Yan'an area in north China (Jones 2007, 2009) that was given the political task of promoting the party-state during the socialist era, this chapter examines how this folk traditional performance in contemporary rural daily lives neither resists nor colludes with the state; nor does it cater to urban tourism or consumption. I argued that the folk cultural practitioners have opened up a quasi-religious space for rural villagers to express their new needs and communal concerns. I examine how the revival of such traditions remains connected to the Maoist legacy of mass culture, while responding to agrarian change and translocal conditions in rural communities of Yan'an today. More generally, this revival offers a new perspective on state-society relations and rural conditions in late socialist China.

The data of this chapter are drawn from fieldwork conducted in the Yan'an city and two counties of the area, Ansai and Yanchuan. In Yan'an city, I extensively interviewed five storytellers, who were members of the Yan'an Area Musical Drama Society (*Yan'an diqu quyiguan*) managed by the Hall of Culture. In Ansai County, I consulted with the head of the Ansai Musical Drama Society. In Yanchuan County, I interviewed eleven storytellers of the Yanchuan Musical Drama Troupe. Most of the practitioners had attended training classes organized by the CCP during the socialist era. Some of the older members are especially acclaimed artists. In July 2004, one of these storytellers, Master Xu, allowed me to accompany him on a storytelling trip that lasted for one month, during which we visited eight villages in rural Yan'an. Most of the information in this chapter was gathered during that trip. At the community level, I found that Master Xu neither spoke for the state nor gave extensive storytelling performances. Instead, he had transformed his performance into a series of clandestine religious activities and ritual performances.

Northern Shaanxi Storytelling in Yan'an: From Rural Folk to Sanxian Warrior

During the "Yan'an Period" (1937–1947), the CCP not only launched vigorous socioeconomic developmental programs in the Shaan-Gan-Ning border region, the Communist leaders also began to develop close links and collaboration with folk cultural practitioners as a means of building trust and legitimacy among the masses. Northern Shaanxi storytelling, as a creative form of expressive culture deploying vivid dialects, caught the attention of the CCP in the 1940s.

Northern Shaanxi storytelling was traditionally practiced by blind men who, incapable of raising crops, provided entertainment to remote villages. The musical form is provided by the sanxian, a three-stringed fretless plucked musical instrument that gives out a percussive tone and loud volume.[1] Blending folk songs, ancient stories, village legends, monologues, and local idioms, and accompanied by wooden clappers, pinewood boards, and copper bells, a storytelling performance was "interlaced with songs, rhymes, mimicry, and body movement with dramatic effect" (Wang 1993: 158). A prominent folklorist of northern Shaanxi Province, Wang Yuhua, described its musical style as a fusion of "different musical dramas of *daoqing*, *meihu*, *qinqiang* (various kinds of Chinese opera) and even songs of Daoism, shamanism and funeral rituals" (1993: 6–7). Like most other peasant cultures in the area, however, a northern Shaanxi storytelling performance must be understood as integrated historically with the local ritual ceremonies of temple fairs, lifecycles, rain processions, or shamanic exorcism. The performance therefore not only carried the function of musical entertainment but formed part of communal religious life at the village level. In fact, precisely because of the storyteller's capacity to recite ancient calendrical details, local poetry, and the lyrics of dynastic songs, they were often asked to cure illness in individual households (Wang 1993: 9). Traditionally associated with a large spectrum of religious and ritual activities, storytellers were particularly good at ritual performances to sing "stories for wellbeing" (to secure divine blessings for the community) and to appease deities (Jones 2009: 31–33). Their role as storyteller was often blurred with that of geomancer or supernatural healer.[2]

Despite its ritual and religious functions, northern Shaanxi storytelling was perhaps one of the first few local cultural practices the Communist intellectuals approached and identified as suitable to disseminate the CCP mission and policies in the 1930s. In 1940, the "storytelling group" (*shuoshu zu*) was formed under the Cultural Association of the border government (Hung 1993: 399–400; Wang 1993: 15). Urban intellectuals, such as Lin Shan, worked closely with the storytellers and revised their traditional tales (*jiushu*). Stories that once revolved around the emperor and the general, or around romances between young scholars and beautiful maidens (*caizijiaren*), were reworked into "new stories" (*xinshu*), which emphasized the distress of the country folk and revolutionary changes.[3] Though being turned into party propaganda, the reworked storytelling was not completely focused on political indoctrination or the promotion of party ideology. Instead, it carried a strong emphasis on the cultural enrichment of the poverty-stricken region and aimed mainly to deliver entertainment to remote rural corners. As Wang Yuhua notes, "without the influence of the CCP, rural Yan'an would have been so culturally impoverished that villagers could barely see one monkey comedian a year" (Wang 1993: 7).

Han Qixiang was perhaps the most successful storyteller to emerge from this culture reform movement. Illiterate and blind, he became the most famous folk artist of the Communist era and of northern Shaanxi storytelling (Wang 1993: 214–236). Han's signature piece, *Fanshenji*, an autobiographical account of how his fate was "turned around" (*fanshen*) by the Communist liberation, was performed for thousands of people (Shaanxisheng Quyizhi Bianji Bangongshi 1985; Hung 1993: 395–426). During Mao's time, Han's performance helped to win popular support for the Communist government. He was given the honorable title of "sanxian warrior": "his sanxian [was] like a gun, his singing like bullets and his scripts like an arsenal" (Wang 1993: 310–318).

Still, one brilliant storyteller was not enough: ideally, many Han Qixiangs would be needed to roam the countryside and spread the gospel of Communism (Hung 1993: 408). To realize this goal, a massive reorientation was undertaken: in 1946 alone, 273 out of a total of 483 storytellers in China attended "retraining classes," and more than 50 traditional tales were rewritten (Yuan et al. 2001: 25–38). After 1949, the Hall of Culture sponsored and organized folk practitioners to form opera troupes (*jutuan*). Approximately 500 reformed storytellers went to remote rural areas and performed in the Yan'an region. Master Xu recalled that, during Mao's era, the production brigade leader would announce the arrival of a storyteller through the village broadcast (*cun guangbo*) and the commune members would rush out to attend the popular recital, "Wanggui and Li Xiangxiang."[4] Often staged in winter during which farm work was less intense, northern Shaanxi storytelling was a major show in rural collective life, mixed with the dissemination of party-state policies. But even during the high time of socialism, not all storytellers joined the government-sponsored opera troupes (Jones 2009: 55).

The practice of storytelling continued into the reform era. In 1977, the Yan'an Area Musical Drama Society was established to recognize the contribution of northern Shaanxi storytelling to the creation of the modern Chinese state. Financed by the city government as an nonprofit danwei (*shiye danwei*) under the Hall of Culture, the Society continues to train storytelling artists and to provide performances in government-sponsored night shows, cultural programs, and festivals.[5] In rural Yan'an after Mao, folk storytelling practitioners have reverted to catering to religious audiences at temple festivals, even though they continue to promote government campaigns in their performances (Cao 2005). The following case with Master Xu demonstrates the highly ambivalent form and meanings of folk cultural practice in today's rural Yan'an.

A Performance in Heijiawa Village

When in July 2004 I accompanied Master Xu on a storytelling trip, the first village that we visited was Heijiawa in Yan'an's Guantuan County, an impoverished community with a rough terrain and poor transportation. The village had a population of three hundred, with an annual income of 2,000 yuan per capita. In the summer, the younger generation was mostly absent, working as migrant laborers in the city. There remained only about one hundred men and women, all older than forty, together with no more than twenty small children. Upon arrival, Master Xu and I were housed with the village leader, Li, who was also host of that night's performance. By eight o'clock, a crowd of about forty villagers had gathered at the village leader's cavehouse. Many secured a seat on the *kang*—a raised concrete platform occupying the center of the cavehouse.[6] People crossed their legs, rested their arms on their knees, and pushed their hands into their sleeves—signature posture of the "old Shaanbei." Instead of taking his position on a platform above his listeners, Master Xu retreated to an unoccupied corner. Some members of the audience could not see him after he settled down. When Master Xu started playing, however, everyone could see the swinging movement of the embroidered sachet (*xiangbao*) hanging from the instrument and its amplified reflection on the wall.

As was the case with the other storytelling events that I had attended, Master Xu played while the audience continued with their own activities: the elderly dozed, women chatted, and babies cried. After ten minutes of playing, Master Xu started to sing the lyrics, which appear at the beginning of this chapter. He sang of a new prosperity (*xin xiaokang*) in rural Yan'an, with tap water, concrete roads, televisions, and gas stoves, and he attributed these developments to the leadership of the party-state. The instrumental music then continued for about fifteen minutes, when its tone changed from comforting to solemn. Master Xu began speaking again, this time in prayer:

> Oh, I call on you, gods and goddesses, those in the mountain ranges, those in the forest, those by the pool and those in the cosmic palace. Gods and goddesses, please line up in two rows. As the sanxian's voice rises, the Buddha goes to the lotus leaves and the temple of green shade. In the middle of the sea stands the God Guanyin. There are others who stand by the sun, by the cloud and the spirit pavilion. Under the big trees are the Black Tiger God, the guardian of eternal punishment, the Monkey King riding on his magical cloud, the God Erlang hiding in the cave and the Goddess NiangNiang riding on a boat. When the dragon raises its head, the God Sanhuang comes. Gods and goddesses, please listen. I call on your names to come down to our place. I pray to you with my spoken wish (*kouyuan*), and in return I am giving you a story performance. This is a story of well-wishing. Please ensure that the elderly members of the Li family have longevity and fortune. Worship is like water running in the Yellow River and reciting scriptures in the South Mountain. Oh, the host, Mr. Li, is a businessman. Please protect his safety when he travels and ensure that all his children take the examination for college. Oh, please let

them be happy throughout this year. Gods and goddesses, please take away their suffering throughout this year and let no sickness come to the family; but if they are sick, please protect them from getting worse. Buddha, please show your power so that evil influences stay away from the family. Please take care of their children at school and make sure that they like studying. Please let them score the highest when taking the examination and let their names appear on the school honor roll. When they grow up, please let them go to Beijing to perform the waist-drum performer or to become a government official. These are our wishes: safety at the heart and no sickness. Please light up the fire mountain to ward off evil influences, and please ensure that the fire continues so that we are protected for twelve months, for 30 days, for 12 hours. Gods and goddesses here tonight, we will offer you a story. [The tone of music changes.]

Historically and even today, northern Shaanxi storytellers perform a "gratitude for a wish fulfilled" (*huankouyuan*) ritual in rural Yan'an when a family has promised a local deity a storytelling performance in return for the fulfillment of a wish. The ritual involves elaborate preparation: setting up a shrine, burning incense, bowing to the sky, and inviting deities to the performance. Both the form and content of the prayer—made to invite and welcome gods and popular pantheons, and to drive away inauspicious forces—were similar to those of the recitation or liturgy historically used in rites and rituals in northern Chinese villages (Yuan et al. 2001: 145–146; Jones 2009: 31–41). The subsequent storytelling is both an offering to the deities and a public entertainment. The ritual simultaneously performs several functions. First, it is a way for the family to reward a deity who has answered their prayer. Second, it is an occasion when the family receives blessings. Lastly, it is a communal entertainment—neighbors are invited to share in the wishes expressed.

That night in Heijiawa Village, Master Xu told a story about a hungry wolf that tricked a man into making friends with a beast. As the story unfolded, the man who was tricked was eaten alive—a warning to the audience to beware of tricks and traps. However, not all the audience members were listening to Master Xu's tale: some villagers were chatting and some children even started to fight. Unlike a show on stage, where the performer demands everyone's attention, a storytelling event is more of a social gathering or an evening of relaxation for those with sore muscles. Still, that night at Heijiawa, there were some fervent admirers of the tale. When Master Xu chanted his conclusion accompanied by his instrument's hypnotic rhythm around midnight, the audience shouted, "No! Tell us another one! We want

FIGURE 3.1. A northern Shaanxi storytelling performance by Master Xu inside a cavehouse.

more!" Despite his exhaustion, Master Xu straightened his back again and chanted another short piece before the crowd dispersed happily around one o'clock in the morning (Figure 3.1).

Religious Rites in the Name of Propaganda

Visually impaired due to suffering from meningitis in childhood, Master Xu remains an easygoing, practical, and dedicated man, happily married with three children. With his residual vision, he has trekked alone on the Loess cliffs and hilly paths to deliver performances in many villages in the Yan'an region. In the 1980s, in recognition of his contribution to the enrichment of socialist life for rural residents, he was given the status of urban citizen of Yan'an; along with five other storytellers, he has since received a basic monthly salary of 1,000 yuan per month from the Yan'an City Hall of Culture. Now in retirement and in his sixties, Master Xu has continued to visit various rural villages every summer. He called these storytelling trips "going down to the countryside" (*xiaxiang*), a term that was formerly used to describe state-orchestrated initiatives to send urban residents/intellectuals to rural areas for reeducation, propaganda, and knowledge exchange during the Maoist period. When he spoke of going down to the countryside, I interpreted this to mean that he saw himself as a propagandist going to a rural village for the promotion of the state, even though I suspected that his intention was simply to have more performances and so to earn more income.

Indeed, our itinerary in 2004 was very much contingent on the bureaucratic operation of the rural government. Before entering any village, we had to meet with the rural township government, the highest level of rural administration. There, Master Xu would produce his propaganda certificate and state his plan: which villages he was intending to go to and how many days he was going to spend in each. Since I was accompanying Master Xu, I was also requested to show my ID to the local bureaucrats and state the purpose of my research. At the individual village level, we confirmed to the local party cadre that we had notified (*dazhaohu*) their superior, so it was clear that our visits were approved. Upon leaving each village, Master Xu received a memo, either from the village committee leader or the local party cadre, containing the date of visit and the amount of money paid. The memo served the Yan'an Hall of Culture and the township government as proof that the storytellers were "doing their propaganda job."

To my surprise, Master Xu was at Heijiawa Village to perform a "gratitude for a wish fulfilled" ritual, even though he began the performance with a "propaganda" piece that glorified the party-state. He spent the next two days in the village reading the palms of the villagers for free. Parents keen to know the condition and future of their children (who were unmarried and/or working far from home), lined up to hear what Master Xu had to say.

In the second village, Wangqu, Master Xu was asked to stage a ritual performance for the protection of small children from sickness and inauspicious influences (*baosuo*) (Figure 3.2). The parents told me that they wanted the ritual because their little baby was always crying and colicky at night, and they wondered if some evil spirits might be bothering him. The ritual was held at noon. It involved setting up a shrine, burning incense, and preparing a bowl of grain. Master Xu held a bell, started chanting, and held a locket over the small baby many times. When the incense finished burning, Master Xu stopped chanting and hung a locket tied with colorful strips for the child; then he gave a yellow triangle packet to the parents. In return, the parents gave Master Xu a red packet with payment inside and a pair of new shoes and asked the child to call him "godfather" (*ganba*). Locals believe that children who have gone through the ritual are better protected from the attack of evil spirits and will grow healthily (Jones 2009: 35–38).

In the third village, Master Xu staged a storytelling performance during the day as usual. At night, however, the village committee leader Wang came

FIGURE 3.2. A storyteller performed the ritual of *baosuo* with a bell, a chopper, a small arch, and two arrows.

to where Master Xu was staying and asked him to help his mother, who had been diagnosed with breast cancer a few years earlier and had stayed at home without getting further treatment. The disease, however, caused great pain to the woman in her seventies. Seeing his mother suffering, Wang hoped that Master Xu could do something. Master Xu told Wang honestly that he could not give much help because breast cancer was a serious illness. All that he could do was to stage a ritual and ask for the protection of the deities. Master Xu then set up a shrine, burnt some incense, and asked the protective deities to come down. After the ritual initiation, he asked Wang to give him some rice wine. First, he poured some wine for the deities into the little cups in front of the shrine. Then he asked Wang's mother to take off her clothes. Master Xu then gulped down half a bottle of wine and blew it on the woman's chest. Chanting spells, Master Xu rubbed the old woman's breasts with more wine. After the ritual, the village leader Wang thanked Master Xu repeatedly. From their farewell conversation, I could tell that Master Xu had known the family for a long time and that he performed the ritual not for money but to help the old woman.

Master Xu and I stayed longest in the sixth village, Wangjiagou, which was situated in a remote mountain location. Since Master Xu and I mostly walked between villages, I lost track of the direction after Heijiawa, but I guessed that Heijiawa was the village closest to the main paved road and that all the other villages after it were located farther away from both the rural administrative center and urban center. In fact, whenever I asked Master Xu about our location, he gave me the answer, *"hou gou,"* meaning the back of the valley.

Wangjiagou contained about thirty sparsely located households. As with the previous village, most of the residents were elderly. The party cadre who came to greet us told me that some of the households have relocated to other villages and some have moved to the city of Yan'an for business. The remaining villagers were mainly elderly and middle-aged people. Villagers continued to grow corn, potatoes, and millet, but the grain was only for their own consumption, as loading it for sale was too costly. Early in the morning of the second day, I found that Master Xu did not come to Wangjiagou for storytelling at all. Before dawn, we woke up and hiked to the top of the hill, where a temple festival was being held. The hike alone took about one and one-half hours, and the slope was very steep, but the villagers passed me by quickly, shouldering boxes of tools, water, offerings, and props for the big event. On the top of the hill stood a temple constructed a few years ago, and the deity worshipped there was the Efficacious Black Tiger Official (*Heihulingguan*).

The Black Tiger Official was a deity responsible for guarding the entrance of Baiyun Mountain, a mountain in northern Shaanxi believed to accommodate hundreds of gods and goddesses of Daoist, Buddhist, and Confucian traditions. Local legends depict him as riding a black tiger and capable of alleviating epidemic diseases (Guo 2000). In today's Yan'an, many spiritual mediums claim that they have been possessed by the Black Tiger Official deity. These spiritual mediums attract followers and give spiritual divinations. In return, the followers donate money, build temples for the deity, and hold annual temple festivals. The temple festival held on top of Wangjiagou Village was one of these.

In the Wangjiagou temple festival, the male spirit medium, addressed as "horse lad" (*matong*) in Yan'an, sat by the offering shrine. He greeted the followers of the temple association and talked extensively with them. The leader of the temple association, who received us, was the old party secretary of the village, and he told me that he had been acquainted with Master Xu for a long time, since the socialist era. About one hundred people from surrounding villages came to the festival, which lasted for two days. People came mainly to receive a blessing, for healing, or to ask about their marriage prospects and fortune; but another purpose in attending the festival was to participate in a local rite known as "passing through the obstacles" (*guoguan*). This rite has a simple setup of an elongated chopper one and one-half meters wide, with the handle connected to a wooden base. Presided over by the temple association leader, the rite was held at noon when enough people were in the queue. Next to the shrine where incense was burning, the temple association leader chanted incantations meant to drive away bad spirits and secure more protection for the children. Then the leader moved the chopper up and down, creating some noise from the blade. Children seven to ten years old wore a rope adorned with dried grass hanging down from their waist. When the leader raised the chopper from the ground to head level, a child would go through it and stop there. The leader would then put down the chopper quickly so that the dry grass was cut off. I saw parents or grandparents waiting happily on the other side of the chopper to give their children a cracker to eat. Most would also burn incense at the temple shrine and give some money to the leader afterward. The temple association leader told me that the big chopper had been blessed by the deity and was thus considered efficacious in dispelling the inauspicious forces holding on to small children, especially those who were vulnerable to illness (Jones 2009: 37–38).

During the temple festival, Master Xu sat in the corner next to the shrine, playing his sanxian and singing the whole time. Sometimes a few elderly villagers surrounded him and listened to his performance, but most of the time he was just singing without an audience. The temple association leader told me that Master Xu's performance was meant as an offering to the deity. The music and singing from the storytelling performance thus formed part of the local ceremonial and cultural networks of the surrounding villages. If the association had had a larger budget, they might invite a drama troupe, but the leader said that Master Xu had been with them for years and he would continue to invite him.

New Desires and New Problems in Rural Yan'an Today

Much has been written about the serious rural-urban divide and regional developmental imbalance in China since the 1990s (Wang and Hu 1999; Sun 2004a, 2004b; Chen and Chun Tao 2004; Berstein and Lu 2003). Agriculture has been considered "a losing business" with inflation raising the price of necessities, from education to fertilizer, and the state putting much more capital investment in cities. Farming has become utterly unprofitable for most, and the villagers' land of production has become a land of subsistence. Sociologist Huang Ping even maintains that "scavenging in the city is better than farming" (2003: 12–33). The result is the migration of 200 million rural residents to urban coastal cities. Migrant workers face numerous challenges, such as long working hours, low wages, the need to leave their children in the rural homeland, and the difficulty of making ends meet in the cities (Chan 2001; Pun 2005; Fan 2008).

Though some measures have recently been introduced to correct this inequality, these were not evident during my stay in Yan'an in 2004. In the rural communities, the majority of the inhabitants were small children, young wives, and the elderly. Most villagers between the ages of eighteen and forty-eight were working in other provinces. Those who continued to farm had reverted to primitive means of farming, such as carrying loads of straw on their back or milling wheat by physically pushing a traditional grinder.[7] Unprofitable farming, combined with the lack of basic infrastructure like paved roads, water pipes, and sewage systems, reinforced the severe underdevelopment of the rural area. However, the movement of people, urban images, and information never ceased. Young villagers coming back to rural hometowns bring new consumption values and urban styles (Liu 2000; Gaetano and Jacka 2004). Tim Oakes and Louisa Schein argue that mass mobility exposes the highly uneven and differentiated effects inherent in processes of development. Not everyone can move, and those who stay behind are confronted with even greater problems of insecurity and deprivation (Oakes and Schein 2006). As a result, as Stephen Jones notes, "the traditional rituals that had revived in the area became among the few remaining embodiments of community values" (2009: 10). I would add further that the spiritual, rather than the folk storytelling, aspects of the practice have become valorized because they speak to a rural community that has drastically transformed in relation to new forms of urban development, desires, and new problems.

The massive departure of rural residents in search of urban jobs has resulted in a dramatic transformation of traditional rural family structures and values. Once village couples start working in cities, they have to leave their children behind with their grandparents, who must then add child-rearing to their other responsibilities. In addition, when young migrant workers are immersed in urban settings, traditional notions of success, morality, and family are often challenged. In the villages I visited, many young migrant women and men find it difficult to marry and return to their rural roots after living in the city, but their parents find it hard or even shameful when their children in their late twenties or even thirties have not yet married. At the same time, even married migrant workers are burdened by complicated translocal relationships. As more couples work in different cities and some leave their spouses in the rural home, extramarital relationships and divorce have become new rural problems.

Indeed, Master Xu had been called to Heijiawa Village to perform rituals essentially because Li, the host and village leader, had discovered that his new daughter-in-law had run away with another man while working as a migrant laborer in south China. The Li family asked Master Xu to encourage the local deities to hasten the return of their daughter-in-law, and hoped that the storytelling performance would be a stronger offering to the deities than just burning incense. It should be noted that, in rural Yan'an, acquiring a daughter-in-law is a stressful undertaking: the groom's family must have enough money to pay the brideswealth and to build a new house for the couple (Liu 2000: 66–71). In remote and economically depressed villages, families often find it very difficult to attract a daughter-in-law and a runaway daughter-in-law is a great hardship. Nonetheless, the event also reflects changing gender values among rural women working away in the city, who find new opportunities, partners, and individual development outside of rural domestic households (Cheng and Ma 2005, Ma 2006: 45–105).

In addition, traveling has become one of the most important activities in rural villages today. Instead of staying put and farming, villagers leave their villages constantly, and most of the younger members even reside permanently in distant cities. It is no wonder that the traditional wish for safe journeys has increased in importance. As almost every rural villager now either makes trips or depends on their younger children to maintain a livelihood elsewhere, Master Xu's prayers that the deities "give safety when the family travels" become ever more relevant.

Third, spiritual need thrives in rural communities today. Instead of attributing the spiritual revival to a simple return to the storytelling tradition from before the 1940s, I relate it to the huge movement of labor, objects, and emotions between the rural and urban areas. Because such movement is highly uneven, and because of the widening cultural distance between remote rural areas and the city, the villagers left behind are in the condition of always waiting for news of their family members. This is especially true for aging parents yearning for their children who are working away. Knowing that their children are likely to be subjected to harsh working conditions and negligible remuneration, these parents ease their worries through the gratitude rituals.

My point is not that northern Shaanxi folk storytelling has revived because of depressing rural economic conditions. Rather, I wish to emphasize that the revival of storytelling practice becomes one of the rare social and communal occasions for rural villagers to get together where they can openly discuss all kinds of major rural developmental contradictions: lack of elderly care, split households, and youth who find no career development in remote rural hometowns and who encounter much difficulty surviving in cities. Whenever Master Xu sings at a temple festival, villagers know that there is a short emergence of a "public agrarian sphere" where villagers can enjoy more lively communal interactions and seek more personal and familial concerns (Chau 2006: 11). For sick rural residents such as Wang's mother, the coming of a storyteller means both spiritual healing and psychological comfort. For others, it means getting together with one's neighbor and having some fun and excitement together.

In short, folk storytelling occasions are valuable not so much because villagers are getting more religious or that the practice is a time-honored heritage. Rather, folk storytelling has become what Megan Moodie called "platforms for articulation," where local citizens draw traditional cultural resources to discuss pressing concerns of split households among left-behind elderly and young wives in remote rural communities in a translocal age (2008: 462–463).

Conclusion

Popular religious revival is not only a rural phenomenon but is equally rampant in today's urban prosperous Yan'an city, as evident in the thousands of annual urban pilgrims who hike up the Qingliang mountain to celebrate the Daoist temple festival of the 8th day of April in the Chinese lunar calendar. There, I witnessed people lining up to tell Master Xu and other storytellers their names, residences, and concerns and to hear a quick, five-minute version of a "story for wellbeing" or to fulfill a vow (Jones 2009: 84–87). In his book, *Miraculous Response*, Adam Chau has argued that religious practice, economic interests, regional fame, local governmental legitimacy, and communal interests often meet in large-scale temple fairs where local state and local religious leaders collaborate with each other (Chau 2006). However, if a large-scale government-sanctioned temple festival allows open worship and profit making, and results in "red hot sociality" (*honghuo*)—a state of excitement for social events—the village ritual performances that I witnessed in remote rural Yan'an were very different. In villages in between the isolated valleys, the sent-down propagandist Master Xu was transformed into a more versatile character, presiding over a variety of healing services and rituals in the "gray religious market" where the local state officials kept a half-open eye on the many informal, illegal religious and cult practices.[8] There, the villagers were keen to articulate personal fortune and navigate the gaps created by mass migration and the existing rural-urban divide, rather than merely to look for some excitement through traditional rites.

Indeed, storytellers like Master Xu, who is entrusted with the ability to engage with supernatural forces, are in great demand today. In a way, Master Xu resembled the historically prevalent yet localized figure of the "incense head" (*xiangtou*), an individual endowed with religious knowledge who engages supernatural forces and is actively sought by rural villagers to treat minor ailments (Dubois 2005: 65–85). In other ways, however, Master Xu was not exactly a religious figure; his late socialist network and Maoist storyteller persona still mattered greatly. Master Xu repeatedly stressed that his business of going down to the countryside was intricately linked to his late socialist network and previous propagandist identity. He said that had he not gained the various official approvals or used the social network along the previous administrative hierarchy of the People's Commune, he would not have been able to come down annually to the individual households. Observing his interactions with local villagers, especially with the village party cadres or village leaders along the route, I also sensed that Master Xu's religious "ability" or his "localized religious knowledge" derived not only from the ritual tradition of northern Shaanxi storytelling but also from his status as a government sponsored figure (*gongjiaren*) and a recognized individual (*shouren*). In fact, villagers cannot trust just anyone when fraudulence in the remote rural society is rampant. The ritual of hanging lockets for small children, for instance, calls for highly reliable and respectable "godfathers" among left-behind young wives and small babies. In this context, Master Xu's credibility and respected status were especially valued. His storytelling performance not only connotes a social opportunity where people share problems, receive diagnoses, or go through spiritual rites; it also highlights the niche for a reliable religious resource with a "professional reputation" (Dubois 2005: 83). I once saw Master Xu meet with a rejection of his storytelling performance, but that was because the village leader to whom we talked was new and had no knowledge of him as an ex-propagandist.[9]

In conclusion, northern Shaanxi storytelling can be considered a quasi-religious resource with late socialist characteristics, which responds to new social and communal desires in the context of a great rural-urban divide. For the local party cadre, township-level bureaucrats, and the villagers left behind, the coming of storytellers meant the provision of cultural entertainment. A performance continued to be a break for many in the busy summer. The spiritual activities associated with storytelling were particularly welcome because they helped to alleviate anxiety at the community level. Ironically, however, it was the ambiguous identity of the storyteller, with his late socialist reputation, that made him a credible religious resource catering to translocal desires in today's marginalized rural corners.

Northern Shaanxi storytelling was originally designed as part of a government-sponsored cultural enrichment mission to poverty-stricken rural areas. Today's rural Yan'an no longer faces starvation, but encounters very different challenges. Separated families, an aging population, and abandoned farming activities have all bred new anxieties and desires. The folk cultural practitioner turned state propagandist no longer goes around to share a socialist vision: instead, he delivers a variety of spiritual services that are much needed by the remaining rural residents. The combination of his ex-propagandist identity with his current spiritual service, however, provides an ironic commentary on the underdevelopment for rural communities in Yan'an, the very place where earlier Communist leaders had vowed to instigate good governance, social equity, and the new future of a socialist China.

CHAPTER 4

Folk Cultural Production with Danwei Characteristics

Folk Storytelling and Public Relations Activities

Hit the counter top and move forward. Let us promote the quality control system.
Product quality is important and all leaders should ensure the working of the system.

Speaking of quality, talking of quality; product quality is the key
Good quality control earns applause
Bad quality control leads to disaster.

Low quality copper and bricks result in building collapse
Low quality furnaces cause big explosion
Low quality vehicles and planes make traffic accidents
Low quality drinks and well water lead to multiple social issues

Demand quality consumption
Demand quality production
Demand quality service
Demand especially quality construction
The issue of quality is key to millions of products and thousands of companies.

This northern Shaanxi storytelling piece, entitled "Quality Control System Spreads to Millions," was sung in the evening of August 25, 2004, in the courtyard of a state-owned workers' residence in Yanchuan township, by the Yanchuan Musical Drama Troupe. The piece was followed by a short story about a man, Zhang, who was cheated into buying expensive drugs but later found out they were all fake. The piece ended as follows:

People with black hearts cheat people with fake products
Fake fertilizers, fake pesticides
Fake food, fake medicine
Fake seeds and fake cement
Fake recruitment and fake school admission
Fake friends and fake couples
Selfish and greedy thoughts hurt people, the heaven and the earth
People should be alert about the fakes
Everyone learns the Law of Quality Control to facilitate the Great Development of West China
Implement the Law of Quality control benefits [for] our country and us
Learn the law, use the law, know the law to build a happy family

In a hot evening, sixty workers and their families from the Engineering and Machinery Factory, a major SOE of Yanchuan county, Yan'an, enjoyed the show in their open-air residential courtyard, with some standing and some sitting on small wooden stools. Under only one big light bulb, four storytellers in their fifties and sixties performed with traditional Chinese instruments: *pipa*, sanxian, and wooden clappers. They started with a few stories on quality-control legislation and subsequently changed to a traditional Chinese story performance entitled "Muguiying." The traditional story concerns a woman warrior named Muguiying who, in the Song Dynasty, fought against the Xia ethnic people with good archery skills and thoughtful strategies. Storytellers' singing, amplified through several standing microphones, captured the attention of the worker audience.

Putting together news headlines on fake products, legislation on quality control, and a traditional Chinese story in one folk storytelling performance in an SOE residential setting reveals a peculiar nature—yet extremely common form—of folk performance in Yan'an. In this example, the northern Shaanxi storytellers put together two seemingly unrelated tasks in one setting: singing for the government's Bureau of Quality Control to promote the recent legislation; and staging a traditional storytelling entertainment for the audience.

Such a performance is definitely different from most Western understanding of Communist party-state propaganda, which in the past was often associated with totalitarian, manipulative messages surrounding national political campaigns and, in recent years, with policies that satisfy the citizens' needs for stability and a harmonious society. Political scientist Anne-Marie Brady argues that the CCP today is actively constructing a "state Confucianism" by joining the popular revival of Confucianism in rural society and promoting the study of it, from colleges to cadre political training, in order to reinforce Chinese moral values of filial piety and virtuosity (2012: 60–75). She thinks that the CCP's selective mobilization of Chinese traditional thoughts is a party-state effort to forge the "Chinese model" (*zhongguo moshi*), a form of governance that rejects Western liberal democracy but incorporates Chinese tradition within modernity (2012: 57–75). However, the storytelling performance cited earlier did not seem to easily fit in such a mobilization plan of appropriating folk culture for social control and governance purposes.

The performance is also quite different from conventional understanding of a folk musical performance, which appeals to audiences by stressing the traditional, the pristine, and the historical elements in both its contents and forms. American Chinese photographer Yan Qingzhao, for instance, once described the northern Shaanxi storytelling cultural form as "an ancient folk art that has curiously lived on in this aged and beautiful earth of the Loess." Yan wrote, "If you happen to see a blind storyteller, please slow down your pace. Do not miss him. Listen to the stories they moan with a peaceful mind. You might find what you have been seeking in your life" (Yen-Burgermeister and Yang 2004: 145). Nostalgic representations of folk storytelling—as reflecting a simple, slightly mysterious, yet natural form of rural life in which one will find truth and wisdom—is common among urban photographers, writers, and folklorists. The storytelling performance discussed earlier, however, addressed one of the most controversial social problems of Chinese society today—faked products—with a disapproving tone.

This chapter examines the practice of folk tradition as coming from the danwei of state-owned enterprises and government departments at the local county level in economically less developed Yan'an. Using the case of northern Shaanxi storytelling, I show that the practice of folk tradition engages heavily with work-unit messages and, sometimes, national ideology promotion. Such folk performance is different from the understanding mentioned earlier of party-state propaganda, which aims to achieve thought control or morality cultivation. Instead, I show the ways in which folk cultural production today concerns complicated political, commercial, and social relations with work units that existing literature seldom addresses. My major argument is that the production of folk tradition is increasingly adapted to danwei public relations events and campaigns, while, at the same time, danwei events also become the spaces wherein traditional folk art forms find new developments, audiences, and visibility in the age of urbanization and marketization.

The data of this chapter are drawn from fieldwork in Yanchuan county, east of Yan'an city in 2004, 2008, and 2012. I participated in the annual training of the Yanchuan Musical Drama Troupe held every August in Yanchuan town center. I interviewed all twelve members of the troupe and I went with them to ask for performance opportunities at various work units. I also interviewed one of the most renowned storytellers in Yan'an, Cao Boyan, and the region's most authoritative and prolific storytelling scriptwriter, Cao Bozhi.

The Yanchuan Musical Drama Troupe

A typical small town center of inland China, Yanchuan town center is at the valley bottom, cut into two halves by a river and surrounded by hills and ridges where arrays of cavehouses line up. In 2004, it had two to three main streets of small restaurants, noodle stations, cell-phone outlets, photograph shops, one supermarket, two banks, and other small vendors of housewares, baked goods, groceries, and clothing. All the other small alleys were mud paths, and most buildings here were five to seven stories, built in the early 1980s. The most prominent structures were the city government office and two hotels, standing amid hundreds of cottage-height brick structures and cavehouses. The Yanchuan primary and secondary schools, with new building structures and nice facilities, were located in the less busy and residential side of the town. A few bridges connected the two sides. But most crossed the main bridge, where it was a very busy marketplace in the morning. Food vendors sold congee, noodles, steamed buns, and all kinds of cooked food. Peasants in the surrounding village spread products on the ground for sale: fruits, nuts, animal leather, poultry, meat, Chinese herbs, clothing, hardware, and agricultural tools. Amid people buying and bargaining, traders loaded their donkey with carts of goods on and off of the bridge. As compared to Yan'an city in the same year, Yanchuan county remained much less urbanized and its residents were mostly working in the agricultural sector.

It was a hot day when Mr. Cao and I arrived at Yanchuan town center. The sun was so strong that most people went inside for shade, leaving the street empty. As we walked toward the end of the main street, the road revealed its unpaved and rough soil surface. Quickly, we made a right turn into a dark and filthy alley, where a shabby building, the South Gate Hostel, was located and where the Yanchuan Musical Drama Troupe conducted their annual training. When I entered the room of the storytellers, there was a second of grayout due to the sharp contrasts of light. But the heavy smell of urine mixed with strong tobacco smoke quickly brought me to my senses. I found myself standing in a room in which two *kangs* occupied all of the eighty square feet, leaving a narrow passage in the middle. Twelve blind men, old and young, were lying down or sitting on the *kang*, some gently played their instruments. The storytellers sensed that people had come in. One of them rolled his eyes, showing clouded eyeballs with less distinct pupils. He asked, "Who is it?" Mr. Cao immediately raised his voice, "It is me!" Later I asked how Mr. Cao knew all the blind men so well. He smiled, "I grew up listening to their stories."

Every year, the twelve visually challenged storytellers stayed at the South Gate Hostel to conduct their month-long training because the owner here offered the troupe a discounted rate—only 2 RMB a night each. Normally, these storytellers lived in different villages sparsely scattered in the county countryside. During the one month in town, the objective of the troupe was to find as many performance opportunities as possible at various danwei—government departments, state-owned and private enterprises—in order to earn income collectively. After the training, they would go back to their own villages and sing for individual temple festivals or stage the ritual of "gratitude for a wish fulfilled" for rural households (see Chapter 3).

Performance Scheduling at Work Units

In the morning of August 10, I woke up early to find that the storytellers, who had practiced for about a week, proceeded to "schedule a story performance" (*dingshu*) in town. The troupe sent out three to four representatives as a team, with at least one member with residual eyesight, to find work units interested in sponsoring a performance. The troupe leader kindly allowed me to join their trip. That morning, Master Gao and Master Chen had very specific targets: the Yanchuan county government building.

Some government danwei were waiting for the annual visit of these storytellers that morning. As soon as we went into the Statistics Bureau of the county government building, a woman officer warmly greeted us and poured us some tea. From their friendly conversations, I could sense that they had known each other for a long time. After some chatting, she gave the storytellers a piece of paper with themes related to the launching of the county census work. She told me that the bureau was happy to give lyrics and scripts, based on their upcoming census launch, and have the troupe stage performances in rural villages during the national census period. She joked that the storytellers would serve as "promotion officers" before the census workers actually go in and collect information at individual households. Her explanation was that many elderly in the rural area might not understand the meaning of census work by just watching the news headlines on television. And the census could be done much more effectively if villagers enjoy a performance and understand some details before the official launch. We left happily from the Statistics Bureau after a performance was successfully scheduled that day.

Later, we met with the staffs at the Education Bureau. Obviously, the storytellers had scheduled a performance with the Yanchuan schools before this trip. In that summer, one of the biggest audiences the troupe performed for was at the Yanchuan County Primary School. At the campus playground, the event drew an audience of over one hundred teachers and schoolchildren. It started with the school president speaking of northern Shaanxi storytelling as a regional traditional art form and the significance of students understanding it as a cultural heritage. The major program of the night was a storytelling version of the renowned folk legend, "*Baoliandeng*" (Lotus Lantern). The legend tells of a courageous young boy struggling to rescue his mother, a goddess penalized and imprisoned for her decision to marry a mortal. The schoolchildren enjoyed the story until nine o'clock at night. During the break, I saw some children carry the blind storytellers to bathrooms in a highly respectful manner.

I could imagine it was not very difficult for storytellers to schedule a performance with the county primary school. As a major work unit at the county level, the primary school can host a storytelling performance either as cultural education or as an extracurricular activity. It was also legitimate for schools to promote northern Shaanxi storytelling as a local tradition and now an intangible cultural heritage. In fact, the storytellers had promised they would come back next year after the performance that night.

Another very successful performance was at the SOE of the Yanchuan County Engineering and Machinery Factory mentioned at the beginning of the chapter. The storytellers had scheduled a performance at the Quality Control Bureau before and related officers had given the troupe singing scripts on avoiding fake products in order to promote the quality-control legislation. The performance drew about sixty people to the courtyard of the state-provided factory residence. Storytellers told me that they had had performances at this enterprise almost every year for more than a decade. The Engineering and Machinery Factory as a major county SOE always invited the storytellers for its annual staff event. That night, the storytellers promoted the law of quality control and the "Great Development of West China," a national development campaign that extended state and private investment into northwestern China.[1]

SOE workers in Yan'an usually have a high social status, good welfare benefits, and lifelong job security. Many SOEs organize entertainment events, even traveling tours and trips, to cultivate workers' loyalty to the enterprise. With economic reforms and market competition starting from the 1990s, however, some of the less competitive SOEs were having problems with attracting enough business contracts. Some of these unprofitable SOEs thus put older employees in an arrangement of early retirement, a condition in which workers continue to receive a large portion of salary and the original welfare package, without having to work at the danwei. The Yanchuan County Engineering and Machinery Factory was one of these SOEs with a number of staff members in the condition of early retirement. The performance that night therefore turned out to be a great gathering among those who continued to stay and those who no longer had to report to duty. It almost worked like a reunion party, where workers gave big hugs to and reconnected with each other and let their children run around with peers. The performance could in no way alleviate the sadness of looming layoffs, but it allowed the "early retirees" to sing and gather as proud SOE workers again. Most importantly, everyone enjoyed the featured northern Shaanxi storytelling as the core entertainment. That night, folk storytellers magically combined the promotion of quality-control legislation, consumers' rights, national campaigns, the enterprises' images, and staff entertainment in a single event.

But the storytellers were not always successful in their attempt to win a performance opportunity. That day at the Yanchuan government building, we were rejected twice. First, at the office of the Communist Youth League, Master Gao kindly stated the purpose to the two young officers, presented the propaganda certificate, and waited. The officer who covered his face with a newspaper, however, uttered the word "No." But since none of us were intending to leave, the officer put down his newspaper and waved his hand, saying "Go away, we don't want it." Yielding no response, he softened his tone a bit and said "We've got only four people in this department and we do not have the budget for you." The group stayed silent for a long while. Master Chen then sat on a couch, followed by Master Gao, who lit a cigarette and offered one to the officer, who naturally accepted it. For the next ten minutes, the three of them smoked, but no one talked. The office atmosphere was quiet, tense, and smoky. Finally, the officer put down 50 yuan on the couch. The two storytellers looked at the banknote and said, "we have twelve people, 50 yuan is not enough for us. We want to have a performance." Another five minutes of silence passed. Then the three of us left without taking the money.

We did not leave the government building but went directly to another wing of the building and stopped at the local branch office of the All China Women's Federation, the state feminist organization. At the office, three women staff members were busy gardening, spreading around potting soil and leafy plants on the floor. We squatted down together with them to talk. Master Gao initiated the conversation by suggesting possible performance

FIGURE 4.1. Storytellers gathered to schedule a performance at the Yanchuan government office.

themes related to the one-child policy, such as "A girl is equally precious as a boy" and "Man is responsible for the one-child policy." We did not have much luck that time either. The three women coldly repeated what we had heard at the Communist Youth League office and waved us away.

There was another occasion when I went with three storytellers to the county office of China Telecom, the second largest telecommunication company in China, in hopes of scheduling a performance. It was a spacious, bright, and clean office on the second floor of a modern building in the Yanchuan town center. A young junior clerk received us and repeated that he could not make any decision without the manager. But the storytellers "occupied" the office and insisted that they should be given a performance opportunity. After much waiting and inquiry, storyteller Master Luo blew up, saying, "We have visited you five times. Every time your manager was not here. I think your manager is hiding and you are just covering for him! You have no sense of sympathy for the disabled." In a split second, he changed to a political tone: "We are still living in a socialist society. Therefore the enterprise's concern toward the disabled is reasonable and legitimate (*lisuo dangran*). I would not come if we are living in a capitalist society. We all know that a capitalist society is a brutal one and no one cares about the other. But we are not living in capitalist society yet, are we?"

Master Luo's outburst might sound awkward, but to a large extent it reveals some of the core values these storytellers see in their cultural production: the rights of the disabled to make a living and the danwei's social responsibility to support such right. The room was silent for a short while and the young clerk was dumbfounded by such an accusation. Sensing the weight of the issue, he called the manager immediately and demanded to see the storytellers' propaganda certificate. After verifying the "official" identity of the storytellers, he gave them 120 yuan without asking for a performance.

As I will elaborate in later sections, folk tradition performance is heavily linked to the work-unit system, its business, public relations activities. and—to a certain extent—its social responsibility. This is especially true for folk cultural production in small towns and cities of the country. The following section reviews a brief history of the Yanchuan Musical Drama Troupe, where most of the northern Shaanxi storytellers in Yanchuan are from, and its complex socialist and commercial relationship with government and danwei in today's Yan'an.

Northern Shaanxi Storytelling: A Socialist Cultural Arrangement

The Yanchuan Musical Drama Troupe was established in 1964, with four men—Hao Neng, Ji Fengxiang, Hu Xingcai, and Feng Yuelin—who first underwent storytelling training in Yan'an. After the training, they went back to the Yanchuan countryside to perform, singing stories that echoed the national class struggle education and the "Learn from *Leifeng*" movement (*Leifeng* was a model soldier always willing to sacrifice for public or national interests). The troupe repertoire included "Lei Feng Participate[s} in the Army" and "Machine Gun," along with traditional pieces. Later the troupe grew to ten people and started to sing the renowned storyteller Han Qixiang's works, such as *"Fanshenji," "Liuqiao Reunion,"* and *"Big Victory at Yichuan."* During the Cultural Revolution, the troupe changed their name to "Musical Drama Propaganda Troupe for Mao Zedong Thoughts" (Cao 2005: 186–190).

In order to better understand the effects of storytelling during the 1960s and 1970s, it is useful to turn to those documents that commemorate Han Qixiang, the most famous northern Shaanxi storyteller during Mao's period (Han 1985; Hu Mengxiang 1989; Li 1993). Han Qixiang helped win popular support for the Communist government's policies by singing about the distress of the country folk and promoting revolutionary changes. In his reflections on his own life, Han Qixiang was proud of the empowerment his stories gave to audiences. He wrote, "Every time I finished performing my stories, I would hear daughters telling their parents, 'You cannot sell me. If you do so, I will sue you.' Or a wife would tell her husband, 'Don't abuse me anymore, or else I will learn from the role model Zhang Yulan (who defied her husband and joined the Communist-led local election)'" (Han 1993: 296). In one essay commemorating Han, Lin Shan, an urban intellectual, who worked with Han closely, recalled the "profound impact" of Han's storytelling: "There was a peasant, last name Lau, in *Yangjiayao* village. He was so deeply moved after hearing Han's story of a brave soldier named Liu Sihu that he immediately asked his wife to make a pair of shoes and sent them to the front line of the battlefield. Another case concerns a village that, after hearing the story "Against Sorcery and Promoting Hygiene" (*fanwushen jiangweisheng*), initiated a hygiene team to clean the village ditches and combat flies" (Lin 1993: 269).

While it is highly probable that these writings exaggerated the success of and audience reactions to Han Qixiang's storytelling, they did reveal to a large degree that northern Shaanxi storytelling was quite well received at the local level. The folk tradition with social reform contents engaged heavily with down-to-earth topics such as villagers' religious practices, marrying customs, and community welfare. It also touched boldly on sensitive issues of domestic violence and women's rights. Military plots with brave soldiers as characters were certainly stories of sensation and attraction, too. And in the context of remote and hilly rural Yan'an in the 1960s where people were barely mobile and barely had enough food to eat, one could imagine that they could not wait to see a storytelling performance! Folklorist Fu Peiyuan went so far as to characterize storytellers as those who "processed literature, history and all kinds of knowledge and messages, giving the mountain inhabitants [*shanliren*] the most precious news, like giving them light in their heart or a pair of wings for their thoughts" (Fu 2000: 33).

During Mao's time, northern Shaanxi storytelling became a socialist cultural arrangement that provided a low budget yet popular local entertainment. The arrangement fulfilled several tasks simultaneously: cultural enrichment of work units and rural communities, the employment of disabled people, and the need of the state to promote and reach out its policies. Although it has the word "propaganda"(*xuanchuan*) in this title, and it did promote government's policies, the storytelling troupe was really quite different from the Western stereotype of a censorship machine, deployed by the totalitarian state to control and influence the masses. There is no doubt that many of its story topics were connected to national class struggle, patriotism, or anti-imperialism movements. But when translated into a local peasant genre, a storyteller's performance must engage people's everyday concerns in order to stay attractive. In many ways, storytelling blurred the boundary between state policy promotion and cultural entertainment, making political topics palatable, even attractive. Putting the visually impaired into a musical drama troupe was also a smart social welfare policy design. As Master Zhang proudly remembered for me:

> We were propagandists (*xuanchuan yuan*). We went down to villages in a team of six. As soon as we went to a Commune, the production brigade leaders settled us in different individual families. Those who fed us got the amount of grain (two *liang* per day) reimbursed by the brigade. The Hall of Culture wrote us recommendation letters and held the brigade responsible for finding our way along the route to the next brigade. We could earn work points for performing in the area and get food ration at our village.

I could feel strongly a sense of empowerment and honor from Master Zhang when he recalled the performance experience, in which storytellers were warmly welcomed and guided along the singing tour. His desire to "disseminate" the new nation's policies means that folk cultural performances during the Maoist era were not rendered as some propaganda imposed by the party-state for social and political control (Schein 2000: 176–184). More importantly, cultural workers were not necessarily losing their creative autonomy. This is especially the case when folk storytellers came from peasant villages and lower-class backgrounds. Their roles became that of promoting a sense of hope and mobility for the oppressed groups or for a united future instead of for party-state indoctrination (Schein 2000; Mittler 2012; Hung 1994).

Such socialist cultural arrangements have slowly transformed since the People's Commune ceased to operate in the beginning of the 1980s. Today, the Yanchuan Musical Drama Troupe is still affiliated with the Hall of Culture, which continues to issue them performance certificates. The certificate allows the troupe to keep performing in rural villages and work units by proving their disability status (Figure 4.2). Folk storytellers somehow continue the legacy of the socialist cultural arrangement to stage performances at various danwei in the market era. But, as shown earlier, some work units are no longer willing to pay for a performance today, especially when their work is not about outreaching to the masses.

However, northern Shaanxi storytelling has not become obsolete in today's market economy. Instead, it is getting ever more popular and, in some cases, built an even tighter relationship with some danwei. In the following,

FIGURE 4.2. The Yanchuan Musical Drama Troupe.

I delineate how the folk practice further transforms and becomes intertwined with various work-unit or danwei public relations events in new ways.

Danwei Events, Folk Tradition, and National Ideology

In Yan'an, one can see a storytelling performance during many kinds of occasions: government-sponsored Lunar New Year parades, danwei night shows, danwei staff gatherings and award ceremonies, and, certainly, temple festivals in rural communities. As a folk genre that highlights peasant vernacular, humorous lyrics, fast tempo, and traditional *sanxian* music, it continues to be very popular at the local level. Cao Boyan, for instance, one of the most renowned storytellers in Yan'an, is someone who has performed on the most prestigious television program, "The Spring Festival Gala" (which features the best folk cultural performances from the country), broadcast by the Chinese Central Television Channel in Beijing. He has sung in front of former Chinese President Hu Jintao as well as on stage in many foreign countries. He has his own DVD album on sale in major department stores in the Yan'an region, and he is highly visible in all kinds of media in Yan'an.

In both 2004 and 2008, I got the chance to interview Cao Boyan at his work unit, the Yan'an Musical Drama Society in Yan'an city. As an educated, visually normal, and professionally trained storyteller, Cao Boyan has made northern Shaanxi storytelling well known by mixing the national language Putonghua in the vernacular singing, making it more understandable across provincial dialectic differences. In recent years, he has even taken the musical genre to France, Belgium, the Netherlands, Vietnam, and South Korea (Cao 2011: 473). When talking about his career, he proudly told me that he was so busy with all the work-unit invitations that he had hardly enough time serving his own work unit. At his own work unit, Cao received a modest monthly salary of no more than 2,000 RMB, associated with housing, medical, and pension welfare. But a single invited performance in other work units or companies could pay him more than his monthly salary.

In 2008, Cao shared with me a lyric he was working on for a staff appreciation event called "Alleviate Earth Quake Disaster, Look Forward to the Olympics, Increase Productivity" at a big oil company in Yanchang county, east of Yan'an city. The program title sounds strange. But it was in July 2008 when we talked, just after one of the most disastrous earthquakes in human history, which killed nearly seventy thousand people in Sichuan province, Southwest China. In August of the same year, however, the Beijing Olympics was ready to open. The Chinese state was faced with the enormous stress of disaster alleviation and yet expecting to host one of the most important international events. Around this time, the oil company invited Cao Boyan to stage a folk storytelling performance for its mining workers. The song is entitled, "Praise Workers," and I cite the lyrics Cao wrote as follows:

> Earth Quake in Sichuan province. The whole country is in pain
> Unite to resist the quake and alleviate the disasters
> Oil workers please show your care
> When disaster strikes, help comes from everywhere
> Oil miners and quake survivors please connect your hearts together
> We express our deepest consolation
> Together we build new homes for them
> The effect of the quake is yet to know
> Look forward to the Olympics with joy
> The Olympics is going to start soon
> The human resource department in the factory has made
>   this arrangement
>
> I bring the most genuine concerns from your leaders
> To greet you the front line workers
> Bring along tea, bring along sweet

Bring along as well this spiritual food

Sisters and Brother workers you have worked so hard
You have made a contribution to safe production
For production, you weather in rain, wind and cold
For production, you get drench in heat and sweat
For production, you leave your rural hometown
For production, you cannot see your families throughout
    the seasons.
Your safe production brings us security
Your hard work brings us good supply
Oil miners are like tigers, fighting with a roar
Model workers and outstanding soldiers come from you
This year alone you have produced millions of tons
You have made much effort for the oil field

Brothers and sisters your effort is no little
Everyone in the factory knows
I don't need to go into details
The following few stories show my respects to you
(my own translation)

Similar to the aforementioned "Quality Control System Spreads to Millions," this "Praise Workers" piece shows the complicated role and meanings of folk storytelling performance today. Sung in traditional storytelling style, with sanxian music and the clapper's beat, the piece put together some very diverse topics: mourning for the earthquake, welcoming the Beijing Olympics, and praising the miner workers' productivity. In the context of a staff appreciation event, the latter part of the lyrics, which recognizes the miners' labor, makes a lot of sense. But why include the Sichuan earthquake and the Olympics, too? Cao Boyan explained to me that the earthquake part was meant to raise donations from workers. Right after the Sichuan earthquake, there were donation calls everywhere for quake alleviation. All kinds of danwei—government departments, private companies, and even schools—competed to donate as much as possible. They even held press conferences about their donation amount. The first part of the song is therefore designed to encourage workers to make a donation, hoping to increase the company's donation fund and hence its enterprise charity image. But to mention only the disastrous quake and the fundraising makes such a staff appreciation event a bit awkward. Thus, the Olympics is included in the song to alter the depressing tone. It is also an obligation for danwei at all levels, especially government departments and major SOEs, to promote the Beijing Olympic Games in 2008 in order to steer a sense of unity and commitment. As a major SOE in Yan'an, the oil company was expected to enthusiastically promote the Olympics. No wonder the lyrics refer to the human resources department (*laosi bu*) of the company, which is responsible not only for personnel matters but also for making sure that the party agenda gets to work units.

Staff appreciation events happen everywhere in the world. Oftentimes they are coordinated to develop the company values of team building, commitment, and competitiveness. Other times, they are meant to bring staff members together for a relaxing gathering. In China, however, such an event is a little more complicated, especially one organized by a major danwei, which continues to promote to its workers the latest party-state values and national campaigns. As late as 2000, some major danwei continued to hold political education gatherings among workers in Yan'an. That trend is diminishing today and it is almost nonexistent in private enterprises. But the political work and ideological education are not simply obliterated. Instead, the political task of danwei to disseminate party-state values or an official message is becoming more subtle and increasingly integrated into other events. This is the reason why a danwei's staff appreciation event, apart from promoting the company's agendas, often includes the party-state's latest campaigns and slogans (Li 2015; Liu 2015).

The political task is not easy. Government departments and SOEs generally find it hard to connect national or ideological slogans to local conditions—not to mention to a company's context. The slogan of "harmonious society," a concept the Hu-Wen administration promoted to address the rising levels of discontent in rural areas in relation to the widening rural-urban divide, for instance, can be quite strange if promoted in a commercial context. But it makes a lot of sense in a cultural program when "harmonious society" is related to persuading workers to donate to the conationals after the earthquake, therefore translating the slogan into a more generic advocacy to unify people across different provinces. Another example concerns the promotion of the national campaign of "the Great Development of West China" in 2004 Yan'an. During the performance at the Engineering and Machinery SOE staff quarters, for instance, the promotion of this national campaign did not raise much interest among the laid-offs because local workers hardly see how they could benefit from any potential investment opportunities. They perhaps liked the promotion of quality-control legislation more even though they clearly knew that the reason behind the prevalence of faked products had much to do with the lack of necessary actions from the local authority. The singing of northern Shaanxi storytellers, in contrast, reinvoked nostalgia of the Maoist past when grassroots SOE workers enjoyed more exclusive, stable, and secured jobs. Their performance of the traditional Chinese warrior story "Muguiying" was ultimately what attracted many to stay for hours that night. In such occasions, the folk tradition element stood out and overshadowed the national and government messages.

Indeed, danwei now actively conduct what they call "public relation activities" (*gongguan huodong*) in order to reach out to the media and to the public. Both government danwei and private enterprises need publicity occasions to promote their brands, company images, new campaigns, and products. A press conference with only speeches draws no audience. Public relation activities can include sponsoring other events, giving away free product samples, or throwing a staged performance. This explains why in Yan'an, northern Shaanxi storytelling often becomes the core program of such activities. It fits well in public relation activities as it promotes the work unit's business while also staging good shows for everyone. Its spoken music form, like a form of rapping, transforms formal speeches and ideological slogans into enjoyable lyrics, rhyming prose, and local dialects. No wonder when I asked Cao Boyan why he got so many invitations, he answered straightforwardly, "for promotion (*xuanchuan*)!"

Conclusion: Folk Tradition in Contemporary China

The production of folk tradition in today's China is largely independent of the party-state control, both in its art form and content. Its linkages and relations with some of the local government campaigns and danwei business, nonetheless, have become stronger. Today folk tradition production must increasingly adapt to various promotional events, press conferences, and staff events of various danwei. At the same time, danwei events, which promote very practical enterprise messages and some national ideologies, ironically become the spaces wherein traditional folk art forms find new developments, audiences, and visibility in the age of urbanization and marketization. This is the case not only for folk storytelling but also for folk paper-cutting. Successful paper-cutting artists are those who can collaborate with danwei well. Artists would make folk paper-cutting designs, based on certain danwei's branding, into special paper-cutting albums. A lot of danwei like to place orders for such tailor-made albums and use them as company gifts or souvenirs for business partners. One can imagine how paper-cutting artists work closely with certain danwei, such as local tourism departments, museums, and historical sites, to increase sales. Many artists are also eager to be invited to danwei events to stage live paper-cutting shows for more visibility.

In the end, it is hard to judge whether the work units deploy folk tradition performance for their enterprise agendas or the folk practitioners have made use of the work-unit platform for tradition revival. It is a mistake to view folk tradition as simply a tool of the party-state propaganda. Even though the staging of a folk storytelling carries with it some nationalist ideological messages, they are often mentioned in a passing, ritualistic manner, and are often dwarfed by the core content of the traditional performance. It is therefore more productive to attend to the mutual interpenetration and agenda contestation among the local state, danwei, and folk cultural practitioners in the process.

In this chapter, I showed that the revival and renewed interest in folk tradition is now linked to late socialist danwei institutions, their agendas, and enterprise business and culture. Folk storytelling fits well with many work-unit events and campaigns and is becoming more popular in Yan'an. But one major feature differentiates folk danwei propaganda from its precedent during the Mao era—the absence of class politics. During Mao's time, caring for the impoverished and disabled was the responsibility of urban work units and the People's Commune in the rural areas. Having blind men stage folk storytelling in the past blended together the work-unit social responsibility, employment of the disabled, staff entertainment, and political persuasion of the masses. The sense of caring socially marginalized groups has faded today, as shown by Master Luo's outburst at the China Telecom. Blinded, older, and lower-class storytellers thus found it increasingly difficult to survive in today's environment. Much like laid-off workers from state-owned enterprises who protest for the right of employment, they keep trying to claim entitlements and recognition as veteran cultural workers of the state, though often in vain (Lee 1998b). Instead, those who are entrepreneurial and talented enough to fit a traditional performance into an existing work-unit agenda fare very well. The fading of class politics and the inclusion of more entrepreneurial, corporate, and marketing elements in late socialist folk cultural production, certainly, corresponds to the similar socioeconomic change of contemporary Chinese society. The continual relevance of party-state policies and national politics in the production of folk traditions, nonetheless, speaks of the continuing negotiations among different forces in and beyond folk cultural production.

CHAPTER 5

Spirit Cults in Yan'an

Surrogate Rural Subjectivity in the Urbanizing Rural

In mid-September 2003, two months before I entered my host Aunt Fang's cavehouse at the hilltop of Mojiagou village, she was seriously injured in a car accident. She was thrown out from a bus she was getting on when another bus hit from behind. She was flung up in the air, flipped upside down, and fell unconscious after hitting her head on the newly paved concrete road. Some in the surrounding villages witnessed the accident but no one spent too much time thinking about it. Villagers were busy harvesting before winter and, indeed, before the government would take away their farmlands for the construction of a party cadre school on the same site. Aunt Fang's accident articulated more than just an individual misfortune of rural residents adapting to an emerging urban landscape of highway and traffic, but it also heralded the beginning of a much more powerful urbanizing force that rapidly swept across rural Yan'an in the next ten years.

The Urbanizing Rural: Vanishing Farmlands and Villagers' Identity

During the seventy days Aunt Fang was hospitalized, the family's fields were not taken care of, no one was cooking, and their pigs and cows were so starved that they knocked down the fences and ran away. Uncle Fang recalled with bitter humor, "I had *Kang shifu* (instant ramen noodles) everyday."[1]

The Fangs quickly resumed farm labor after Aunt Fang was discharged at the end of November. During the bitter cold winter while I was staying as a guest, the couple never rested. They had numerous tasks to accomplish: trim a few acres of apricot trees at the mountain back, shoulder home the cutout tree branches for fuel, chop hundreds of cornstalks into cow feed, dig frozen human feces from the outdoor "toilet" to fertilize the fields. I later found out such winter labor was nothing when compared with the real agricultural labor in the spring. During the summer of 2004, the Fangs woke up every day before dawn and came back home after nine o'clock at night. In their own farmland, they were busy sowing, fertilizing, irrigating, harvesting, and then carting and selling green vegetables near the city all day long. Dinner was not served until ten, sometimes eleven, at night.

Around March 2004, Aunt Fang started to complain about her back pain and numbing hands. Excruciating pain kicked in whenever she had to make flour dough for meals and hand-wash the laundry. Many times she stared at her hands as if that would trace the invisible knots that bothered her. Residents of rural household registrations, however, were not entitled to medical facilities in the city. This institutionalized inequality explains a popular saying in rural Yan'an before 2009: *"nengsi buneng bing"* (you can die, but you can't get sick).[2] Luckily, Aunt Fang could see the doctor at the City Hospital because she could get the medical payment reimbursed by the bus company.

After an x-ray check, the doctor concluded that she had a spinal spur, affecting nerves on her back and hands. He gave her a prescription painkiller and recommended physical therapy once a week for ten weeks. The doctor remarked before we left, "work less (*shao laodong*)." Aunt Fang responded to his advice only after we stepped out of the hospital, "I am a farmer (*shoukuren*). How can I work less?"

Aunt Fang would not have imagined the professional farmer identity, *shoukuren*, she has proudly claimed for her whole life, would vanish so fast. Literally translated into "someone who can bear bitterness," *shoukuren* is a northern Shaanxi dialect term referring to those who make a living by growing crops. Whenever she is asked what she does for living, Aunt Fang has spoken proudly of herself as a *shoukuren*. But Aunt Fang would not "bear bitterness" very soon. Indeed, "the lack of farm work" would soon become a permanent state faced by all Mojiagou villagers (Figure 5.1). Aunt Fang naturally did not think about it then. In fact, shortly after finishing the pills, she decided to go see a spirit medium and took me along.

This chapter joins ongoing debates on folk popular religion in China and engages discussions of spirit possession in the larger anthropological scholarship. It focuses specifically on spirit cults in Yan'an and connects such major practice of the rural folk society to the broader environment of urbanization of the rural area. By spirit cults, I refer to forms of popular folk religious practice that involve people consulting spirit mediums for healing or divination when they are possessed by a deity. Such consulta-

FIGURE 5.1. Villagers digging up wells on farmland to bargain for more government compensation.

tion takes place mostly inside private cavehouses. Spirit cults in the region vary greatly in their practices and ritual forms. Most are not associated with temples even though some of them involve followers constructing temples for the deities concerned. Considered as informal sects categorized neither as legal nor illegal, spirit cults mushroom in rural corners of Yan'an and attract quite significant numbers of followers.

In this chapter, I show that spirit cults in Yan'an work as a form of folk rural discourse as they capture and recognize the rapidly disappearing and increasingly destabilized subject position of "peasant" in the age of urbanization of the rural area. By urbanization of the rural area, I refer not only to the movement of rural villagers massively migrating to cities to find jobs and opportunities, but also a process in which existing rural villages and farmlands rapidly transform into highways, industrial parks, and towns with shopping malls. The process often involves the appropriation of farmlands from rural villagers by local governments in the name of public interests. In such expropriation, the government provides only minimal compensation to the disposed while securing lucrative land deals with outside investors (Lora-Wainwright 2012). In the case of Mojiagou village in Yan'an, villagers' farmland was expropriated directly by the Yan'an city government to build a large campus for the Communist Party members' political education.

I see folk religion not as a traditional body of unchanging knowledge and practice. I suggest that folk religion now constitutes a new form of rural discourse. This new discourse enables the urbanizing rural subject, who is increasingly distanced from knowledge and practices specific to rural areas, labor, landscapes, households, and communities, to once again find his or her "rural" identity and belonging. In other words, I take spirit cults as that major site through which rural norms, values, dispositions, and desires are not only displayed and enacted, but de facto produced and reconstructed in the urbanization of the rural area. I argue that folk religion becomes one of the most important sites of folk discourse and practice, through which the urbanizing rural subject of China is recognized.

The data used in this chapter are drawn from fieldwork in Yan'an, conducted respectively in 2004 and 2008. I talked to eight mediums who involve spirit possession in their religious behaviors, with some seeming to be more in control of the process (Eliade 1964: 4–7, 499–500; Bowie 2000: 190–201) and some talking about it as if they were being forced into it (Bourguignon 1991). I also have talked to more than fifty villagers who practiced spirit cults in their routine religious activities.

Popular Religion and Spirit Possession in and out of China

Earlier scholarship on popular religion in Chinese society has focused on describing temple activities and organizations, while later works have focused on analyzing how the religious sphere mediates between state and society (Grootaers 1952; Yang 1961; Gamble 1963; Jordan 1972; Wolf 1974; Sangren 1987; Siu 1989; Shahar and Weller 1996; Feuchtwang 2001; Overmyer 2003). But since "religion in Chinese society" has been a target of state control spanning from the late Qing empire through the Republican and the Communist periods, its scholarship is inevitably drawn to the study of those effects of the state or political authority vis-a-vis responses from religious specialists, society, and institutions (Duara 1988; Dean 1998; Anagnost 1994; Chen 1995; Bruun 1996). In other words, existing scholarship has looked at state legislation, repressive measures, and various religious reforms to achieve modernization and to eradicate local religious authority. At the same time, scholars have examined how religious societies constantly resist state actions and reinvent themselves. A dominant "popular religion as resistance" thesis points out that the resurgence of community ritual actions indicates a desire on the part of villagers to rediscover local communities' cultural and historical meanings that had been suppressed by modern governance. Jing Jun's study on the revival of a Confucius hall in a village in Gansu province, for instance, suggests an ardent communal energy to reassert its lineage power, reclaim its physical space, and retrieve its collective memories destroyed under the Maoist era (Jing 1996, 2000). Kenneth Dean's *Lord of the Three in One* presents a complex picture of how local rituals, cult practices, and their contemporary revival could provide a means of resisting the hegemonic discourse of the state on religion (1998). Eric Mueggler's work (2001) shows how the Lolo (Yi) minority of rural Yunnan resisted the government birth control policy and violence by refashioning the suppressed spirit possession practice into a form of healing. Thomas Dubois's work (2005) puts emphasis on the ways "specialized localized knowledge" constituted religious practices and how, in turn, these religious practices formed a closed local cultural sphere in North China.

But recent studies have shown that the resistance argument might be oversimplifying the reality, as it has assumed an undifferentiated entity of "local" or "community" reclaiming power from a hegemonic state. These studies instead support the argument that the state and community at the local level are not dichotomous entities but they often interpenetrate each other. Paul Katz, for instance, has shown how local government often needed to collaborate with temple association leadership in order to gain legitimacy (Katz 2003). Stephan Feuchtwang and Wang Mingming show that political leadership was played out in religious terms (Feuchtwang and Wang 1991). Most recently Adam Chau has argued that the revival of popular religion in northern Shaanxi province did not involve only the imagined "peasant community" but multiple interests of local elites and local government (2005: 251). This scholarship shows that popular folk religion is a "public agrarian sphere," in which local religious groups, local elites, and the local state bargain, and contest the power and interests of each other.

Possession cults as resistance tactics have also been a major topic of debates in anthropological studies of religion outside of China. The resistance thesis is most elaborately upheld by I. M. Lewis's classic account in *Ecstatic Religion* (2003). Lewis argues for a differentiated understanding between "central possession religions" and "peripheral cults." Central possession religions involve shamans holding key ritual and political roles in society as well as religious leaders seeking to augment spiritual and mundane power through recourse to the authority of the gods. Peripheral cults, however, attract marginal members of society, particularly women or politically impotent men, and involve spirits and deities not necessarily recognized by mainstream religious authority. Peripheral cults therefore tend to subvert the moral code of the social dominant. Analyzing the cross-cultural association of women with ecstatic possession, Lewis suggests seeing peripheral cults as "thinly disguised protest movements directed against the dominant power relations" (1971: 31). This perspective views cult practices as an indication of the malfunctioning of the social system or marginal groups' tactics to resist a society's inability to treat its members.

As insightful as these studies are, they easily gloss over many issues. Lewis's resistance thesis tends to view peripheral cults as embodying a kind of repression and those who practice them as backward, irrational, unhappy members of the society (Lewis 2003: 27). Such a perspective overlooks the complex issues of power relations at the local level and often generalizes the existence of certain hegemonic orders. The state-society integration accounts often focus on the mutual dependency among the local state, the elites, and the rural society in the making of large-scale public religious events. It cannot quite adequately explain the more marginalized and clandestine incidences of deity cults held in private settings.

The crucial questions remain to be asked. In spirit cults activities where state penetration is minimal, and local economic interests and public morality are not at stake, what do the spirit cults offer? How do people understand their practice? Must peripheral cults be read as an antihegemonic move against a repressive state? What is being said and done in such ritual performances? What kind of experience and sociality are produced through such practices?

In this chapter, I depict in detail two ritual performances of a spirit medium in rural Yan'an: dancing deity (*tiaoshen*) and elevating luck (*fuyun*). I analyze the relationship among words, images, and the power of healing, and their relationship to symbolic healing (Firth 1967; Dow 1986). I do not view spirit medium as representing "a protest against the established order" (Gluckman 1965: 109) and do not agree with an instrumental understanding of it in which followers utilize the cult practice to pursue particular personal or collective interests (Lewis 1971). My argument resonates with Bruce Kapferer's insight on sorcery in Sri Lanka (1997) and that of Janice Boddy's work on *zar*, spirit possession in Africa (1989). Both see spirit cults as integral to a wider complex of practice.

I argue that the practices of spirit cults in contemporary Yan'an constitute a new form of folk discourse, which reproduces and reconstructs specific systems of rural knowledge, symbols and technical know-how, and a range of ritual practices in an urbanizing environment. I also argue that such discourse produces what I call "surrogate rural subjectivity" among participants of spirit cults. The word *surrogate* is defined as "a substitute, especially a person deputizing another in a specific role." By surrogate rural subjectivity, I mean that the subjectivity enabled by the folk religious discourse substitutes the one previously constituted by daily agricultural labor, cavehouse households, village environment and experiences, and language. Spirit cults as a contemporary rural discourse provide the occasions for the expression and experience of disappearing rural communal relations and folk values and practices. Without assuming that believers are atomized victims against the malfunctioning social structures, I see cult practices as "cultural acts for villagers themselves within a specific social context" (Boddy 1989). I will show that their meanings go beyond generating "liminality" for participants to produce a process of renewal (Turner 1967, 1969). I highlight the effects of spirit cults in enhancing communal sociality, reinvigorating interpersonal exchange, and providing a group with an identity, though not in a functionalist sense as if cult practices naturally reintegrate believers in "normal social structures" (Turner 1969; Crapanzano 1977).

The Black Tiger Diety in Rural Yan'an

In Yan'an and northern Shaanxi province, local cult activities and worship practices have long existed. During both the Republican and socialist periods, the governments were keen to eradicate the many cult activities in the area because they were seen as "parasites of society" or "upholders of superstition." After 1949, foreign missionaries were expelled and cultic and heterodox sects were banned. Only five religions—Buddhism, Daoism, Islam, Catholicism, and Protestantism—were incorporated into official national associations. Still, popular religious life prospered during the politically peaceful period of the 1950s, especially on the North China Plain, mainly because of its distance from central government control (Freedman 1974). Popular religious and cult activities experienced some interruption for a decade during the Cultural Revolution but even the Communist antisuperstition efforts were primarily confined to a small number of urban centers (Chau 2003).[3]

In the reform era of the 1980s under Deng Xiaoping's leadership, popular religion was once recast by the Chinese state as signifying a "backward peasantry whose ideology lagged behind the historical development of China's progress toward socialism." Religion, nonetheless thrived along with economic development and relaxed political control. Today, the Chinese government endorses Confucianism, Buddhism, Daoism, and popular religious practices such as life-cycle rituals and ancestral worship "based on protective deities in domestic shrines and community temples, which has long provided community identity and cohesion, and support for traditional social values" (Overmyer 2003: 2). But spirit medium practices are generally understood as *heterodox*, characterized by "heterogeneous beliefs, myths, and values that have been transmitted by popular lore and by symbols" and involving spectacular spiritual possession performances and rituals (Shahar and Weller 1996: 1).[4] They thrive by borrowing deities' names direct from the constitutionally approved traditions and yet are practiced in very different manners. Unlike more mainstream religious revivals such as the Mazu worship or Daoism, in which local governments are involved, spiritual cults barely exist on the verge of the "gray" religious economy, sometimes even shifting to the illegal "black religious market" (Yang 2006).[5] Today, when Yan'an locals say that they believe in *shenshen*, a local dialect term referring to a variety of big gods and small deities, they explicitly admit to joining a range of illegal, but widely practiced, cult activities.[6]

Aunt Fang took me to see one of them, south of Yan'an city, in a rural neighborhood called Hewanjiagou village. This was after she finished her painkiller prescribed by the city doctor. We stepped into a stone cavehouse without any signs outside and a big front yard; a woman sat at the door. The woman obviously recognized Aunt Fang and she let us walk through the door curtain. The room inside was bright and modern, with lots of burgundy-colored flags hanging on the walls that read, "Grateful for the benevolence of god (*ganxie shen en*)," "Goddess Guanyin reincarnated (*guanyin zaishi*)," "Savior (*jiuming Enren*)." Aunt Fang swiftly took me through another door, which led into a bigger space.

I was stunned: the place was packed with at least forty visitors. We squeezed through the crowd and stood closer to a big *kang*, about six feet wide and ten feet long, where the spirit medium was diagnosing a patient. Crossing his legs, the spirit medium sat on the edge of the *kang* while the patient sat across from him. He asked the patient for his birthday and hour of birth in the Chinese lunar calendar, where he was from, and what his problem was. The patient said he had bad luck and wanted to know the reason. The spirit medium stayed quiet for a while, his mouth muttering and his fingers spinning.

Suddenly, the spirit medium rose up on the *kang*. He picked up two big cleavers and started to speak in a very strange voice. Then he turned to his audience and started to dance vigorously and spectacularly. "Cling, cling, cling," the spirit medium hit and slid the cleavers against each other, making a high pitch and threatening sounds. Roaring, he used the flat side of the cleavers to forcefully hit his own chest and at the same time hit the blades of the cleavers together, giving an illusion that the blades were incising his body. While we all held our breath, he suddenly jumped off the *kang* and prostrated on the floor. He turned still and stiff for a minute, and then he abruptly banged the cleavers on the floor, scaring those whose feet were just an inch away. He raised himself up again; this time, he used the side of the cleavers to hit his head. The noise of hitting, his solemn expression, and his rolled-up eyeballs were petrifying.

"This is to scare away the devils and wretched deities harassing this man. He is the Black Tiger deity (*heihulingguan*)," Aunt Fang whispered in my ears, explaining the animalistic growl and gestures of the possessed man.

After the dance, which lasted about two minutes, he went back to the sitting position and started to give a prescription. His language was, however, completely unintelligible. A woman in red was sitting beside him, quickly interpreting out loud and jotting down his words on a piece of paper. One was in unintelligible speech, another in Shaanbei dialect, and both were spoken so fast that I hardly followed. Still, I could hear that the patient was told to prepare a list of things: a red color thread, some rice, and a few other items and bring them for the next visit to evict the bad spirits entirely. The patient was then directed to another woman at the door entrance to take his oral prescription—medicine powder in a triangular yellow packet.

It took about three hours of waiting in line before Aunt Fang and I could finally move to the consultation position on the *kang*. There, I could look at the spirit medium clearly. He was a middle-aged man, of medium build, with tanned skin and spiky gray hair. In spite of the last few hours of dancing and roaring, he looked just like an ordinary peasant in the area. Aunt Fang told him about her bus accident and wanted to know if the back pain and hand numbness had anything to do with evil spirits. He pondered for a while, during which his eyeballs were rolled up, giving others the impression that he was eyeless. His eyeballs, filled with red veins, however, blinked to hint at some mysterious vision, warning others not to look into it. He muttered for a little while and concluded that Fang's problem was a real disease, not a cursed disease (*xiebing*). Although he said she should follow the doctor's advice, he gave a prescription of seven packs of "spiritual medicine," some for burning and some for oral intake. He said that the medicine would guard Fang's family against any future danger. At around 5 o'clock in the late afternoon, we left the place after paying a fee of 80 RMB.

The first thing we did upon before stepping into the cavehouse home was to burn a pack of spiritual medicine at the door entrance. Aunt Fang was very meticulous about and familiar with these procedures. She asked me to organize and mark the prescription packs in numerical order. And in the next seven days, she followed the prescription religiously. At night, as I helped wash her back with the medicine, which was burned and mixed with rice wine and some pot ashes, she told me she had been a "follower" of the "Black Tiger God" for about ten years since he had healed her son's kidney problem. Aunt Fang said that his magic was very efficacious (*ling*) and his followers were from all walks of life, in and outside of the Yan'an area.

Seeking Spirit Mediums in Yan'an

The world of spirits, and their ability to possess individuals and cause illness are common beliefs in rural Yan'an. The Black Tiger deity, among many local powerful deities, was a major deity responsible for guarding the entrance of *Baiyunshan*, a mountain in northern Shaanxi, which accommodated hundreds of gods, goddesses, and deities of Daoist, Buddhist, and Confucian traditions. Local legends have seen the deity as always riding a black tiger, capable of alleviating epidemic diseases, and have therefore transformed him into a local deity of cures and healing.

I did not get the chance to do interviews with the Black Tiger deity medium because I did not reside in the area where he lived and could not get into the network of people around him. But I interviewed seven other spirit mediums close to Mojiagou village, as well as relevant patients and neighbors. They went through crisis-type misfortune or illness initiation, an "unsolicited altered state of consciousness" that afflicted them first, drove them into solitude, and demanded them to become mediums. Like many of the shaman experiences cross-culturally, the possessing spirits eventually become the young mediums' main tutelary spirits, which pave their careers as mediums and affect their lives in many ways (Peters 1982: 23). According to spirit mediums I talked to, possession is a state induced by the spirit's entry into the body, which displaces or shifts the person's human self to another perceptual plane. It is a "radical discontinuity of personal identity" (Bourguignon 1991: 12). But all possession is an induced state, which means it is not unpremeditated outside of the ritual context. The mediums also induce and control the possession through ritual processes such as "speaking in tongues" or burning incense (Peters 1982; Boddy 1989: 134–144).

Local residents often address the spirit medium as a "horse lad" (*matong*). They believe that when a deity possessed the medium, the deity mounted the horse (*qima*) and descended from the horse (*xiama*). The horse as an idiom signifies the descent of a spirit from heaven and is not specific to Shaanxi; it is shared by spirit mediums in other societies (Beattie and Middleton 2004; Debernardi 2006). By addressing themselves as "horse lads," spirit mediums invoke the image and metaphor of their body being "turned into a site of origination" to be prepared for spiritual transformation (Morris 2000: 122).

Some might attribute the popularity of spirit mediums to the lack of affordable medical service in rural China. But Yan'an people who sought spirit mediums attribute their visits to "weird disease" (*xiebing*), caused by bad spirits taking away their souls and hence incurable by modern doctors. The local villagers' concept of well-being and illness approximates what Csordas calls the "tripartite person," in which the person is a composite of body, mind, and spirit. Bodily illness, emotional distress, and adverse effects of the evil spirit are "holistically" related, even though each requires different healing genres and elements of techniques for treatment (Csordas 1994: 39). Physical illness, for instance, could provide an entry point for evil spirits, though in some other cases, affliction by an evil spirit might be the primary cause of physical illness. In either case, successful therapy requires a biomedical method, emotional healing, and eviction of external evil spirits, all of which are coherently related.

Deity Dancing as a Spectacle: Deity Presence and Cure

My experience with spirit cults in Yan'an was that they created a new kind of social space where people mingle together and share their experiences of inauspiciousness and health problems regardless of social status or whether they are rural or urban, haves or have-nots. But it is not just the social leveling that spirit cults enable; it is the proliferations of folk discourse and practices that are crucial.

Within such space, one major feature was watching a spectacular folk performance together. The dance of the Black Tiger deity was an example. Locals call such an occasion "dancing deity" (*tiaoshen*). Before I saw it, I have been asked many times, "Have you seen a deity in dancing using a heavy, three-pronged wrought-iron sword (*sanshandao*)? It is really worth seeing!" All villagers I talked to unanimously said the "dancing deity" is a must-see! Many recalled with vivid images, "the medium used a heavy chopper and a steel rod that weighs about ten catty to hit his own body but was not injured!" Interestingly, when people mentioned "dancing deity," they never spoke of it in a frightening manner, but with great excitement. Mr. Cao, an old brigade leader of Mojiagou village, recalled seeing one: "her (the spirit medium) feet were bound, tiny and pointy, but when she tip-toed on the ground, dancing with a heavy steel rod, she moved faster than everyone else!"

Dancing deity is indeed a powerful show or a "dramatic spectacle" (Firth 1967: 202). The power of the spectacular is mixed with the power of healing. That day in the cavehouse of the Black Tiger deity medium, not only was the audience absorbed in the dance, they queued to watch the performance again and again. In the process, we heard the spirit medium repeat the formulaic procedure of asking a list of questions from the clients and muttering spiritual prescriptions. At the same time, patients were put in situations one after another where they were urged to recount experiences of inauspicious encounters and uncomfortable bodily symptoms. Everyone got to hear about everyone's problems, recommendations, and prescriptions from the beginning to the end. Instead of seeing a doctor in a private clinical setting, spirit mediums treat patients collectively and through dramatic scenes. In a way, the cure is associated with the public and collective sharing, watching, and hearing. It was in the repetitive speaking, roaring, and muttering of the spirit medium, and under a public witnessing, that the efficacy of deity power is expressed and publicly endorsed.

The spectacle of the medium's dance is more than mere entertainment. It is, as Kapferer says, "a demonstration of the totalizing power of god, or even a mimetic presence of their divine energies. Through the mediation of the spectacle of dance, human beings and the gods are brought into touch" (1997: 128). The dance could be articulated as a representation of the Black Tiger deity's appearance and that was indeed how Aunt Fang understood it—scaring away the evil spirits. And if the dance was god performing, it was also presented in a form of "gift" to the audience. In this way, the audience not only received treatment or protective force from the deity, but their watching together constituted "an auspicious gaze," which was "a central act of worship in which human beings see and are seen by the deity" (Kapferer 1997: 128).

If the medium's dance symbolizes a building, demonstration, and revelation of the Black Tiger deity's power, the eventual placing of patients close to the mediums and their dialogues have had meanings beyond simple medical or psychotherapy consultation. In the medium's cavehouse, everyone was a spectator. But everyone must be a spectator long enough to be able to get to the position of diagnosis. There on the medium's *kang*, Aunt Fang was seated not exactly as a patient, or a passive, weak, sick person. Quite the contrary, the person who finally gets to see the medium face to face, must be sober, reflexive, and articulate enough to turn one's problem and experience into a narrative—and be able to present it in public. For Aunt Fang, she must come to terms with the ill fortune the bus accident had brought to her and make a connection with her back pain. The speaking out was not always an easy task for many. Some broke down and were unable to continue. Some spoke without enough details that the mediums had to ask more questions to sort out what happened. Some concerns were straightforward and simple. Others could be complicated and involved ancestral history. Nonetheless, all were critical moments when individuals came to articulate their experiences, actions, and life situations.

Analyzing the sorcery rite of Suniyama in Sri Lanka, Bruce Kapferer argues that human beings are treated as the focal center of the universe in religious rituals, in which the victim becomes the embodied potency of what may be described as the "constituting consciousness of humankind: a consciousness formed in the process of action and a consciousness on the threshold of further constituting action" (1997: 157). Similarly, I understand Aunt Fang's dialogue with the medium as a critical moment of self-reflection, where she became the focal point of the broader, urbanizing, rural world she is situated in. Her account of the bus accident was not about telling an objective event. It was an active, subjective remaking and re-understanding of one's own crisis experience, and a conscious connecting of it to practices of extrahuman energies or sociopolitical forces. If speech is an act of consciousness constitutive of the process of coming into being (Kapferer 1997: 158), the dialogue between Aunt Fang and the medium was a consciousness constitution act. The process helped Aunt Fang refocus her reality, articulate the external and internal forces surrounding her, and reinforce her agency to control the event's effects on her body.

Aunt Fang may have seen and spoken directly to the Black Tiger deity and witnessed and felt his power. But these acts and the consciousness formed through these acts would not be meaningful without the subsequent ritual practices. All the symbolic meanings and power must involve the body "as both the instrument and the site of practice" (Kapferer 1997: 177). It was in the repetitive practices of the deity's advice, of studying the details of his prescription paper and mixing his medicine with the right ingredients, and of anointing it on the body at the right moments of the day that the power of the deity became present and real. Belief is certainly important, but it is "the body as belief" that really matters. With the body as a site of practice, the "technology of ritual"—the liturgical repetition, obsession with details, precision, and conventions—turns belief into a dynamic and embodying process (Kapferer 1997: 178).

In short, not only are the mediums' dance rituals and speech acts crucial to spirit cults in Yan'an. Patients' reflections and postvisit practices are all crucial to the content of belief and cult experience. In the following, I discuss a spirit cult in Mojiagou village in particular as constructing a new kind of communal gathering and sociality in the changing rural community.

The Ritual of "Elevating Luck" (*fuyun*) on the Eighth Day of the Lunar New Year

During the Chinese New Year in 2004, the Fangs' split household condition paused as the children who work away came home for a family reunion. The second daughter, working as a nurse in Xi'an, the only son studying in Yulin county, and the youngest daughter—studying in Shanxi province—had come home. The elder and third daughters, both working in Shenzhen, south China, could not join due to high travel expenses. The Fangs got busy with the three children around and cooking a lot, and we spent most of the time staying home and watching television. I thought various New Year ritual observances would occur at the village level but none did. The main event was a large-scale New Year parade centrally organized by the city government at the city center on the fifteenth day of the Lunar New Year. Before that, there was barely any festive ambience at the village level.

The eighth day of the Lunar New Year (*chuba*) was as quiet as previous days. When the family sat comfortably in front of the television after lunch, I went out to visit another villager, Mr. Mo and his family, who stayed home, idle, as everyone else did. We chatted for a while about his elder daughter working in south China as a factory worker. When I was ready to leave, as it was getting dark, Mr. Mo said, "Stay here. There is a thing tonight."

After an hour, Mr. Mo took me to walk up the hill a bit and we went into the cavehouse of his brother, elder Mo. The next forty-five minutes were, perhaps, the most bizarre in my life. Four people were sitting inside, all surrounding a small coal burner. A dim lamp, hanging from the ceiling, shaded everyone's face, giving the space an eerie ambience. The wife of elder Mo, sweeping the floor and disposing of paper fragments in the burner, ignited a fire and obliged everyone to bend backward. At the same time, elder Mo's granddaughter, who was mentally disabled, made some hearty laughs one minute and some melancholic wails another.

The tension slowly diminished as more people came in. All were members of Mojiagou village, people that I ran into every day, and most belonged to the Mo lineage. There were some strange female faces; I later figured out that they belonged to the Mo lineage but were married to men in neighboring villages. Some were surprised that I was there but most did not react. After about ten people came in, elder Mo set up a small shrine on a table, where a bowl of millet was used to hold three sticks of incense and two small yellow flags on the side. Behind the incense container, a piece of cloth was put up on which many local gods' and deities' names were written. An empty metal basin for burning was placed underneath the shrine.

Meanwhile, the wife of elder Mo climbed up onto the *kang* and sat down on a red cloth with gold color embroideries. Then she started having hiccups periodically, with her eyes closed. The sound and speed of her hiccups grew and eventually became some loud coughing, which lasted for a few minutes. As her cough grew worse, her face became red and twisted. Just as I thought she was going to throw up, her cough abated and all of a sudden, she was speaking in a different voice.

"You have invited Niangniang (the queen) to the earth. The earth door and the heaven door are open now. Niangniang has come down to the earth. Niangniang loves prosperity. Niangniang loves the people. Do you understand? Niangniang loves everyone. So what is the matter?"

"Niangniang, please give us direction. We want Niangniang to take away adversity and give us luck," a man next to her said.

"Who are you and how old are you?" Niangniang asked.

"My name is Yue Seng."

"How old are you?"

"44."

"What month?"

"November 15th."

"How about you?"

"My name is Li Yan."

"I am 27, October 23rd, a rooster."

"Your fortune is very good. But I will raise it for you. You must burn the yellow paper and shatter it. You should bury it in a shrub of the woods, and I will give you luck. You must also shred this string and bury it."

"Let me see if I can take adversity away. I will put all the disaster, adversity, and tragedy deep in the mountain and down in the woods. Everything is cleaned up. I will make a new path for you, so that you can go from north to south, east to west. And when you walk, you will run into a living Wealth God (*caishen*). I am giving you good luck so that good fortune substitutes for bad one, and an up fortune for a down one. After this, your back is no longer in pain."

"I am now calling the horse. And you should whirl the yellow paper around yourself. It will not only raise your fortune but also let you run into a Wealth God alive. You will feel well at home and outside and through the four seasons. Your foot will trace the Wealth God and I will pave the way for you. I will give you good luck until the end of June and in the middle of October, and a fortune star will fall on you. I will also let your children run into good luck. No matter where you go, in and out of home, you will have good luck. Niangniang will secure your safety. I will secure your baby and your elderly. I will also call and settle with your Door god [a major deity believed to guard at individual households doors to keep evil spirits away] so that everyone is protected. Look how Niangniang takes care of you."

"Everyone is taken care of. Kowtow and burn the paper," the man next to Niangniang instructed.

Another five people went through the similar ritual in which the *Wangmu Niangniang* (the Queen Mother of the West) gave divination. The whole event lasted for about two hours and everyone took away several packs of spiritual medicine at the end. They were similar to the yellow triangular paper wrap Aunt Fang obtained from the Black Tiger deity medium. The attendants also donated some money before leaving.

When the event was over, it was close to ten o'clock at night. I ran back to the Fang's family, fearing they might worry about my whereabouts, only to find out that a stranger was leaving. Aunt Fang told me that he was a spirit medium who gave a blessing for the whole family and I had missed a *fuyun* ritual staged at home!

Worship, Healing, and Bonding in Spirit Cults in Yan'an

Wangmu Niangniang, known in English as Xi Wang Mu or the Queen Mother of the West, is an ancient Chinese goddess whose origin can be traced in the ancient book of *Guideways of Mountains and Seas (shanhaijing)*, in which she was a ferocious goddess with the teeth of a tiger. She was later adapted into Daoist tradition and transformed into a goddess of life and immortality (Cahill 1993). In Chinese popular religion, Queen Mother of the West is a prominent figure capable of dispensing prosperity, longevity, and eternal bliss. She is actively sought by followers for healing, fortune telling, and, in Mojiagou during the New Year, for elevating luck (*fuyun*).

The ritual of elevating luck enables people to make wishes of prosperity, good luck, affluence, and good health, and it is usually held on the eighth day of the Lunar New Year. Many in Yan'an would choose this date to worship gods or deities they are devoted to. Some choose to visit the state-sponsored Daoist temple on top of Yan'an city hill.[7] Some villagers in Mojiagou opted to celebrate this date with their own communal deity—the Queen Mother of the West—whose medium was elder Mo's wife. In her own cavehouse, elder Mo's wife went into an "altered state of consciousness" after vigorous hiccups and coughing (Bourguignon 1991) after which villagers received her "word gifts" as divination (Csordas 1994: 47). The Mo villagers not only heard words of wisdom and fortune, they also collectively experienced the revelation of the Queen Mother, descended from heaven to earth, through the medium's speech acts.

Spirit cults in Yan'an present potent relationships between images and ideas. In both the Black Tiger God dancing and the Queen Mother of the West's divination, the power of magic and healing work through powerful speeches and imagery. While the Black Tiger deity showed much of its might through the medium's dancing, fighting, and roaring, the Queen Mother of the West conveyed its power through the medium's incantations and spells.

Unintelligibility characterizes the formulaic and archaic ritual language of the two spirit mediums. These excerpts of the Queen Mother of the West's divination were recorded and transcribed by a local student at Mojiagou village, who could extract and write down only some parts of her speech. Even the Black Tiger deity needed an onsite interpreter to tell the clients his prescriptions. But as Marilyn Ivy argues, it is not the content of the medium's incantations that leads to the desired effect of the ritual performance, but purely the form of the incomprehensible utterance. Writing about *kuchiyose* in Japan, uttered by *itako* (mediums who are healers) at Mount Oscore, Ivy argues that the unintelligibility of the itako's chants not only makes them believable, but "magical." The spirit medium's muttering and chanting effects "a dissociation between signifier and signified," leading the language to be unbound as the chanting foregrounds itself as pure utterance, divorced from meaning (Ivy 1995: 169–178). The form, instead of the content, of the speech compels beliefs. In a different light, Thomas Csordas uses the term "glossolalia" to describe the healing minister's speech when the healers "are opening themselves to divine revelation, and when they want to surrender control of the healing process directly to divine action" (Csordas 1994: 46). The medium's unintelligible speech enables the patient to be immersed in and overwhelmed by divine power.

The fortune-elevating ritual conjured up a very clear imagery: believers' bad luck is exorcised and buried in the deep woods and their good luck is visualized by the daily practice of walking. The ritual works not only through speech, but also through objects. The paper and red string each believer burned is close to what Bruce Kapferer calls the "objectification of consciousness" (Kapferer 1997: 161–163). The ritual objects first symbolized the believer; then, after the act of whirling above his head—as if absorbing something—it shifted to symbolize bad luck; and subsequently through the act of burning it, it became the evil spirit to be exorcised. The image of good luck was clearly represented through the local landscape of four directions (east, south, west, north), roads, cavehouse doorsteps, daily practices of walking to and from home, and images of a "living Wealth God." Ritual objects such as the Black Tiger deity's cleavers and the yellow triangular spiritual medicine packs are vested with power. Inscribed by the spirit medium's speech, they "act like incantations" and make the speech rituals magical and efficacious (Mauss 1972: 77–78).

Together, these ritual objects, the speech acts, the practices of burning paper and kowtow, and the associated imagery involve believers in a cosmic passage so that they are reoriented to feel in control of their action again. The practices of burning paper make them know that the evil spirit is evicted and one is able to reestablish a sense of safe boundaries and harmonious relations with humans, demons, and gods.

Women Becoming Spirit Mediums in the Nineties

After a year of talking extensively to many, followers and otherwise, within and outside of Mojiagou village, I figured that the cult worship for the Queen Mother of the West really started in the few villages surrounding Mojiagou around the mid-1990s. A few female mediums claiming to possess the Queen Mother of the West emerged. Some of them were widows. All of them went through a traumatic experience of either mental or physical sickness that triggered their first trance. After that initiation, all claimed that there was a big urge within themselves to speak (*chukou*) for the deities concerned when they saw people suffer.

Elder Mo's wife started her medium career after a serious mental illness in the 1980s. She recalled for me that she had had mental problems as early as during the Maoist years. She said she often had to ask for sick leave under the People's Commune system, in which everyone worked for the collectivity. Uncle Fang also remembered that she was no model worker of the time. Gaining more popularity in the late 1990s, she has gradually attracted followers within and surrounding Mojiagou village.

The prominence of women in peripheral possession has been a topic of discussion within the scholarship on Chinese and East Asian religion, which has centered on explaining the division between male mediums engaged in more formalized rituals and female mediums who are possessed by marginal deities or household gods (Jordan 1972; Kendall 1985; Lee 2010; Young 1994). I will not elaborate further surrounding the discussions but would speculate that elder Mo's wife gave more relevant and personal divinations than other deities precisely because she knew her followers well in the village. The Mo villagers consulted her for various issues: inability to conceive a baby, suffering from diseases, or suspicion of inauspicious forces. She was the best consultant when things happened in the village, and she could channel the deity's advice directly to those concerned. I therefore agree with Cline's recent findings that female spirit mediums often give useful advice and personal guidance on private matters, particularly women's childbirth matters, because such intimate and caring advice, with a kind of religious authority, is nowhere to be found in the rural area (Cline 2010: 548).

The rise of the cult for Wangmu Niangniang in rural Yan'an coincides with the beginning of the marginalization of rurality in Yan'an, when young sons and daughters started to leave rural hometowns in great numbers, leaving their children and parents at home. The decade of the nineties was only the beginning of rural to urban migration and rural social change. In the

2000s, everyone in rural Yanan came to understand the meaning of "all that solid melts into the air": villages were uprooted, residents were relocated, highways replaced farmlands, and cavehouse architecture disappeared. After the announcement of the urban planning in the region, Mojiagou villagers were compensated with a lump sum from 50,000 to 80,000 RMB per person in 2005, based on the size of the farmland they were allocated. The remuneration was seen as quite generous, at least in the years before 2005 when the price of vegetables was only 0.5 RMB per catty (500 grams). In only a few years time, however, the same amount of money purchased far less. Villagers ardently complained about the loss of farmland and their livelihood. At the same time, those households living close to the main road started to open small businesses and make more money, while the majority of the remaining households needed to find other means to maintain the rising cost of living.

New inequalities have been introduced within the village, and existing rural residents have been propelled into a new, unfamiliar way of making a living. In this context, traditional values and desires of getting rich and longevity are newly embedded in the current state-led urban development, agrarian decline, and vanishing rural community life. A communal spirit medium such as Wangmu Niangniang is perhaps demanded more than ever for her provision of spiritual and religious services (exorcism, divination, spiritual counseling) in this time of great social change. In this context, the popularity of spirit cults reflects a "counter-reality," where salient social values and cultural orientation are played out, reassessed, weighted differently than in everyday life, and opened up to other interpretations (Boddy 1989: 156–157).

The Production of a Surrogate Rural Subjectivity

In *Gender Trouble* (1999), Judith Butler argues that what we take to be an internal essence of gender is in fact the effect of a "repeated stylization of the body, a set of repeated acts within a highly rigid regulatory frame that congeal over time to produce the appearance of the substance, of a natural sort of being" (43–44). Butler refuses to see the female subject as a coherent or foundational category for feminist theory and practice, because such an assumption ignores the very social conditions that govern and enable the emergence of any politically qualified subject. She argues that the emergence of any subject, such as a woman, is necessarily dependent upon the performative reiteration of specific norms, such as speaking and behaving in certain manners, within a tightly regulated framework of femininities.

Such a framework provides the conditions of recognition through which a subject emerges as legitimate (1995: 36).

Along with Butler's logic and theorizing, I argue that spirit cults produce a unique folk discourse, which in turn enables the production of what I call surrogate rural subjectivity in the context of urbanization of the rural area. By *surrogate rural subjectivity*, I mean to highlight the subject of rural villagers as an unstable category in today's Yan'an, when many migrate to work in cities, live in an urban environment, lose their farmlands, and engage in nonagricultural careers. Spirit cults, in turn, generate those social conditions or social happenings that enable the (re)emergence of a new rural subject, even a surrogate one.

One such social condition or happening is a distinct form of sociality. In Mojiagou, no one would talk about the Queen Mother of the West publicly, and there has never been any promotion of her events. Yet followers would know what would happen on certain dates: where to go, at what time, and how to react at ritual performances. During the time of the temple construction, followers helped out and nonfollowers within the village would not bother to ask any questions. Ever since I was introduced to the elevating luck ritual, I started to relate to villagers differently. I have been able to learn about many individual and family problems, which I would otherwise be unaware of. For example, one villager had a stroke in the hot summer of 2004 and asked the medium of Queen Mother of the West to stage a healing ritual. He told me about this when I passed by his field—not because I noticed anything unusual, but only because he wanted to share with those in the circle. Similarly, I learned of Fei, who had fallen from a tractor, and his experience of the ritual of soul-calling, through Fei's brother. Throughout my stay in the village, I learned of various updates of villagers from elder Mo's wife, and from there I went around to those households and chatted with the people concerned. Word of mouth spread within the cult circle, and followers were more aware of fellow followers' family and health conditions and their children's careers and marriage prospects.

The rituals of giving divination, elevating luck, or soul-calling generate intimate relations and subtle interactions among followers. As opposed to the "red-hot sociality"—the heightened excitement, happy ambience, loud noises, and crowded intermingling among attendants—that Adam Chau finds at the officially endorsed and large-scale temple festivals (Chau 2006: 163–165), the sociality and communal relations that spirit cults generate are inconspicuous, delicate, and—sometimes—mysterious. The rituals of spirit cults are not occasions of open houses but rather by invitations only. Organizers also constantly watch out for suspects who might expose such gatherings to the government. The sensations surrounding spirit cult activities are therefore prudent and never overtly exciting. Followers mingle with each other in a low-key and cautious manner, yet also show mutual concerns and support. Such confined intimacy and discreet sociality certainly reinforce the magical efficacy, religiosity, and bonding surrounding the cult. At the same time, they transform and reconstitute traditional lineage bonding in a changing rural community.

Another social happening surrounding spirit cults practices is grassroots organizing. Apart from attending ritual performances, part of being a cult follower is to help plan and build a temple for the tutelary deities. Temple construction could be initiated when the deity appears in the medium's dream, and the medium in turn mobilizes followers to build a temple. It might also come from followers who receive the signs. The scale of the construction and the subsequent maintenance often depend on the medium's healing power and the number of followers and their fundraising capacity. When planning a temple, followers sort out among themselves forms of division of labor, leadership, informal networking, and volunteering based on rural folk organization rules and conventions.[8] The experience and process involved are not just about being religious, but about attaining culturally specific know-how concerning forms of inviting and appeasing deities, interacting with mediums while they are in a state of spirit possession, and so forth. Much technical knowledge and practices are also involved concerning temple building and the social skills of coordinating followers and their labor. On top of the collective and communal organizational level, the process includes personal understanding and appreciation of the deity dancing, feeling the deity's presence, and relating cult divination with one's well being. In other words, followers learn and share associated cultural knowledge and relevant techniques and pass on ritual understandings. Practicing spirit cults are therefore really about putting oneself in village social life again, exchanging folk ritual knowledge with each other, and learning to practice a series of cultural specific skills and norms.

The peculiar context under which this discreet sociality and folk organizing take place is crucial. In the context of urbanizing existing rural villages, many no longer reside in a rural hometown, only a few young villagers know how to grow crops, and even fewer would identify themselves as *shoukuren*. To those work-away migrants, like Aunt Fang's children, spirit cult occasions and spaces embody an annual yet unfamiliar ritual experience and rare communal sociality. In these occasions, young work-away rural villagers exchange with older followers ritual knowledge and folk cultural beliefs associated with the rural landscape, cavehouse architecture, and popular local history. As these rural backgrounds and landscapes rapidly vanish and rural migrants no longer engage with agricultural labor, spirit cult activity becomes a special folk cultural space and time that is constitutive of a new rural subject position.

Contemporary discourse and practice of spirit cults therefore provide that major framework that reorganizes rural life experience and worldviews, mobilizes folk organizations, reproduces communal sociality, and governs folk religious practices and beliefs. Spirit cult practices reproduce and recuperate increasingly forgotten folk religious rituals and values. Within the cult ritual contexts, one no longer questions but learns about the following: "What counts as inauspicious force?" "What makes a good life in a rural village?" "What makes an efficacious deity?" These questions might seem strange to an urbanite, but they are indeed what Butler would call the "conditions of intelligibility" by which the subject of a rural villager could become culturally recognized (Butler 1993: xi). The conditions of intelligibility are those norms, beliefs, and practices that are "presuppositional" for the production of a subject and subjectivity. These norms and practices form part of the rural everyday lives that are formative to rural villagers' worldviews, ritual common sense, language, and practice.

The folk cultural space created by spirit cults complicates the understanding of a public agrarian sphere generated by popular religious revival (Chau 2006: 9–11). Adam Chau shows that both the local state and the local community in post-Mao rural China actively revive folk religious activities to gain income and legitimacy. He shows that the temple institutions, the open popular religious events, and the increasing number of religious visitors have created a public agrarian sphere. In this sphere, worshippers find recognition of and interactions among fellow villagers, form a ephemeral co-presence (red-hot sociality), and construct a shared sense of well-being that they attribute to the divine power of the deities (2006: 166–168). Chau's notion of a public agrarian sphere is nonetheless conceptually anchored in the assumptions of a rural area still occupied with agricultural labor and that villagers' identities remain relatively fixed, localized, and stable. The contemporary practice of spirit cults, even though it generates a similar sense of co-presence and collectivity, signifies a change of some underlying assumptions: the vanishing of rural farmland, agrarian decline, and the disappearance of farm work and rural livelihood.

The contemporary practice of spirit cults therefore simultaneously constitutes such a "public agrarian sphere" and thrives along with its "vanishing." By vanishing, I reinvoke Marilyn Ivy's analysis of marginalized cultural practices as those that are on the verge of disappearing and yet produce effects through deferral, displacement, and repetition (1995). To understand spirit cults as a discourse and practice of the vanishing is to see how they simultaneously recognize the loss of the existence of rural environment and

FIGURE 5.2. A newly built temple for the spirit deity *Heihulingguan* in rural Yan'an.

FIGURE 5.3. The Fangs sitting on couches inside their new urban apartment.

FIGURE 5.4. Aunt Fang standing in front of the village's farmland. In 2004, when the picture was taken, greenhouses with white plastic roofs were scattered along the farmland.

FIGURE 5.5. The newly built Chinese Communist Party school stands where the Mojiagou farmland used to be (photo taken in 2012).

agrarian culture as much as they also revive and recuperate them. The result is what I call the production of surrogate rural subjectivity, which villagers assume when watching an occasional and spectacular deity dancing, getting an annual spiritual divination, and socializing with fellow followers in a cavehouse healing session amid urbanizing lives, habits, and practices. Such surrogate rural subjectivity, though fleeting and ephemeral, revives that sense of loss of traditional rural sociality and community.

When I returned to Mojiagou again in 2011, a gigantic school building—surrounded by gardens and trees—for the political education of Communist Party members replaced all farming fields. A new site of a commercial complex, new urban parks, and an extension of the Yan'an University campus and other tourist sites replaced several preexisting villages of the region. I saw Aunt and Uncle Fang, who were now landless. They continued to grow some vegetables in their cavehouse courtyard for family consumption. They also started to earn income by doing brickwork for companies constructing the city's growing tourism sites. Fei, the young man who went through the soul-calling ritual because he was hurt while driving his farm truck, is no longer farming. He now lives on the government compensation he received in exchange for his farmland being taken away. He plays cards at home with friends every day and makes a living by gambling and from the interest derived from small-scale loans he makes to others from his principal compensation. All of them continue to attend divination rituals of the cults of which they are members.

In this chapter, I show that spirit cults as a major form of folk tradition, retaining some of the most localized knowledge, representations, and practices due to their historical resistance to intellectual mediation and state reform, are subjected to numerous contradictions and reinterpretation today. But it is in the vanishing of rural environment and community that spirit cults thrive and produce new folk discourse and new rural subjects. Urbanizing villagers recognize both the sense of loss generated by the changing rural community and the concomitant feeling of the impossibility to really recover the original rurality; they keep reconstructing their tradition.

Conclusion

In this book, I have emphatically argued that the meanings of folk cultural revivals in contemporary Yan'an are woven together by multiple actors and various political, economic, and social forces and initiatives. I call the production and consumption of folk revival discourses and cultural practices in post-2000 Yan'an "hyper-folk" to capture the distance between what is celebrated today as "Chinese folk tradition" and what was understood as exclusively peasant culture in the past. Hyper-folk enables one to examine the various governmental, intellectual, urban, and communal forces shaping and constituting the contents and meanings of today's Chinese tradition, as opposed to its previous meanings largely determined by either local customs or national political campaigns. Most importantly, hyper-folk points to the rapidly vanishing of material referents or origins of all kinds of folk cultural representations and practices caused by intensified urbanization of the rural areas.

The cultural logic of late socialism is one that converges these political, social, economic, and communal forces and relations and, at the same time, makes their meanings and practices flexible and malleable to fit in various purposes and occasions. Today, one can watch a live performance of folk paper-cutting, which features a woman villager from Xiaocheng making a paper-cut inside her traditional cavehouse, as mediated through a television channel or YouTube and staged by the local government to promote cultural tourism in Yan'an. Similarly, one can appreciate a traditional northern Shaanxi storytelling show at night, sponsored by a danwei, for the promotion of the latest enlisting of intangible cultural heritage. A migrant returnee would line up to consult the communal spirit medium for her marriage prospect, videotape through a smart phone a deity dancing show, and share the divination in her urban apartment with friends in a cosmopolitan city. In each of these occasions, the practice of folk tradition becomes the site of a complex presentation of the local state appropriating local resources for tourism purposes, of work units reviving folk performances for public relations purposes, of locals reenacting localized knowledge and practices for recuperating a vanishing public agrarian sphere, and of urbanites consuming rural values and lifestyles. In each of these, the linkage between both the practice of folk tradition and the condition of the rural area is reinterpreted and reflected upon.

Finally, "Yan'an and folk culture" are used to connote a historical model of the Chinese Communist Party appropriating folk traditions to promote rural reform and national state campaigns. Such a historical relationship has been transformed when the party-state is no longer the sole interpreter of local traditions today. Instead, these two keywords in late socialist China suggest constant contestations among multiple actors and forces in their attempt to mobilize the discourse and practices of traditional rural culture. The meanings and authenticity of Chinese tradition will eventually be determined by the ways local and civil initiatives negotiate with state and capital appropriations and by the ways villagers and urban consumers refashion them.

Notes

Introduction

1. This book takes folk culture as a site of contest politics and dynamic cultural change, on which tradition was debated and reformulated and where multiple parties struggle for discursive power (Mani 1987; Duara 1995). It draws the polemics differently from existing studies on post-Mao tradition revivals, which often focus on aspects of communal resistance and local history or identity building against the hegemonic party-state (Jing 1996; Mueggler 2001; Liu 2000). Instead, it discovers the nature of the complicated alliance and interpenetrations between folk tradition and Communist party-state ideology (Greenblatt 1976). It echoes existing observations that link the production of tradition to contemporary governance and economic benefits (Wang 2001; Chau 2005; Goodman 2006) and modern imaginations (Schein 2000; Oakes and Schein 2006).

2. The CCP was forced to embark on the Long March in 1934 after the Nationalist government launched a large-scale annihilation attack against all Communist elements in the country. To avoid enclosure from combined air and ground attacks, the Communists scaled mountains, forded rivers, and crossed plains to escape. The journey was so arduous that only a tenth of CCP's original force of 100,000 survived. For the official Communist history of the Long March, see "Weida de changzheng" (Bianweihui 2006) and *Zhongguo gongnong hongjun changzheng quanshi* (Junshi kexueyuan junshi lishi yanjiusuo 2006).

3. Ding Ling, an acclaimed feminist and novelist in Shanghai, was a typical example of those thousands traveling to and for Yan'an. Having been a political prisoner under Jiang Jieshi, Ding Ling arrived at the red capital with the help of underground Communists in 1937 and was later appointed to supervise political education in the Soviet (Spence 1981: 270–272). See also (Ding 1984). Many foreign pilgrims also came, such as Norman Bethune, a Canadian thoracic surgeon who arrived at Yan'an in

1938 after his volunteer service aiding the Republicans in the Spanish Civil War. Dr. M. M. Atal, an Indian doctor who joined the Spanish people's fight against Fascism in 1936, led the Indian Medical Mission to China (Basu 2003).

4. Gao found that the political persecution associated with the Rectification Campaign was not limited to cadres and the army, but was extended to students of universities and even primary schools. The number of identified special agents was as high as 75 percent in some of the cadre training groups, 50 percent in the Anti-Japanese Red Army University (*Kangri Hongjun Daxue*), and about 30 percent in the Yan'an University. (Gao 2000: 519–527). One of the major intellectual dissidents, Wang Shiwei, was indicted with the crime of being a Nationalist agent and was later beheaded (Gao 2000: 335). Michael Dutton explains the recurrent tragedies of political persecution within the Communist Party by tracing a sentiment of distrust resulting from the Nationalist purge in 1927, in which the Nationalist military leader Zhang Jieshi betrayed the Nationalist-Communist alliance of the Republican government (1924–1927) and killed thousands of left-wing intellectuals and labor unionists (Chiang 2002). Dutton argues that the purge had since produced sentiments of suspicion and distrust, which became built into Chinese leftist revolutionary politics, leading to the excessive use of physical torture and unjust injuries for finding out possible and imagined traitors. The Yan'an Rectification Campaign is, according to Dutton, already a moderate one in terms of the CCP's "disciplining of its political excess," as the numbers and degrees of unjust persecutions were smaller than in previous internal struggles (Dutton 2005: 78–80).

5. The Yan'an government encouraged power sharing and a less violent form of campaigning for ideological unity. Politically, the "three-thirds system" allowed the CCP to form a power alliance with the national bourgeoisie, local gentry, and other non-CCP elements. The CCP would take only one-third of the positions in all government bodies while the remaining two-thirds were reserved for "people who stand for resistance and democracy whether or not they are members of other parties." Economically, the government put higher taxation on landlords and allowed poor peasants to buy land and become middle peasants (Huang 1995).

6. Rita Felski shows that artists, writers, and intellectuals within the European fin de siècle sought to express their sense of estrangement from an ever more urban and technologized society through an orientation to the feminized past and an explicit cult of the mythic and the nonrational (1995: 50). She argues that the oriental and feminized Other has played a key role in the construction of experiences of temporality and historical consciousness in Western modernity.

7. Here, I am mainly referring to Chen Kaige's film *Yellow Earth* (1984), one of the most representative works in the Chinese fifth-generation cinema. As observed by Chris Berry, the movie features "a representation of the peasantry that is totally contrary to that favored in the days of the 'worker soldier peasant' orientation, when all peasants were represented as mentally prepared, willing followers of revolution." The young girl in the film is still locked in a world of poverty and ignorance, and her father, uninterested in change, forces her to a marriage she does not want (Berry 1992: 52–53). I am also referring to *Heshang*, one of the most controversial television

documentary series in Deng's period (Bodman and Wan 1991: vii). Heshang chooses the Yellow River, the dragon, the Great Wall and deity worship as symbols of the Chinese collective consciousness and explores them as a basis for reexamination of traditional Chinese culture. In the episodes, viewers are called upon to break away from the earthbound culture and to dispense with the dynastic cycle and the defensiveness of a siege mentality (Field 1991: 5). The program associates oceanic culture with industrialized capitalist modernization and the Yellow River silts with the aging agro-civilization. Its central message is to call for China to join the industrial Western civilization of the world, associated with the spirits of freedom, openness, science, and democracy in order to break away from developmental stagnation and cultural stasis. See more discussions surrounding the documentary by the *Bulletin of Concerned Asian Scholars* 1991 23 (3): 1–32. See also Su Xiaokang and Wang Luxiang (1991). See also "Zhishifenzi (Chinese Intellectuals) and Power," Tani Barlow's critique of the intellectuals' enlightening project as trapped in the authority and power of an imagined Western modernity (1991).

8. In the 1980s, the cultural fever discussion developed into a full-blown sociocultural movement for "ideas," "theories," and "methodology," which intellectuals thought would shed light on the nation's cultural agenda and the formula for a market economy. In these different schools of thoughts, themes, and questions—which the May Fourth intellectuals had discussed sixty-years prior—surfaced again, though with far more complexity: Who am I as an intellectual? What is the meaning of Chinese traditional culture? What is its place in the process of modernization? How should China modernize—through a cultural, scientific, or philosophical reflection approach? See Chen (1989), Chen (1991), the journal *Culture: China and the World*, Wang (1996), and Cha (2006).

9. This book cannot adequately address the complicated reasons and heated ideological debates concerning the material underdevelopment of the rural area and institutional rural-urban divide during the Maoist era. My view is that although the newly formed socialist state after 1949 eagerly wanted to overcome the difference between cities and countryside through rapid industrialization, the problem of rural-urban disparity became even more institutionalized and unarticulated because the Maoist state was constantly torn by two divergent and contradictory needs: the need to subject the rural population to hard labor and contribute cheap agricultural products for the new nation's urbanization and industrialization, and the need to deliver a new image of a hopeful rural area. This dilemma led to paradoxical consequences and problematic implementations. For instance, the more the party-state endeavored to maximize the surplus of industrial output, the more it had to acquire agricultural products through a unified procurement system that kept prices for agricultural products at a low level. As this occurred, the state had to impose disciplinary measures on villagers for total extraction of their harvest. Even though the People's Commune system provided villagers with basic medial service and literacy resources, it inevitably became a policing machine that strictly controlled villagers' daily work schedules, private lives, and behaviors to ensure their subordination and their contribution of the harvest.

10. Sun Liping attends to the ways rural villagers gain incremental benefits by specific reform policies at different stages without reducing the "economic reform" to either economist's celebrated market freedom project or an easily generalized neoliberalism in China. He characterizes the economic reform during the 1980s as one that "extends rights and resources previously centralized by the party-state to many" through policies such as redistributing farmland to individual rural households, giving villagers the rights to own and sell their products after meeting the contribution requirement, raising the state procurement price on agricultural products, and allowing peasants to move out of their birthplace, set up rural enterprises, and so forth. Sun, however, criticizes the economic reform in the 1990s as one that "re-centralizes and redistributes resources to the party-state ruling class and economic elites" through privatization policies. It was a time when some failing SOEs were transferred to a few, and millions of state-owned workers lost jobs. At the same time, there was rapid commodification of housing, education, and medical services (2004a, b).

11. Wen Tiejun, an expert on agricultural economics, is the most important figure who articulates the problem of the agrarian crisis in today's China. He promoted the formulation *sannong wenti* (*sannong* is *nongmin, nongcun, nongye*—"peasants," "rural society," and agriculture"; *wenti* means "problem") to fully understand the intertwined historical, political, economic, and cultural factors constituting the current problems. For a more detailed discussion of Wen's view and his advocacy for a new rural reconstruction movement, see Alexandar Day (2008).

12. Jean Baudrillard used the concept of "hyperreality" to understand the media-saturated consumer society, in which fantasy and reality, fake events and real agendas, and consumption and production interpenetrate with each other (1988). Baudrillard's theorization has been insightful in understanding the extensive late capitalist cultural phenomena of simulation, cultural replicas, and media industry's "simulated environments," such as Disney theme parks, award ceremonies, and TV reality shows. He aims to show how people in the postmodern era now live in the age in which reality, technology, and artificial settings are blended together and become so real that people develop intimate relationships with them.

13. The name and concept of Yan'an has a long history. During the Ming and Qing dynasties, Yan'an denoted a large area in northern Shaanxi province, known as Yan'an Fu, with districts of Zichang, Yanchuan, Yanchang, Ganquan, Fuxian, Zidan, Ansai, and Gulin. Under the Nationalist Government from 1911–1933, Yan'an Fu was directly administered by the Shaanxi Provincial Government. The CCP established a Soviet government in the area, calling it a northern Shaanxi Soviet (*Shaanbei Suqu*). After 1949, Yan'an's government was promoted to a Special District government (Yan'an Zhuanqu) but was renamed Yan'an District after 1978. In 1996 Yan'an District was reorganized into Yan'an City, administering twelve counties. For details of existing counties, see the Yan'an government Web site at http://www.yanan.gov.cn/zjya/yagk/xzqy.htm (last accessed on March 1, 2015).

14. For instance, in 2004, Yan'an's GDP was 19 billion yuan. The annual disposable income among urban residents was 6,334 yuan per capita (Yan'an Yearbook Edito-

rial Board 2005: 87), and income among rural residents was 1,953 yuan per capita (Yan'an Yearbook Editorial Board 2005: 158). In the same year, Guangzhou, a coastal city in South China, had a GDP of 411 billion yuan (Guangzhou Yearbook Editorial Board 2005: 43). The annual disposable income among Guangzhou urban residents was 38,053 yuan per capita, and income among rural residents was 16,788 yuan per capita (Guangzhou Yearbook Editorial Board 2005: 454).

Chapter 1. Paper-Cuts in Modern China

1. For motifs, characteristics, and styles of paper-cuts in different regions, see Wang (2006).

2. Shaanxi paper-cuts or Yan'an paper-cuts are often characterized by faces delineated in profile with large, oval eyes. They also often exhibit a balance between solid and cutaway areas of paper, and interior sections are decorated with fringed, circular, triangular, and crescent-shaped cutouts. (Wachs 2004: 17).

3. Ai Qing (1910–1996) is the renowned poet and painter in modern China. He went to school at Hangzhou West Lake Art Academy in 1928 and studied further in France. He returned to China in 1932 and joined the China League of Left Wing Artists (zhongguo zuoyi meishujia lianmeng). With his first poetry anthology, *Da Yan He*, he became famous throughout the country. Ai went to Yan'an in 1941 and became the chief editor of *Poetry Journal* (shikan) there. In 1945, he served as the vice director of the Literature and Arts College at the Shanxi Chahar Hebei North China United Revolutionary University (Jin-Cha-Ji Huabei Lianda) in 1945. After the establishment of the PRC, he was the deputy editor of the national journal *People's Literature*. In the 1950s, he emerged as an important spokesperson for the view that Chinese painting (guohua) should be thoroughly reformed through synthesis with Western art. He and Jiang Feng were close friends; they served a prison term together in the early 1930s and were administrative colleagues in the late 1940s and early 1950s.

4. Jiang Feng (1918–1982) may be considered the most influential figure in the art world of modern China. He became involved in leftist activities at the age of seventeen and in 1930 joined with other leftist art students to launch the Shanghai Eighteen Art Society Research Center (Shanghai yibai yishe yanjiu suo) in 1930. He learned woodblock carving and print techniques at the bidding of Lu Xun. Jiang joined the CCP in 1932, traveled to Yan'an in 1939, and became an instructor in the Lu Xun Academy of Literature and Arts. In 1949, he served as the vice director and secretary of the party committee at the National Arts Academy in Hangzhou, a combination of administrative and party posts that gave him executive control of China's most prestigious art college. He also held high positions in the Art Workers Associations, which oversaw the making and publicizing of art, and in the academic world of the Central Academy of Fine Arts (CAFA). In the 1957 Anti-Rightist Campaign, he was criticized for valuing Western oil painting over classical Chinese painting, sent to labor reform, and removed from his powerful positions in the cultural bureaucracy. Indeed, Jiang Feng was famous for his uncompromising idealism in his approach to art. His belief was that Western-style painting, with its particular techniques of

anatomy, perspectives, and texture, was scientific and therefore the more appropriate means of reflecting the realities and political ideals of the modern era.

5. In 1944, an article by Ai Qing called *"Chuanghua jianzhi"* (Window Flower Paper-Cuts) ran in *Jiefang ribao* (November 16). In 1946, this article was then reprinted in Zhou Yang, Xiao San, Ai Qing et al., *Minjian yishu yu yiren* (Folk Art and Artists), which contained only a very limited number of prints. In 1949, Ai Qing and Jiang Feng revised the volume into *Xibei jianzhi ji* and published it through Shanghai chenguang chubanshe. (Xu 2005: 96).

6. All quotes from Chinese texts are my translations, unless otherwise noted.

7. Jin Zhilin recited this poem at a gathering of his training class students in the village of Ningjiawan, Wuqi county, Yan'an. The students asked Jin about the meanings of *yafeila* (the Chinese abbreviation for Asia, Africa, and Latin America). After this gathering, the training class group decided to give paper-cuts to village households as a Chinese New Year gift. (Zhang 2009: 37–38).

8. In 1958, the Fine Arts School Education Reform Movement was part of the Rectification Campaign to reduce red tape and inertia in the education bureaucracy. In response to this movement, the official journal on fine arts, *Meishu*, issued an editorial entitled "Ally with Workers and Peasants—The Necessary Road of the Revolutionary Artist." In Pi County, Jiangsu province, villagers created twenty thousand paintings in one month's time, earning the title "Mural Painting County" in 1958. (Chen 2000: 65–69; Duan 1999).

9. Jin Zhilin was born in 1928 and graduated from the CAFA, where he studied oil painting under Xu Beihong and Wu Zuoren and Chinese painting under Qi Baishi and Li Keran. Inspired by Gu Yuan in the Yan'an period, Jin visited Yan'an many times from 1948 on to paint the Loess landscape. One of his most renowned pieces *"Nan Ni Wan"* was commissioned by the Chinese Military Museum in 1961; the painting reconstructed the scene of the eight-route army and Yan'an villagers cooperating to open up wasteland for cultivation. But during the Cultural Revolution, Jin was condemned as a counterrevolutionary. In 1973, he became affiliated with the Yan'an city Hall of Culture, where he worked as an art cadre for the next thirteen years. During this time, he participated in the large-scale rural survey on paper-cutting in Ansai county and has since become one of the most important authorities on folk art and paper-cutting in China.

10. According to Jin Zhilin's biography, Jiang Feng responded negatively during the seminar held in conjunction with the 1980 Yan'an paper-cutting exhibit in Beijing. Supposedly, after hearing people speak of the zhuajiwawa paper-cuts as symbols of the worship of reproductive power, Jiang left the seminar as he cursed, "Reproductive organ, bullshit!" (Zhang 2009: 107).

11. "Product after labor" is translated from the Chinese phrase *"laodong zhiyu de chanwu"* (*laodong* means "labor," *zhiyu* means "afterward," *chanwu* means "product"). It refers to the ways paper-cuts were often produced from fragments of scrap papers after or at the end of the domestic labor of needlework and shoemaking.

12. Born in 1952, Lü Shengzhong graduated from CAFA and did his postgraduate study in folk arts. One of his most significant publications, *Chinese Folk Paper-Cuttings*

(1987), was in fact his master's thesis. It drew national attention to the subject, turning him into one of the most influential figures in the field. Lü is an independent artist today, although he continues to teach at CAFA. His iconic design, little red people (*xiao hong ren*), inspired by the paper figurine of *zhuajiwawa*, has been widely exhibited internationally in Europe, the United States, and various Asian countries. His publications are numerous, and he remains one of the most influential modern artists utilizing folk legends and motifs in contemporary China. See www.baidu.com for more of his publication and exhibit details (last accessed on April 30, 2015).

13. For meanings of various propitious images and the use of visual, puns, rebuses, and symbols in Chinese culture, see Murck and Fong (1991), and Bartholomew (2006).

14. See http://baike.baidu.com/view/975614.htm for Ansai figure. See the national figure on national statistics Web site http://www.stats.gov.cn/tjsj/ndsj/2006/indexch.htm (both sites last accessed on March 16, 2012).

15. Along with Ansai paper-cuts, those of Weixian, Fengning Man ethnicity, Zhongyang, Yiwu Lushan Man ethnicity, and Yangzhou, Lengqing, Guangdong, Dai ethnicity were listed together. See the list at http://www.ihchina.cn/inc/guojiaminglu.jsp (last accessed on March 16, 2012).

16. Along with Yanchuan paper-cuts, those of Baotou, Xingan, Xunyi, Huiling were listed together. See the list at http://www.ihchina.cn/inc/detail.jsp?info_id=3361 (last accessed on March 16, 2012).

17. All the exhibits were successfully launched. The Shanghai Biennale 2004 was a widely covered event in September 2004. In November 2004, I saw a special version of this exhibit in the Beijing 798 Art Zone. Later, my friend Tim Choy in the United States saw the same exhibit in San Francisco. Highlights of the exhibits can be found in the foundation catalog; see Lu and Tung (2004).

18. Liu Jieqiong, daughter of Gao Fenglian, was born in Yanchuan in 1967. She started learning paper-cutting from her mother in 1996 and became famous for it quite quickly. Her first picture collection *Liu Jieqiong's One Hundred Ox Images* was published in 1998. Her designs have won awards and are collected by the National Museum of Art in China as well as museums all over the world. Liu has been invited to give paper-cutting demonstrations around and outside of China. Liu, her mother, and her cousin are three of the most renowned paper-cutting artists in Yan'an. In 2010, the three artists were invited to schools in New Zealand to instruct students in paper-cutting skills, art, and the folk culture of Yan'an. See the event at http://big5.sznews.com/culture/content/2010–06/11/content_4668392_4.htm. See also Yanchuan government Web site's introduction of Liu Jieqiong http://yanchuan.678114.com/Html/wenyi/xiehuizuzhi/meixie/20080419EDFD6474.htm (both sites last accessed on March 16, 2012).

19. Runtu is a character in Lu Xun's short story "Hometown." The young Runtu was a lively boy full of aspiration and imagination. He later grew to be a quiet and faceless man, like a wood person, after experiencing economic harshness and the injustices of the Confucian code of ethics. See Lu Xun (1954).

Chapter 2. Narrative Battle

1. In 1997, the United Nations Educational, Scientific and Cultural Organization (UNESCO) began to protect oral and intangible cultural heritage around the world by asking nation-states to submit applications on their local practices. In 2001, 2003, and 2005, the UNESCO proclaimed ninety masterpieces in total, located in seventy countries of the world, now known as the List of the Masterpieces of the Oral and Intangible Heritage of Humanity. After that, UNESCO asked national governments to set up internal systems to continue this task of identifying and protecting intangible cultural heritage. The Chinese state set up its own Intangible Cultural Heritage Project and created the list of 518 items in 2006.

Chapter 3. Traditional Revival with Socialist Characteristics

1. The sanxian is one of the most popular Chinese folk instruments. North Shaanxi storytellers use it as a solo instrument even though it is more commonly used as an accompanying instrument in ensembles in north China. It has a long fingerboard and the body is usually made of snakeskin stretched over a round rectangular resonator.

2. The historical origin of storytellers possessing the ability to cure remains unclear. Master Xu often told me legends about the origins of his practice involving two brothers surnamed Huang (Yellow), one handicapped and another blinded after committing an offense. As they were begging, they created the sanxian to attract an audience. Other origin legends are mentioned in Stephen Jones's work, but they do not explain the spiritual power of the storyteller (Jones 2009: 40).

3. New stories did not necessarily contain socialist rhetoric and content. They could be thoughtful reworkings of traditional tales in which the traditional characters were not eliminated but also not glorified. Instead, common people (*laobaixing*) were valorized and gained greater importance. The "new" stories were rescripted from existing folk songs and stories so that the distinctions between the oppressed and the oppressors become more clear-cut (see Shaanxisheng Quyizhi Bianji Bangonshi 1985, Wang 1993, Yu 2004). The complete list of northern Shaanxi storytelling is available online (http://www.zgya.com/zgya/sbss.htm (last accessed March 9, 2015).

4. "Wanggui yu Li Xiangxiang" is a famous Communist story, which depicts how young lovers fought for freedom from the oppression of the landlords in the Yan'an soviet area.

5. Storytelling performances were transformed from a one-person show to a three-person one in 1951 and later a four-person troupe under the supervision of county-level Cultural and Education Bureaus. The repertoire of musical styles (*diao*) was also increased to more than fifty types. In 1957, a Center of Musical Drama (*quyiguan*) was established in Yan'an city, which incorporated all the storytelling groups (Wang 1993: 15).

6. In earlier days, the kang was used for resting, eating, and social activities; it was not until the 1980s that tables and chairs were introduced. Today, the *kang* is usually located at the back of the cavehouse and functions simply as a bed. In economically

less developed villages like Heijiawa, however, the *kang* continues to be a prominent social space; on the night of the storytelling, it functioned as a seating area for the audience and accommodated about fifteen people.

7. The production brigades used to own tractors, mechanical mills, and other machines during the 1970s, but their equipment was sold or illegally privatized after the economic reform. (Meisner 1999: 463).

8. Fenggang Yang proposed a "triple-market model" to understand the complex religious situation in China: a red market (officially permitting religion), a black market (officially banning religion) and a gray market (permitting religion with an ambiguous legal/illegal status) (2006: 93–122).

9. Jones mentions that storytellers in the 2000s "could do much better on their own without government control" (2009: 74), but my experience with Master Xu reveals that his business in the rural area follows the previous socialist networks. I think that this applies particularly to the older generation of blind storytellers who were not able to develop broader social and business networks.

Chapter 4. Folk Cultural Production with Danwei Characteristics

1. The "Great Development of West China" program was first launched in 1999 to boost economic development of the western part of China, which lagged behind in terms of GDP performance and socioeconomic developments as compared to the eastern part. The program includes six provinces (Sichuan, Qinghai, Gansu, Yunnan, Guizhou, and Shaanxi), five autonomous regions (Tibet, Xinjiang, Ningxia, Guangxi, and Inner Mongolia), and Chongqing municipality. The program aims at extending infrastructure projects and investment projects to these provinces and regions in order to better develop and utilize its natural resources of the region. See David Goodman (2004).

Chapter 5. Spirit Cults in Yan'an

1. Rural villagers normally make noodles from fresh dough every day, and packages of instant ramen noodles are a cheap and less preferred fast food consumed only outside of one's household.

2. The situation has improved since 2009 after the Chinese state introduced the rural cooperative medical insurance. Rural villagers need only to pay a small monthly fee to have access to diagnosis, medicine, and hospitalization services.

3. All religious sites were closed down during the Cultural Revolution. Many temple buildings were torn apart, statues of gods and religious artifacts were smashed, and religious scriptures were burned. Still, some took great risks to save scriptures, sculptures, and buildings in the name of preserving antiques or cultural heritages (Lang 1998).

4. For an excellent discussion on the historical and translingual construction of the distinctions between religion and superstition in modern China, see Mayfair Young (2008).

5. Recall from Chapter 3 that Yang Fenggang (2006) proposed to use a triple-market model to understand the shifting religious situations in socialist and post-socialist China: a red market (officially permitting religions), a black market (officially banning religions), and a gray market (allowing religions with an ambiguous legal/illegal status). He argued that the heavy state crackdown of popular religion and informal spiritual practices did not lead to religious demise or eradication of religion but a dynamic tripartite religious market, with the emergence of a huge gray market.

6. The Chinese state clearly stipulates that only "normal" religious activities are protected. In 1996, the CCP and the State Council tightened control over the building of temples and outdoor Buddha statues. In 1999, Falun Gong was banned as an "evil cult," and its core leaders were jailed. In the years after that, the Chinese state adopted many ordinances and administrative orders on banning heretic cults and legitimized the crackdown to even *qigong* groups, a form of physical exercise, meditation, and healing. See Yang 2006: 100–101.

7. The Communist government allowed the Daoist shrines on Yan'an city's Great Serenity Mountain (*Taihe Shan*) to go through two restoration efforts between 1956 and 1960, showing the state differentiation of Daoism from other religious sects (Chau 2003: 42).

8. Adam Chau has noted that the organization techniques, social skills, and cultural know-how involved in temple associations have been historically used in many other rural social institutions, including building a family house and staging life-course events such as weddings, funerals, and so forth (Chau 2006: 144–145).

Glossary

Baosuo: Literally translated as "wrap" and "lock," *baosuo* is a popular ritual performance for the protection of colicky or physically weaker children from sickness and the influence of inauspicious spirits. In Yan'an, a storyteller or geomancer would hold a bell and a locket over the concerned small baby many times while chanting. At the end of the ritual, the storyteller would hang a locket tied with colorful strips around the child's neck. In return, the parents gave the storyteller a pair of new shoes and asked the child to call the ritual holder "godfather."

Danwei: Translated into "work unit," *danwei* is the most important term in China since 1949. During Mao's era when the Chinese economy was planned, all sectors from manufacturing factories and service industries to government institutions became state-owned and all units were uniformly called "danwei." Through nationalizing the private sectors and building the danwei system, the Maoist government wanted to recover the national economy quickly from war destruction and boost the new nation's industrialization and modernization. Only residents born of non-agricultural households could land at a danwei, which was not only a job, but also was associated with an extended package of housing, medical, educational, and child-care provisions, as well as career opportunities. Throughout the 1980s, when Deng Xiaoping allowed rural residents to work as low-end laborers of various urban sectors, the meanings of danwei started to change as migrants' employment was not guaranteed lifelong and was not associated with any urban welfare provision. In the 1990s, many state-owned enterprises went out of business because of structural adjustment policies, and also because of lack of competitiveness as China started integrating with the global market. Millions of urban residents lost their danwei positions. Today, Chinese people continue to refer to the place of employment in state-owned enterprises and government departments as danwei.

Fuyun: Translated as assisting or elevating luck, the *fuyun* ritual enables people to make wishes of prosperity, good luck, affluence, and good health on the eighth day of the Lunar Chinese New Year. Some choose to organize the ritual by inviting deities they are devoted to while some choose to visit the state-sponsored Daoist temples to burn incenses and make their wishes.

Kang: A *kang* is a raised concrete platform occupying the center of the cavehouse where people sleep, eat, and conduct all kinds of social activities. It is often connected to the household stove, and smoke from cooking would go through the built-in tunnels and warm up the *kang*. In earlier days, a family of five to six would sleep on a big *kang* together at night. Households with more income would have two separate *kang*s that separated adults from children, or men from women. It was not until the 1980s that tables and chairs were introduced. Today, the *kang* is usually located at the back of the cavehouse and functions simply as a bed.

Kouyuan: *Kouyuan* is literally translated as "spoken wishes." In northern Shaanxi, people make spoken wishes to deities they worship and are obligated to return gratitude for a wish fulfilled. People often return gratitude by staging a storytelling or opera performance so that both deities and humans can enjoy a show and receive blessings.

Sanxian: The *sanxian* is a three-stringed Chinese lute, one of the most popular Chinese folk musical instruments. North Shaanxi storytellers use it as a solo instrument even though it is more commonly used as an accompanying instrument in ensembles in north China. It has a long fingerboard, and the body is usually made of snakeskin stretched over a round rectangular resonator.

Shoukuren: Literally translated into "people who can bear bitterness," *shoukuren* is a northern Shaanxi dialect term referring to those who make a living by growing crops. Farmers would say that they are *"shouku de"* (to bear bitterness) if they are asked what they do for a living.

Tiaoshen: *Tiaoshen* is the ritual of the dancing deity, in which the spirit medium uses the religious paraphernalia of a three-pronged wrought-iron sword (*sanshandao*) and makes dramatic bodily movements. Worshippers watch the performance in order to feel and receive the healing power of the deity.

Yangge: *Yangge* is a traditional folk song-and-dance ritual originally associated with the Chinese New Year's ritual celebration. The Chinese Communist party reformed it into a political medium to promote socialism.

Yaodong: A dugout from a vertical side of a hill, the *yaodong* is the most common type of dwelling in the north China area. In the arid climate of the Loess, the yaodong keeps a living space warm in the cold season and cool in the hot season. Its cross section is similar to a cave: a rectangle in the lower part connected to a semicircle in the upper part. The width at the floor is about four to five meters. Windows and doors can be installed only at the opening of the yaodong and the frames are usually made of wood. Today, people build yaodongs with stones to reinforce the dwelling structure and to prevent it from collapsing from a landslide or heavy rainfall.

References

Ai, Qing. 1949. "Chuanghua Jianzhi: Xibei Jianzhiji Daixu (Folk Window Flower: Preface for *Collection of Northwestern Paper-Cuts*)." In *Xibei Jianzhi Ji*, edited by Ai and Jiang, 1–5. Shanghai: Chenguang Chubanshe.
Ai, Qing, and Feng Jiang, ed. 1949. *Xibei Jiangzhi Ji (Collection of Northwestern Paper-Cuts)*. Shanghai: Chenguang Chubanshe.
Ai, Sheng. 1998. *Liu Jieqiong Jianzhi Bainiutu (One Hundred Ox Patterns by Liu Jieqiong)*. Xi'an: Shaanxi Renmin Meishu Chubanshe.
An, Zhubao. 2002. "Ansai Jianzhi (Ansai Paper-Cutting)." In *Yan'an Wenshi Vol. 5 (Yan'an Literary History Vol. 5)*, edited by Peiyuan Fu, 236–238. Yan'an: Zhengxie Yan'anshi Weiyuanhui Wenshi Ziliao Weiyuan Hui.
Anagnost, Ann. 1987. "Politics and Magic in Contemporary China." *Modern China* 13 (1): 40–61.
———. 1993. "The Nationscape: Movement in the Field of Vision." *positions: east asia cultures critique* 1 (3): 585–606.
———. 1994. "The Politics of Ritual Displacement." In *Asian Visions of Authority: Religion and the Modern States of East and Southeast Asia*, edited by Laurel Kendall, Helen Hardacre, and Charles Keyes, 221–254. Honolulu: University of Hawaii Press.
———. 1997. "Making History Speak." In *National Past-Times: Narrative, Representation, and Power in Modern China*, 17–44. Durham: Duke University Press.
Andrews, Julia. 1994. *Painters and Politics in the People's Republic of China, 1949–1979*. Berkeley: University of California Press.
Ansaixian Difangzhi Bianzuan Weiyuanhui, ed. 1993. *Ansai Xianzhi (Ansai Gazette)*. Xi'an: Shaanxi Renmin Meishu Chubanshe.
Ansaixian Weiyuanhui Wenshi Ziliao Yanjiu Weiyuanhui, ed. 1989. *Ansai Jianzhi Yishu (Ansai Paper-Cutting Art)*. Yan'an: Yan'an Daxue Yinshuachang.
Ansaixian Wenhua Wenwuguan, ed. 1999. *Ansai minjian jianpin jianzhi (Fine Selections of Ansai Folk Paper-Cuts)*. Xi'an: Shaanxi Renmin Meishu Chubanshe.

Apter, David, and Tony Saich. 1994. *Revolutionary Discourse in Mao's Republic*. Cambridge: Harvard University Press.

Bakhtin, Mikhail. 1993. *Rabelais and His World* [1941], translated by Helene Iswolsky. Bloomington: Indiana University Press.

Barlow, Tani. 1991. "Zhishifenzi (Chinese Intellectuals) and Power." *Dialectical Anthropology* 16 (3-4): 209–232.

Bartholomew, Teresa Tse. 2006. *Hidden Meanings in Chinese Art*. San Francisco: Asian Art Museum of San Francisco.

Basu, B. K. 2003. *Call of Yanan: Story of the Indian Medical Mission to China 1938–43*. Beijing: Foreign Languages Press.

Baudrillard, Jean. 1988. "Simulacra and Simulations." In *Jean Baudrillard: Selected Writings*, edited by Mark Poster, 166–184. Stanford: Stanford University Press.

Beattie, John, and John Middleton. 2004. *Spirit Mediumship and Society in Africa*. London: Routledge.

Benjamin, Walter. 1968. *Illuminations: Essays and Reflections*. New York: Schocken Books.

Berry, Chris. 1992. "'Race': Chinese Film and the Politics of Nationalism. *Cinema Journal* 31 (2): 45–58.

Berstein, Thomas, and Lu Xiaobo. 2003. *Taxation without Representation in Contemporary Rural China*. Cambridge: Cambridge University Press.

Boddy, Janice. 1989. *Wombs and Alien Spirits: Women, Men and the Zar Cult in Northern Sudan*. Madison: University of Wisconsin Press.

Bodman, R. W., and Pin P. Wan. 1991. Introduction and Translators' Foreword. In *Deathsong of the River: A Reader's Guide to the Chinese TV Series Heshang*, written by Xiaokang Su and Luxiang Wang, translated by Pin P. Wan and R. W. Bodman. Ithaca, N.Y.: Cornell University East Asia Program.

Bourdieu, Pierre. 1990. "Appendix: The Kabyle House or the World Reversed." In *The Logic of Practice*. Stanford: Stanford University Press.

Bourguignon, Erika. 1991. *Possession*. Long Grove, Ill.: Waveland Press.

Bowie, Fiona. 2000. *The Anthropology of Religion: An Introduction*. London: Blackwell.

Brady, Anne-Marie. 2008. *Marketing Dictatorship: Propaganda and Thought Work in Contemporary China*. Lanham, Md.: Rowman and Littlefield.

———. 2012. *China's Thought Management*, edited by Anne-Marie Brady. Abingdon, Oxon: Routledge.

Bruun, Ole. 1996. "The Fengshui Resurgence in China: Conflicting Cosmologies between State and Peasantry." *China Journal* 36: 47–65.

Bulletin of Concerned Asian Scholars 23 (3): 1–31.

Butler, Judith. 1993. *Bodies That Matter: On the Discursive Limits of "Sex."* London: Routledge.

———. 1995. "Contingent Foundations: Feminism and the Question of 'Postmodernism.'" In *Feminist Contestations: A Philosophical Exchange*, edited by Judith Butler, Seyla Benhabib, Drucilla Cornell, and Nancy Fraser, 35–57. London: Routledge.

———. 1999. *Gender Trouble: Feminism and the Subversion of Identity*. London: Routledge.

Cahill, Suzanne. 1993. *Transcendence and Divine Passion: The Queen Mother of the West in Medieval China*. Stanford: Stanford University Press.
Caillois, Roger. 1984. "Mimicry and Legendary Psychasthenia," translated by John Shepley. *October* 31: 17–32.
Cao, Bozhi. 2005. *Shaanbei Shuoshu Gailun*. Hong Kong: Huaxia Culture Art Publishing House.
———. 2011. *Shaanbei Shuoshu Juan (Shaanbei Storytelling Collection)*. Shaanxi: Shaanxi Renmin Chubanshe.
Cha, Jianying. 2006. *Bashi Niandai Fangtanlu (The Eighties: Dialogues)*. Beijing: Sanlian Shudian.
Chan, Anita. 2001. *China's Worker under Assault: The Exploitation of Labor in a Globalizing Economy*. Armonk, N.Y.: M. E. Sharpe.
Chan, Kam Wing. 1994. *Cities with Invisible Walls*. Hong Kong: Oxford University Press.
Chang-tai, Hung. 1985. *Going to the People: Chinese Intellectuals and Folk Literature 1918–137*. Cambridge: Council on East Asian Studies, Harvard University.
———. 1993. "Reeducating a Blind Storyteller: Han Qixiang and the Chinese Communist Storytelling Campaign." *Modern China* 19 (4): 395–426.
———. 1994. *War and Popular Culture: Resistance in Modern China*. Berkeley: University of California Press.
Chatterjee, Partha. 1993. *Nationalist Thought and the Colonial World: A Derivative Discourse?* Minneapolis: University of Minnesota Press.
Chau, Adam. 2003. "Popular Religion in Shaanbei, North-Central China." *Journal of Chinese Religion* 31: 39–73.
———. 2005. "The Politics of Legitimation and the Revival of Popular Religion in Shaanbei, North-Central China." *Modern China* 31 (2): 236–278.
———. 2006. *Miraculous Response: Doing Popular Religion in Contemporary China*. Stanford: Stanford University Press.
Chen, Guide, and Chun Tao. 2004. *Zhongguo Nongmin Diaocha (Report on Chinese Peasantry)*. Beijing: Renmin Wenxue Chubanshe.
Chen, Kuide. 1991. "Wenhua Re: Beijing Sichao Ji Liangzhong Qingxiang (Culture Fever: Background, School of Thought and Two Kinds Of Tendencies)." In *Zhongguo Dalu Dangdai Wenhua Bianqian 1978–1989 (Cultural Transformations in Contemporary Mainland China, 1978–1989)*, edited by Chen Kuide, 46–71. Taipei: Guiguan Tushu Gufen Youxian Gongsi.
Chen, Lai. 1989. "Fulu: Sixiang Chulu De San Dongxiang (Appendix: The Three Orientations in the Outlets of Thought)." In *Zhongguo Dangdai Wenhua Yishi (Cultural Consciousness in Contemporary China)*, edited by Gan Yang, 581–587. Hong Kong: Sanlian Shudian.
Chen, Lisheng. 2000. *Xinzhongguo Meishu Tushi: 1949–1966 (Illustrated History of New China: 1949–1966)*. Beijing: Zhongguo Qingnian Chubanshe.
Chen, Nancy. 1995. "Urban Space and the Experience of Qigong." In *Urban Spaces in Contemporary China: The Potential for Autonomy and Community in Post-Mao China*,

edited by Richard Kraus, Deborah Davis, Barry Naughton, and Elizabeth J. Perry, 347–361. New York: Cambridge University Press.

Chen, Ruilin. 1991. *Zhongguo Minjian Meishu Yu Wuwenhua (Chinese Folk Art and Shamanic Culture)*. Beijing: Xinhua Chubanshe.

Chen, Shanqiao. 1989. "Ansai Ren yu Jianzhi Yishu (Ansai People and Paper-Cuts Art)," 218–234, in Ansaixian Weiyuanhui, 1989.

Chen, Yousheng. 1992. "Minjian Jianzhi Suobaohande Shengzhi Chongbai Yuanshi Neihan Chutan (Preliminary Study on the Primitive Meaning of Reproduction Worship in Folk Paper-Cutting)." In *Zhongguo Minjian Jianzhi Yishu Yanjiu (Chinese Folk Paper-Cutting Art Studies)*, edited by Chen Jing, 250–252. Beijing: Beijing Gongyi Meishu Chubanshe.

Cheng, Helen Hau Ling, and Eric Ma. 2005. "Naked Bodies: Experimenting with Intimate Relationships among Migrant Workers in South China." *International Journal of Cultural Studies* 8 (3): 307–328.

Chiang, Kai-shek. 2002. *Jiaogong Yu Xi'an Shibian (Purging the Communists and the Xi'an Incident)*. Guoshiguan shenbianchu. Taibei: Guoshiguan.

Chow, Rey. 1991. *Women and Chinese Modernity: The Politics of Reading between West and East*. Minneapolis: University of Minnesota Press.

Clifford, James, and George Marcus. 1986. "Introduction: Partial Truth." In *Writing Culture: The Poetics and Politics of Ethnography*, edited by James Clifford and George Marcus, 1–27. Berkeley: University of California Press.

Cline, Erin M. 2010. "Female Spirit Mediums and Religious Authority in Contemporary Southeastern China." *Modern China* 36 (5): 520–555.

Comaroff, Jean. 1994. "Epilogue: Defying Disenchantment: Reflections on Ritual, Power and History." In *Asian Visions of Authority: Religion and the Modern States of East and Southeast Asia*, edited by Laurel Kendall, Charles Keyes, and Helen Hardacre, 301–314. Honolulu: University of Hawaii Press.

Comaroff, Jean, and John Comaroff. 2000. "Millennial Capitalism: First Thoughts on a Second Coming." *Public Culture* 12 (2): 291–343.

———. 2009. *Ethnicity, Inc*. Chicago: University of Chicago Press.

Crapanzano, Vincent. 1977. Introduction. In *Case Studies of Spirit Possession*, edited by Vincent Crapanzano and Vivian Garrison, 1–39. New York: John Wiley.

Csordas, Thomas J. 1994. *The Sacred Self: A Cultural Phenomenology of Charismatic Healing*. Berkeley: University of California Press.

Dang, Ronghua. 1989. "Ansai Xin Nongmin Wenhua Yundong Guanghui De Shinian (The Glorious Decade of the Ansai New Peasant Culture Movement)." In *Ansai Jianzhi Yishu (Ansai Paper-Cutting Art)*, edited by Ansaixian Weiyuanhui Wenshi Ziliao Yanjiu Weiyuanhui, 5–8. Yan'an: Yan'an Daxue Yinshuachang.

Day, Alexander. 2008. "The End of the Peasant? New Rural Reconstruction in China." *boundary 2* 35 (2): 49–73.

Dean, Kenneth. 1997. "Ritual and Space: Civil Society or Popular Religion?" In *Civil Society in China*, edited by Timothy Brook and B. Michael Frolic, 172–194. New York: M. E. Sharpe.

———. 1998. *Lord of the Three in One: The Spread of a Cult in Southeast China*. Princeton: Princeton University Press.

Debernardi, Jean. 2006. *The Way That Lives in the Heart: Chinese Popular Religion and Spirit Mediums in Penang, Malaysia*. Stanford: Stanford University Press.

Dicks, Bella. 2004. *Culture on Display: The Production of Contemporary Visitability*. Berkshire, England: Open University Press.

Ding, Ling. 1984. "Xu Yan (Prologue)." In *Yan'an Wenyi Congshu (Yan'an Literary Anthology)*, edited by Yan'an Wenyi Congshu Bianweihui (Editorial Committee of Yan'an Weiyi Congshu). Changsha: Hunan Renmin Chubanshe.

Dow, James. 1986. "Universal Aspects of Symbolic Healing: A Theoretical Synthesis." *American Anthropologist*, New Series 88 (1): 56–69.

Duan, Jingli, ed. 1999. *Huxian Nongminhua Chunqiu (History of Huxian Peasant Paintings)*. Beijing: Zhongguo Dangan Chubanshe.

Duara, Prasenjit. 1988. *Culture, Power, and the State: Rural North China, 1900–1942*. Stanford: Stanford University Press.

———. 1991. "Knowledge and Power in the Discourse of Modernity: The Campaigns against Popular Religion in Early Twentieth-Century China." *Journal of Asian Studies* 50 (1): 67–83.

———. 1995. *Rescuing History from the Nation: Questioning Narratives of Modern China*. Chicago: University of Chicago Press.

———. 1998. "The Regime of Authenticity: Timeless, Gender, and Natural History in Modern China." *History and Theory* 37 (3): 287–308.

Dubois, Thomas David. 2005. *The Sacred Village: Social Change and Religious Life in Rural North China*. Honolulu: University of Hawaii Press.

Dutton, Michael. 1998. *Streetlife China*. Cambridge: Cambridge University Press.

———. 2005. *Policing Chinese Politics: A History*. Durham: Duke University Press.

Eliade, Mirea. 1964. *Shamanism: Archaic Techniques of Ecstasy*, translated by Willard Trask. Princeton: Princeton University Press.

Epstein, Israel. 2003. *I Visit Yenan: Eye Witness Account of the Communist-led Liberated Areas in North-west China*. Beijing: Foreign Languages Press.

Fairbank, John King, and Merle Goldman. 2006. *China: A New History*. Cambridge: Harvard University Press.

Fan, C. Cindy. 2008. *China on the Move: Migration, the State, and the Household*. New York: Routledge.

Fan, Juncheng. 2001. "Shaanbei Shuoshu Zhiwojian (My View of Shaanbei Storytelling)." In *Han Qixiang de Daolu (The Road of Han Qixiang)*, edited by Wang Yuhua, Fan Juncheng, and Yuan Futang, 139–146. Xi'an: Jianming Yinwu Youxiang Zeren Gongsi.

Fan, Zuogang. 1987. *Nongcun Jingshen Wenming Jianshe Xintan (New Explorations into Building Rural Spiritual Civilization)*. Beijing: Nongye Chubanshe.

Fang, Lili. 2003. "Ansai De Jianzhi Yu Nongmin Hua (Ansai Paper-Cuts and Peasant Painting)." *Wenyi Yanjiu* 3: 122–130.

Feidaosuke, H. 1993. "Fangzhongguo Minjian Yishujia Han Qixiang (Visiting Folk Artist Han Qixiang, translated by Zhong Aifan and Deng Chengzhi)." In *Hongguo*

Quyizhi: Shaanxi Juan, Yan'an Diqu Fence (Chinese Musical Drama Record: Shaanxi Volume, Yan'an Area Edition), edited by Wang Yuhua, 273–288. Yan'an: Yanan Ribaoshe.

Felski, Rita. 1995. *The Gender of Modernity*. Massachusetts: Harvard University Press.

Feng, Jicai. 2010. *Xiangtu Jingshen (Spirit of the Rural Soil)*. Beijing: Zuojia Chubanshe.

Feng, Sanyuan. 2005. "Huanghe Wenhua Yu Xiaocheng Minjian Yishu Cun (Yellow River Culture and Xiaocheng Folk Art Village)." In *Guanzhu Muqinhe: Zhongguo Feiwuzhi Wenhua Yichan Minjian Jianzhi Guoji Xueshu Yantaohui Wenji (Keeping a Close Eye on Our Mother River: Collection of Essays from The International Symposium of the Intangible Cultural Heritage of China and Chinese Folk Paper-Cutting)*, edited by Qiao Xiaogang, 326–331. Taiyuan: Shanxi Remin Chubanshe.

Feng, Shenggang. 1989. "Jianzhi 'Sanhua' (Three Types of Paper-Cuts)." In *Ansai Jianzhi Yishu (Ansai Paper-Cutting Art)*, edited by Ansaixian, 229–237. Yan'an: Yan'an Daxue Yinshuachang.

Feuchtwang, Stephan. 2000. "Religion as Resistance." In *Chinese Society: Change, Conflict and Resistance*, edited by Elizabeth Perry and Mark Selden, 161–177. London: Routledge.

———. 2001. *Popular Religion in China: The Imperial Metaphor*. Richmond: Curzon Press.

Feuchtwang, Stephan, and Mingming Wang. 1991. "The Politics of Culture or Contest of History: Representation of Chinese Popular Religion." *Dialectical Anthropology* 16 (3–4): 251–272.

Field, Stephen. 1991. "He Shang and the Plateau of Ultrastability." *Bulletin of Concerned Asian Scholars* 23 (3): 4–13.

Firth, Raymond. 1967. "Ritual and Drama in Malay Spirit Mediumship." *Comparative Studies in Society and History* 9 (2): 190–207.

Frazer, James. 1911. *The Golden Bough, Part 1, the Magic Art and the Evolution of Kings*. 3rd Edition. London: Macmillan.

Freedman, Maurice. 1974. "On the Sociology Study of Chinese Religion." In *Religion and Ritual in Chinese Society*, edited by Arthur Wolf, 19–42. Stanford: Stanford University Press.

Fu, Peiyuan. 2000. *Yan'an De Minsu Wenhua (Folk Culture in Yan'an)*. Yan'an: Yan'an Ribaoshe.

———, ed. 2002. *Yan'an Wenshi Vol. 5 (Yan'an Literary History Vol. 5)*. Yan'an: Zhengxie Yan'an Shi Weiyuanhui Wenshi Ziliao Weiyuanhui.

Gaetano, Adrianna, and Tamara Jacka, ed. 2004. *On the Move: Women and Rural-to-Urban Migration in Contemporary China*. New York: Columbia University Press.

Gamble, Sidney. 1954. "Ting Hsien: A North China Rural Community." New York: International Secretariat, Institute of Pacific Relations.

———. 1963. *North China Villages: Social, Political and Economic Activities before 1933*. Berkeley: University of California Press.

Gao, Hua. 2000. *Hong Tai Yang Shi Zen Yang Sheng Qi De: Yan'an Zheng Feng Yun Dong De Lai Long Qu Ma (How Did the Red Sun Rise? The Process of Yan'an Rectification Movement)*. Hong Kong: Chinese University Press.

Gao, Xiaoxian. 1994. "China's Modernization and Changes in the Social Status of

Rural Women." In *Engendering China: Women, Culture, and the State*, edited by Gail Hershatter, Christina K. Gilmartin, Lisa Rofel, and Tyrene White, 80–100. Cambridge: Harvard University Press.

Gluckman, Max. 1965. *Custom and Conflict in Africa*. Glencoe, Ill.: Free Press.

Goodman, David. 2001. "Contending the Popular: Party-state and Culture." *Positions* 9 (1): 245–252.

———, ed. 2004. *China's Campaign to "Open Up the West": National, Provincial and Local Perspectives (The China Quarterly Special Issues)*. Cambridge: Cambridge University Press.

———. 2006. "Shanxi as Translocal Imaginary: Reforming the Local." In *Translocal China: Linkages, Identities and the Reimagining of Space*, edited by Tim Oakes and Louisa Schein, 56–73. London: Routledge imprint of Taylor and Francis.

Greenblatt, Sidney. 1976. *People of Taihang: An Anthology of Family Histories*. New York: International Arts and Sciences Press.

Griffiths, Michael, Malcolm Chapman, and Flemming Christiansen. 2010. "Chinese Consumers: The Romantic Reappraisal." *Ethnography* 11 (3): 331–357.

Grootaers, Willem. 1952. "The Hagiography of the Chinese God Chen-Wu." *Folklore Studies* 11 (2): 139–181.

Gu, Hao. 2003. "Chenzhong De Gantan—Ansai Minjian Meishu Xianzhuang Kaocha (Deep Sigh: A Study of the Current Situation of Ansai Folk Art)." In *Youxing Yu Wuxing: Zhongguo Minjian Wenhua Yishu Lunji (Form and Formless: Collection of Essays on Chinese Folk Culture Art)*, edited by Li Jinlu, 560–564. Wuhan: Hubei Meishu Chubanshe.

Guangzhou Yearbook Editorial Board. 2005. *Guangzhou Yearbook 2005*. Guangzhou: Guangzhou Yearbook Publisher.

Guldin, Gregory. 2001. *What's a Peasant to Do? Village Becoming Town in Southern China*. Boulder: Westview Press.

Guo, Yuhua. 2000. *Yi Shi Yu She Hui Bian Qian (Rituals and Social Change)*. Beijing: She hui ke xue wen xian chu ban she.

———. 2003. "Xinling De Jitihua—Shaanbei Qicun Nongye Hezuohua De Nüxing Jiyi (The Collectivization of the Mind—Women's Memory of Agricultural Collectivization in Qicun, Shaanbei)." *Zhongguo Shehui Kexue* 4: 79–92.

Han, Qixiang. 1985. *Han Qixiang Chuantung Shumu Suanbian (Selections of Han Qixiang's Traditional Stories)*. Shaanxi: Huxian Yinshuachang.

———. 1993. "Meiyou Gongchandang Jiumeiyou Wo Han Qixiang—Tantan Wo De Shenghuo Chuangzuo (If There Is No Communist Government There Is No Han Qixiang—Speaking of My Life and Creative Work)." In *Zhongguo Quyizhi: Shaanxi Juan, Yan'an Diqu Fence (Chinese Musical Drama Record: Shaanxi Volume, Yan'an Area Edition)*, edited by Wang Yuhua, 288–304. Yan'an: Yan'an Ribaoshe.

Han, Xiaorong. 2005. *The Chinese Discourses on the Peasant: 1900–1949*. Albany: The State University of New York Press.

Hawley, Meeker. 1971. *Chinese Folk Designs: A Collection of 300 Cut-paper Designs Used for Embroidery Together with 160 Chinese Art Symbols and Their Meanings*. New York: Dover Publication.

Hei, Jianguo, ed. 1999. *Gao Fenglian: Xibu Jianzhi Zuopinji (Gao Fenglian: Collection of West China Paper-Cutting)*. Tianjin: Tianjin Renmin Chubanshe.

Hinton, William. 1966. *Fanshen: A Documentary of Revolution in a Chinese Village*. Berkeley: University of California Press.

Hobsbawm, Eric, and Terence Ranger, ed. 1983. *The Invention of Tradition*. Cambridge: Cambridge University Press.

Hoffman, Lisa. 2010. *Patriotic Professionalism in Urban China: Fostering Talent*. Philadelphia: Temple University Press.

Holm, David. 1991. *Art and Ideology in Revolutionary China*. Oxford: Clarendon Press.

Hu, Angang. 2007. *Economic and Social Transformation in China: Challenges and Opportunities*. New York: Routledge.

Hu, Bo. 1989. "Xuexi Minjian Meishu de Jiaoxue Shijian (Teaching Experience in Learning Folk Art)." In *Ansai Jianzhi Yishu (Ansai Paper-Cutting Art)*, edited by Zhongguo Renmin Zhengzhi Xieshang Huiyi Shaanxisheng Ansaixiang Weiyuanhui Wenshi Ziliao Yanjiu Weiyuan.

Hu, Mengxiang. 1989. *Han Qixiang Pingzhuan (A Critical Biography of Han Qixiang)*. Beijing: Zhongguo Minjian Wenyi Chubanshe.

Huang, Philip C. C. 1995. "Rural Class Struggle in the Chinese Revolution: Representational and Objective Realities from the Land Reform to the Cultural Revolution." *Modern China* 21 (1): 105–143.

Huang, Ping. 2003. "China: Rural Problems and Uneven Development in Recent Years." In *China Reflected*, edited by Lau Kin Chi and Huang Ping, 12–33. Hong Kong: ARENA.

Hung, Chang-Tai. 1985. *Going to the People: Chinese Intellectuals and Folk Literature, 1918–1937*. Cambridge: Council on East Asian Studies, Harvard University.

———. 1993. "Reeducating a Blind Storyteller: Han Qixiang and the Chinese Communist Storytelling Campaign." *Modern China* 19 (4): 395–426.

———. 1994. *War and Popular Culture: Resistance in Modern China, 1937–1945*. Berkeley: University of California Press.

Ivy, Marilyn. 1995. *Discourses of the Vanishing: Modernity, Phantasm, Japan*. Chicago: University of Chicago Press.

Jameson, Fredric. 1991. *Postmodernism, or, the Cultural Logic of Late Capitalism*. Durham: Duke University Press.

Jiang, Feng, ed. 1981. *Yan'an Jianzhi (Yan'an Paper-Cuts)*. Beijing: Renmin Meishu Chubanshe.

Jin, Zhilin. 1981. "Introduction to Folk Paper-Cutting in the Yan'an Area." In *Yan'an Jianzhi (Yan'an Paper-Cuts)*, edited by Jiang Feng, 193. Beijing: Renmin Meishu Chubanshe.

———. 1989. "Woguo Minjian Meishu De Zaoxing Tixi (Modeling System in Our Folk Art)." In *Ansai Jinzhi Yishu (Ansai Paper-Cutting Art)*, edited by Ansaixian Weiyuanhui Wenshi Ziliao Yanjiu Weiyuanhui, 179–190. Yan'an: Yan'an Daxue Yinshuachang.

———. 2001. *Zhuajiwawa yu Renlei Qunti de Yuanshi Guannian (Zhuajiwawa and the Primitive Themes of the Human Race)*. Guilin: Guangxi Shifan Daxue Chubanshe.

———. 2002. *Shengming zhi Shu yu Zhongguo Minjian Minsu Yishu (The Eternal Tree and Chinese Folk Culture and Art)*. Guilin: Guangxi Shifan Daxue Chubanshe.

———. 2005. "Zhongguo Minjian Jianzhi De Chuancheng Yu Fazhan (The Transmission and Development of Chinese Folk Paper-Cutting Culture)." In *Guanzhu Muqinhe: Zhongguo Feiwuzhi Wenhua Yichan Minjian Jianzhi Guoji Xueshu Yantaohui Wenji (Keeping a Close Eye on Our Mother River: Collection of Essays from The International Symposium of the Intangible Cultural Heritage of China and Chinese Folk Paper-Cutting)*, edited by Qiao Xiaoguang, 31–39. Taiyuan: Shanxi Renmin Chubanshe.

Jing, Jun. 1996. *The Temples of Memories: History, Power and Morality in a Chinese Village*. Stanford: Stanford University Press.

———. 2000. "Environment Protest in Rural China." In *Chinese Society: Change, Conflict and Resistance*, edited by Elizabeth Parry and Mark Selden, 143–160. London: Routledge.

Johnson, Kay Ann. 1983. *Women, the Family and Peasant Revolution in China*. Chicago: Chicago University Press.

Jones, Stephen. 2007. *Ritual and Music of North China*. Hampshire, U.K.: Ashgate Publishing Limited.

———. 2009. *Ritual and Music of North China, Volume 2. Shaanbei*. Surrey, U.K.: Ashgate Publishing Limited.

Jordan, David. 1972. *Gods, Ghosts, and Ancestors: Folk Religion in a Taiwanese Village*. Berkeley: University of California Press.

Junshi Kexueyuan Junshi Lishi Yanjiusuo, ed. 2006. *Zhongguo gongnong hongjun changzheng quanshi Vol. 1–5 (Complete History of the Chinese Red Army Volumes 1–5*. Beijing: Junshi kexue Chubanshe.

Kapferer, Bruce. 1997. *The Feast of the Sorcerer: Practices of Consciousness and Power*. Berkeley: University of California Press.

Katz, Paul R. 2003. "Religion and the State in Post-War Taiwan." In *Religion in China Today*, edited by Daniel Overmyer, 89–106. Cambridge: Cambridge University Press.

Kendall, Laurel. 1985. *Shamans, Housewives, and Other Restless Spirits: Women in Korean Ritual Life*. Honolulu: University of Hawaii Press.

Lang, Graeme. 1998. "Religions and Regimes in China." In *Religion in a Changing World*, edited by Madeline Cousineau, 149–158. Westport, Conn.: Praeger.

Lee, Ching-Kwan. 1998a. *Gender and the South China Miracle: Two Worlds of Factory Women*. Berkeley: University of California Press.

———. 1998b. "The Labor Politics of Market Socialism: Collective Inaction and Class Experiences among State Workers in Guangzhou." *Modern China* 4 (1): 3–33.

Lee, Rainey. 2010. "Women in the Chinese Traditions." In *Women and Religious Traditions*, edited by Leona Anderson and Pamela Dickey Young, 107–137. New York: Oxford University Press.

Lewis, I. M. 1971 (2003). *Ecstatic Religion: A Study of Shamanism and Spirit Possession*. 3rd Edition. New York: Routledge.

Li, Jing. 2015. "Qiantan Qiye Wenhua Jianshe yu Sixiang Zhengzhi Jiaoyu de Jiehe (Combining Culture of Enterprise with Political Education)." *Dongfang Qiye Wenhua (Oriental Enterprise Culture)* 2015(2): 1–2.

Li, Jinlu, ed. 2003. *Youxing Yu Wuxing: Zhongguo Minjian Wenhua Yishu Lunji (Form and Formless: Chinese Folk Culture Art Essay Collection)*. Wuhan: Hubei Meishu Chubanshe.

Li, Ruobing. 1993. "Wei Renmin Shuochang Yibeizi—Zhuhe Han Qixiang Tongzhi Congyi Wushiwu Zhounian (Forever Sing for the People—The Fifty-Fifth Anniversary Toast for Comrade Han Qixiang's Storytelling Career." In *Zhongguo Quyizhi: Shaanxi Juan, Yan'an Diqu Fence (Chinese Musical Drama Record: Shaanxi Volume, Yan'an Area Edition)*, edited by Wang Yuhua, 310–318. Yan'an: Yanan Ribaoshe.

———. 2001. "Wei Renmin Shuochang Yibeizi—Zhuhe Han Qixiang Tongzhi Congyi Wushiwu Zhounian (Singing for People for Life—Celebrating the Fifty-Five Years of Han Qixiang in Storytelling Art)." In *Han Qixiang de Daolu (The Road of Han Qixiang)*, edited by W. Yuhua, F. Juncheng, and Y. Futang, 94–98. Xi'an: Jianming Yinwu Youxiang Zeren Gongsi.

Lili, Fang. 2003. "Ansai De Jianzhi Yu Nongmin Hua." *Wenyi Yanjiu* 3: 122–130.

Lin, Chun. 2006. *The Transformation of Chinese Socialism*. Durham: Duke University Press.

Lin, Shan. 1945. "Gaizao Shuoshu (Reforming Storytelling)." *Jiefang Ribao*, August 5, 1945.

———. 1993. "Mang Yiren Han Qixiang—Jieshou Yige Minjian Siren (Blind Artists Han Qixiang—Introducing a Folk Poet)." In *Zhongguo Quyizhi: Shaanxi Juan, Yan'an Diqu Fence (Chinese Musical Drama Record: Shaanxi Volume, Yan'an Area Edition)*, edited by Wang Yuhua, 258–270. Yan'an: Yan'an Ribaoshe. [Original: 1949. In *Huabei Wenyyi* 6.]

Link, Perry, ed. 1983. *Stubborn Weeds: Popular and Controversial Chinese Literature after the Cultural Revolution*. Bloomington: Indiana University Press.

Link, Perry, Richard Madsen, and Paul Pickowicz, ed. 1989. *Unofficial China: Popular Culture and Thought in the People's Republic*. Boulder, Colo.: Westview Press.

Liu, Fengzhen. 2003. *Guangjing Riyue*. Changchun: Shidai Wenyi Chubanshe.

Liu, Jieqiong. 2005. "Ganwu Shengming (Understanding Life)." In *Guanzhu Muqinhe: Zhongguo Feiwuzhi Wenhua Yichan Minjian Jianzhi Guoji Xueshu Yantaohui Wenji (Keeping a Close Eye on Our Mother River: Collection of Essays from The International Symposium of the Intangible Cultural Heritage of China and Chinese Folk Paper-Cutting)*, edited by Qiao Xiaoguagn, 345–346. Taiyuan: Shanxi Remin Chubanshe.

Liu, Qiong. 2015. "Xiandai Qiye Dangjian Sixiang Zhengzhi Gongzuo de Chuangxin Guankui (Renewing Party Thoughts and Political Works in Modern Enterprise)." *Dongfang Qiye Wenhua (Oriental Enterprise Culture)* 2005(2): 3–4.

Liu, Xin. 2000. *In One's Own Shadow: An Ethnographic Account of the Condition of Post-Reform Rural China*. Berkeley: University of California Press.

Lora-Wainwright, Anna. 2012. "Rural China in Ruins: The Rush to Urbanize China's Countryside Is Opening a Moral Battleground." *Anthropology Today* 28(4): 8–13.

Lowenthal, David. 1985. *The Past Is a Foreign Country*. Cambridge: Cambridge University Press.

———. 1998a. "Fabricating Heritage." *History and Memory* 10 (1): 31–39.

———. 1998b. *The Heritage Crusade and the Spoils of History*. Cambridge: Cambridge University Press.

Lu, Jie, and David Tung. 2004. *The Great Survey of Paper-Cutting in Yanchuan County*. 25000 Cultural Transmission Center.

Lu, Jie, and Qiu Zhijie. 2002. "Long March: A Walking Visual Exhibition." *Yishu: Journal of Contemporary Art* 1 (3): 55–118.

Lü, Shengzhong. 1987. *Zhongguo Minjian Jianzhi (Chinese Folk Paper-Cuttings)*. Changsha: Hunan Meishu Chubanshe.

———. 2003a. *Zaijian Chuantong Vol. 1 (Goodbye Tradition Vol. 1)*. Beijing: Sanlian Shudian.

———. 2003b. *Zaijian Chuantong Vol. 2 (Goodbye Tradition Vol. 2)*. Beijing: Sanlian Shudian.

———. 2004a. *Zaijian Chuantong Vol. 3 (Goodbye Tradition Vol. 3)*. Beijing: Sanlian Shudian.

———. 2004b. *Zaijian Chuantong Vol. 4 (Goodbye Tradition Vol. 4)*. Beijing: Sanlian Shudian.

Lu, Xun (Lu Hsun). 1954. *Selected Stories of Lu Hsun*. Beijing: Foreign Language Press.

Ma, Eric. 2006. *Jiuba Gongchang: Nan Zhongguo Chengshi Wenhua Yanjiu (Bar and Factory: Cultural Studies of Southern Chinese Cities)*. Nanjing: Jiangsu Renmin Chubanshe.

MacCannell, Dean. 1973. "Staged Authenticity: Arrangements of Social Space in Tourist Settings." *American Journal of Sociology* 79 (3): 589–603.

Mani, Lata. 1987. "Contentious Traditions: The Debate on Sati in Colonial India." *Cultural Critique* 7: 119–156.

Mao, Zedong. 1965. "Talks at the Yenan Forum on Literature and Art." In *Selected Works of Mao Tse-tung*. Vol. 3, 69–98. Beijing: Foreign Languages Press.

Mauss, Marcel. 1972. *A General Theory of Magic*. London: Routledge and Kegan Paul.

McClintock, Anne. 1995. *Imperial Leather: Race, Gender and Sexuality in the Colonial Contest*. New York: Routledge.

Meisner, Maurice. 1999. *Mao's China and After: A History of the People's Republic*. New York: Free Press.

Meng, Yue. 1993. "Female Images and National Myth." In *Gender Politics in Modern China: Writing and Feminism*, edited by Tani Barlow, 118–136. Durham: Duke University Press.

Mittler, Barbara. 2012. *A Continuous Revolution: Making Sense of Cultural Revolution Culture*. Cambridge: Harvard University Asia Center.

Moodie, Megan. 2008. "Enter Microcredit: A New Culture of Women's Empowerment in Rajasthan?" *American Ethnologist* 35 (3): 454–465.

Morris, Rosalind. 2000. *In the Place of Origins: Modernity and Its Mediums in Northern Thailand*. Durham: Duke University Press.

Mueggler, Eric. 2001. *The Age of Wild Ghost: Memory, Violence and Place in Southwest China*. Berkeley: University of California Press.

Murck, Alfreda, and Wen C. Fong, ed. 1991. *Words and Images: Chinese Poetry, Calligraphy, and Painting*. Princeton: Princeton University Press.

Oakes, Tim. 1998. *Tourism and Modernity in China*. New York: Routledge.

———. 2006. The Village as Theme Park: Mimesis and Authenticity in Chinese Tourism. In *Translocal China: Linkages, Identities and the Reimagining of Space*, edited by Tim Oakes and Louisa Schein, 166–192. London: Routledge imprint of Taylor and Francis.

Oakes, Tim, and Louisa Schein. 2006. *Translocal China: Linkages, Identities and Reimagining of Space*. New York: Routledge.

Ong, Aihwa. 1990. "State Versus Islam: Malay Families, Women Bodies and the Body Politic in Malaysia." *American Ethnologist* 17 (2): 258–276.

———. 2007. *Neoliberalism as Exception: Mutations in Citizenship and Sovereignty*. Durham: Duke University Press.

Overmyer, Daniel. 2001. "From 'Feudal Superstitions' to 'Popular Belief': New Directions in Mainland Chinese Studies of Chinese Popular Religion." *Cahiers d'Extreme-Asie* 12: 103–126.

———, ed. 2003. *Religion in China Today*. Cambridge: Cambridge University Press.

Pan, Lusheng. 1992a. "Lun Zhongguo Minsu Jianzhi (On Chinese Folk Paper-Cutting)." In *Zhongguo Minsu Jianzhi Tuji (Chinese Folk Paper-Cutting Anthology)*. Beijing: Beijing Gongyi Meishu Chubanshe.

———. 1992b. *Zhongguo Minsu Jianzhi Tuji (Chinese Folk Paper-Cutting Anthology)*. Beijing: Beijing Gongyi Meishu Chubanshe.

———. 1999. "Zhongguo Jixiang Jianzhi Di Yuyi (Allegorical Meanings of Chinese Auspicious Paper-Cutting)." In *Zhongguo Jixiang Jianzhi Tuji (Illustrations of Chinese Auspicious Paper-Cutting)*, edited by Lusheng Pan and Luxia Chen. Beijing: Beijing Gongyi Meishu Chubanshe.

———. 2006. *Qiangjiu Minyi (Rescue Folk Culture and Art)*. Shandong: Shandong Meishu Chubanshe.

Perry, Elizabeth. 1985. "Rural Violence in Socialist China." *China Quarterly* 103: 414–440.

Peters, Larry. 1982. "Trance, Initiation and Psychotherapy in Tamang Shamanism." *American Ethnologist* 9 (1): 21–46.

Pred, Allan Richard, and Michael John Watts. 1992. *Reworking Modernity: Capitalisms and Symbolic Discontent*. New Brunswick: Rutgers University Press.

Pun, Ngai. 2005. *Made in China: Subject, Power and Resistance in a Global Workplace*. Durham: Duke University Press.

Qiao, Xiaoguang. 2004. *Huotai Wenhua: Zhongguo Feiwuzhe Wenhua Yichan Chutan (Living Culture: Preliminary Researches on Chinese Intangible Cultural Heritage)*. Taiyuan: Shanxi Renmin Chubanshe.

———, ed. 2005. *Guanzhu Muqinhe: Zhongguo Feiwuzhi Wenhua Yichan Minjian Jianzhi Guoji Xueshu Yantaohui Wenji (Keeping a Close Eye on Our Mother River: Collection of Essays from The International Symposium of the Intangible Cultural Heritage of China and Chinese Folk Paper-Cutting)*. Taiyuan: Shanxi Remin Chubanshe.

"Quanjing Yan'an" Editorial Committee. 2008. *Fuxi Guli Yanchuan xian (Fuxi's Hometown: Yanchuan)*. Beijing: Chaohua Chubanshe.

Rabinow, Paul. 1977. *Reflections on Fieldworks in Morocco*. Berkeley: University of California Press.

Ramo, C. Joshua. 2004. *Beijing Consensus*. Foreign Policy Center.
Rofel, Lisa. 1999. *Other Modernities: Gender Yearnings in China after Socialism*. Berkeley: University of California Press.
Ronghua, Dang. 1989. "Ansai Xinnongmin Wenhua Yundong Guanghui De Shinian." In *Ansai Jianzhi Yishu (Ansai Paper-Cutting Art)*, edited by Ansaixian Weiyuanhui Wenshi Ziliao Yanjiu Weiyuanhui. Yan'an: Yan'an Daxue Yinshuachang.
Rosaldo, Renato. 1985. "Where Objectivity Lies: The Rhetoric of Anthropology." In *The Rhetoric of the Human Sciences: Language and Argument in Scholarship and Public Affairs*, edited by Allan Megill, John S. Nelson, and Donald N. McCloskey. Madison: University of Wisconsin Press.
Said, Edward. 1978. *Orientalism*. New York: Vintage Books.
Salamone, Frank A. 1997. "Authenticity in Tourism: The San Angel Inns." *Annals of Tourism Research* 24: 305–321.
Sangren, Stephen. 1987. *History and Magical Power in a Chinese Community*. Stanford: Stanford University Press.
Schein, Louisa. 2000. *Minority Rules: The Miao and the Feminine in China's Cultural Politics*. Durham: Duke University Press.
Selden, Mark. 1995. *China in Revolution: The Yenan Way Revisited*. New York: M. E. Sharpe.
Shaanxisheng Quyizhi Bianji Bangongshi (Musical Drama Editing Office), ed. 1985. *Han Qixiang Chuantong Shumu Xuanbian (Selections of Han Qixiang Stories)*. Huxian: Huxian Yinshuachang.
Shahar, Meir, and Robert Weller. 1996. "Introduction: Gods and Society in China." In *Unruly Gods: Divinity and Society in China*, edited by Meir Shahar and Robert Weller, 1–36. Honolulu: University of Hawaii Press.
Silver, Ira. 1993. "Marketing Authenticity in Third World Countries." *Annals of Tourism Research* 20: 302–318.
Siu, Helen. 1989. "Recycling Rituals: Politics and Popular Culture in Contemporary Rural China." In *Unofficial China: Popular Culture and Thought in the People's Republic of China*, edited by Richard Madsen, Paul G. Pickowicz, and Perry Link. Boulder, Colo.: Westview Press.
Snow, Edgar. 1968. *Red Star over China: The Classic Account of the Birth of Chinese Communism*. New York: Grove Press.
Solinger, Dorothy. 1999. *Contesting Citizenship in Urban China: Peasant Migrants, the State and the Logic of the Market*. Berkeley: University of California Press.
Song, Zhaolin, ed. 2006. *Tushuo Zhongguo Chuantong Xunhua Yu Jianzhi (Illustration of Traditional Chinese "Xunhua" and Paper-Cutting)*. Xi'an: Shijie Tushu Chuban.
Spence, Jonathan. 1981. *The Gate of Heavenly Peace: The Chinese and their Revolution (1895–1980)*. New York: The Viking Press.
Su, Xiaokang, and Wang Luxiang. 1991. *Deathsong of the River: A Reader's Guide to the Chinese TV Series Heshang*, translated by Pin P. Wan and R. W. Bodman. Ithaca, N.Y.: Cornell University East Asia Program.
Sun, Liping. 2004a. *Duanlie: Ershi Shiji Jiushiniandai Yilai De Zhongguo Shehui (Cleavage: Chinese Society since the 1990s)*. Beijing: Social Sciences Publishing House.

———. 2004b. *Shiheng: Duanlie Shehui de Yunzuo Luoji (Imbalance: The Logic of a Fractured Society)*. Beijing: Social Sciences Academic Press.

———. 2007. *Shouwei de Dixian: Zhuanxing Shehui Shenghuo de Jichu Zhixu (Minimal Responsibility: Basic Order of Social Life in Transformational Chinese Society)*. Beijing: Social Sciences Academic Press.

———. 2009. *Chongjian Shehui: Zhuanxing Shehui de Zhixu Zaizao (Reconstructing Society: To Rebuild Social Order in Transformational China)*. Beijing: Social Sciences Academic Press.

Szonyi, Michael. 1997. "The Illusion of Standardizing the Gods: The Cults of the Five Emperors in Late Imperial China." *Journal of Asian Studies* 56 (1): 113–135.

Tang, Beibei, and Luigi Tomba. 2013. "The Great Divide: Institutionalized Inequality in Market Socialism." In *Unequal China: The Political Economy and Cultural Politics of Inequality*, edited by Wanning Sun and Yingjie Guo, 91–110. New York: Routledge.

Tapp, Nicholas. 2000. "The Consuming or the Consumed? Virtual Hmong in China." *Asia Pacific Journal of Anthropology* 1 (2): 73–101.

Taussig, Michael. 1997. *The Magic of the State*. New York: Routledge.

———. 1999. *Defacement: Public Secrecy and the Labor of the Negative*. Stanford: Stanford University Press.

Teng, Fengqian. 1988. "Minjian Jianzhi Chuantong Zhutiwenyang yu 'wuhoulifa' (Traditional and Major Motifs of Folk Paper-Cutting and 'Wuhoulifa')." In *Shaanxi Minjian Meishu Yanjiu Vol. 1 (Shaanixi Folk Art Study Vol. 1)*, edited by Shaanxi Sheng Quncong Yishuguan, 1–37. Xi'an: Shaanaxi Renmin Meishu Chubanshe.

Tiejun, Wen. 2005. *San Nong Wen Ti Yu Shi Ji Fan Si (Rural China's Centenary Reflection)*. Beijing: Sanlian Press.

Tsing, Anna. 2004. *An Ethnography of Global Connection*. Princeton: Princeton University Press.

Turner, Victor. 1967. *The Forest of Symbols: Aspect of Ndembu Ritual*. Ithaca: Cornell University Press.

———. 1969. *The Ritual Process: Structure and Anti-Structure*. Harmondsworth: Penguin.

Urry, John. 1990. *The Tourist Gaze: Leisure and Travel in Contemporary Societies*. London: Sage.

Wachs, Iris. 2004. *Magical Shapes: Twentieth Century Chinese Papercuts*. Tel Aviv: Eretz Israel Museum.

Walder, Andrew. 1986. *Communist Neo-traditionalism: Work and Authority in Chinese Industry*. Berkeley: University of California Press.

Wang, Bomin. 2006. *The History of Chinese Folk Paper-Cut Arts (Zhongguo Minjian Jianzhi Shi)*. Hangzhou: China Academy of Art Press.

Wang, Chaowen, ed. 1993. *Zhongguo Minjian Meishu Quanji (Chinese Folk Art Anthology)*. Jinan: Shandong Jiaoyu Chubanshe.

Wang, Hui. 2003. *China's New Order: Society, Politics, and Economy in Transition*, edited by Theodore Huters. Cambridge: Harvard University Press.

Wang, Jing. 1991. "He Shang and the Paradoxes of Chinese Enlightenment." *Bulletin of Concerned Asian Scholars* 23 (3): 23–32.

———. 1996. *High Culture Fever: Politics, Aesthetics and Ideology in Deng's China*. Berkeley: University of California Press.

———. 2001. "Culture as Leisure and Culture as Capital." *positions: east asian cultural critiques* 9 (1): 69–104.

———. 2005. *Locating China: Space, Place, and Popular Culture*. New York: Routledge Studies on China in Transition.

Wang, Lingyu, and Dang Ronghua. 1988. "Shaanxi Minjian Lianzu Yishu Neihan Chutan (Preliminary Study on Shaanxi Folk Art of Lotus Flower)." In *Shaanxi Minjian Meishu Yanjiu Vol. 1 (Shaanixi Folk Art Study Vol. 1)*, edited by Shaanxi Sheng Quncong Yishuguan, 61–137. Xi'an: Shaanxi Renmin Meishu Chubanshe.

Wang, Ning. 1999. Rethinking Authenticity in Tourism Experience. *Annals of Tourism Research* 26 (2): 349–370.

Wang, Shaoguang, and Angang Hu. 1999. *The Political Economy of Uneven Development: The Case of China*. Armonk, N.Y.: M. E. Sharpe.

Wang, Yanyin, and Yang Yongsheng. 2002. "Huanglong Jianzhi (Huanglong Paper-Cuts)." In *Yan'an Wenshi Vol. 5 (Yan'an Literary History Vol. 5)*, edited by Fu Peiyuan, 249–250. Yan'an: Zhengxie Yan'an Shi Weiyuanhui Wenshi Ziliao Weiyuanhui.

Wang, Yuhua, ed. 1993. *Zhongguo Quyizhi: Shaanxi Juan, Yan'an Diqu Fence (Chinese Musical Drama Record, Shaanxi Volume, Yan'an Area Edition)*. Yan'an: Yan'an Ribaoshe.

"Weida de changzheng" Bianweihui, ed. 2006. *Weida de changzheng (The Great Long March)*. Xi'an: Shaanxi Renmin Meishu Chubanshe.

Weller, Robert. 1994. "Capitalism, Community and the Rise of Amoral Cults in Taiwan." In *Asian Visions of Authority: Religion and the Modern States of East and Southeast Asia*, edited by Laurel Kendall, Helen Hardacre, and Charles F. Keyes, 141–164. Honolulu: University of Hawaii Press.

Wen, Tiejun. 2005. *San Nong Wenti Yu Shiji Fansi (Rural China's Centenary Reflection)*. Beijing: Sanlian Chubanshe.

Wenshi Ziliao Yanjiu Weiyuanhui, ed. 1992. *Yan'an wenshi ziliao Vol. 6 (Yan'an Literary History Archive)*. Yan'an: Yan'an Ribaoshe.

Williams, Raymond. 1976. *Keywords: A Vocabulary of Culture and Society*. New York: Oxford University Press.

Wolf, Arthur, ed. 1974. *Religion and Ritual in Chinese Society*. Stanford: Stanford University Press.

Womack, Brantly. 1991. "Review Essay: Transfigured Community: Neo-Traditionalism and Work Unit Socialism in China." *China Quarterly* 126: 313–332.

Wu, Ka-ming. 2007. "Monuments of Grief: Village Politics in Post-Socialist Rural China." *Ethnology* 46 (1): 41–56.

Xie, Yu, Qing Lai, and Xiaogang Wu. 2009. "Danwei and Social Inequality in Contemporary Urban China." *Res Social Work* 19: 283–306.

Xu, Yiyi. 2005. *Xunchang de Yishu (Ordinary Art)*. Jinan: Shangdong Huabao Chubanshe.

Yan, Hairong. 2003. "Neo-Liberal Governmentality and Neo-Humanism: Organizing Value Flow through Labor Recruitment Agencies." *Cultural Anthropology* 18 (4): 493–523.

———. 2008. "The Emaciation of the Rural: 'No Way Out.'" In *New Masters, New Servants: Migration, Development, and Women Workers in China*, 25–52. Durham: Duke University Press.

Yan'an Diqu Qunzhong Yishu Guan (Yan'an District Mass Art Bureau). 1986. *Yan'an diqu jianzhi Yishu (Yan'an District Paper-Cutting Art)*. Xian: Shaanxi Renmin Meishu Chubanshe.

Yan'an Region Gazette Editorial Committee. 2000. *Yan'an Diqu Zhi (Yan'an Region Gazette)*. Xian: Xian Chubanshe.

Yan'an Yearbook Editorial Board. 2005. *Yan'an Yearbook 2005*. Yan'an: Yan'an Yearbook Publisher.

Yang, C. K. 1961. *Religion in Chinese Society: A Study of Contemporary Social Function of Religion and Some of Their Historical Factors*. Berkeley: University of California Press.

Yang, Fenggang. 2006. "The Red, Black and Gray Markets of Religion in China." *Sociological Quarterly* 47: 93–122.

Yang, Xianrang, and Yang Yang. 2003. *Huanghe Shisi Zou 1 and 2 (Fourteen Walks along the Yellow River, Shang Xia Ji)*. Beijing: Zuojia Chubanshe.

Yang, Xueqin, and An Qi. 1990. *Minjian Meishu Gailun (General Theory on Folk Art)*. Beijing: Beijing Gongyi Meishu Chubanshe.

Yen-Burgermeister, Lynn, and Yang Jiankun. 2004. "Xunfang Yanchuan Mangshujiang (Blind Storytellers in Yanchuan)." *Wenming (Civilization)* 2004(10): 136–145.

Young, Katherine. 1994. Introduction. In *Religion and Woman*, edited by Arvind Sharma, 1–38. Albany: State University of New York.

Young, Mayfair, ed. 2008. Introduction in *Chinese Religiosities: Afflictions of Modernity and State Formation*, 1–42. Berkeley: University of California Press.

Yu, Zhiming, ed. 2004. *Xin Yan'an Wenyi: Minjian Wenxue Vol. 1 (New Yan'an Literature: Folk Literature Vol. 1)*. Beijing: Zhongguo Qingnian Chubanshe.

Yuan, Futang, Wang Yuhua, and Fan Juncheng, ed. 2001. *Han Qixiang de Daolu (The Road of Han Qixiang)*. Xi'an: Jianming Yinwu Youxiang Zeren Gongsi.

Yuan, Zhongtian, ed. 2006. *Yongyuan Di Fengjing: Zhongquo Minsu Wenhua Vol. 2 (Eternal Scenery: Chinese Folk Culture Vol. 2)*. Nanchang: Baihuazhou Wenyi.

Yuval-Davis, Nira, and Flora Anthias. 1989. *Woman-Nation-State*. London: Macmillan.

Zhang, Daoyi. 1980. *Zhongguo Minjian Jianzhi (Chinese Folk Paper-Cuts)*. Jiansu: Jinlin Shuhua Chubanshe.

———. 1999. *The Art of Chinese Paper-Cuts*. Beijing: Foreign Languages Press.

Zhang, Li. 2001. *Strangers in the City: Reconfigurations of Space, Power, and Social Networks within China's Floating Population*. Stanford: Stanford University Press.

———. 2012. "Flexible Postsocialist Assemblages from the Margin." *positions: east asia cultures critique* 20 (2): 659–667.

Zhang, Li, and Aihwa Ong. 2008. *Privatizing China: Socialism from Afar*. Ithaca: Cornell University Press.

Zhang, Tongdao. 2009. *Jin Zhilin de Yan'an (The Yan'an of Jin Zhilin)*. Beijing: Wenhua Yishu Chubanshe.

Zhongguo Qu Yi Yin Yue Ji Cheng—Jiangsu Juan Bian Ji Wei Yuan Hui. 1995. *Zhongguo Quyi Yinyue Jicheng, Shaanxi Juan (Anthology of Chinese Narrative-Singing Music, Shaanxi Volumes)*. Beijing: Zhongguo ISBN Zhongxin.

Zhongguo Renmin Zhengzhi Xieshang Huiyi Yan'an Shi Weiyuanhui Wenshi Ziliao Yanjiu *Weiyuanhui*. 1992. *Yan'an Wenshi Ziliao: Di Liu Ji (Yan'an Literary History) Vol. 6*. Yan'an: [Zhongguo Renmin Zhengzhi Xieshang Huiyi Yan'an Shi Weiyuanhui Wenshiziliao Yanjiu Weiyuanhui]. [Original: Yan'an government. 1992. *Yan'an Wenshi Ziliao: Di Liu Ji (Yan'an Literary History: Vol. 6.)*]. Yan'an: Yan'an Ribaoshe.

Zhou, Lu. 2005. *Gao Fenglian: Huangheben Di Jianhua Poyi (Gao Fenglian: Paper-Cutting Woman on the Yellow River Bank)*. Changsha: Hunan Meishu Chubanshe.

Index

Page references in italics refer to maps and figures. For example *3fo.1* refers to a figure number 0.1 on page 3. *7m2* refers to map 2 on page 7.

Ai, Qing: biographical information, 36, 153n3; and *Northwest China Paper-Cuts* (*Xibei Jianzhi Ji*), 36, 37–38
allegorical and metaphorical interpretations of paper-cut designs: by artists, 31–32; by Communist urban intellectuals, 47–48; and feudal and superstitious elements, 31, 37–38; by Lü Shengzhong, 50; and "window flowers" for weddings and Chinese New Year celebrations, 33, 38, 54. *See also* Ai, Qing; Jiang, Feng; *Northwest China Paper-Cuts* (*Xibei Jianzhi Ji*)
Anagnost, Ann, 15, 19, 67, 125
Ansai county, Yan'an: economic marginalization of, 52; *Fine Selections of Ansai Folk Paper-Cuts*, 52; paper-cutting artists, 52–55, 71; paper-cuts listed on UNESCO's list of intangible cultural heritage, 55; waist-drum performance for photography contest in, 1–2, *3fo.1*, 20–21

Bai Fenglan: paper-cutting taught at the Central Academy of Fine Arts, 47; "Picture of Ox Plowing" (*niu geng tu*), 46, *46f1.7*, 53
Bakhtin, Mikhail, 48
Barlow, Tani, 150–151n7
Baudrillard, Jean, 20, 152n12
bausuo ritual performance, 96, *97f3.2*
Berry, Chris, 150–151n7
Black Tiger Official (*Heihulingguan*): and Master Xu's performance of the "gratitude for a wish fulfilled" (*huankouyuan*) ritual, 94–95; Wangjiagou temple dedicated to, 98, *144f5.2*
Boddy, Janice, 127, 128, 131, 140
Bourdieu, Pierre, 48
Bourguignon, Erika, 125, 131, 137
Brady, Anne-Marie, 106–107
Butler, Judith, 140–141, 143

CAFA. *See* Central Academy of Fine Arts in Beijing
Cao Boyan, 108, 116–118, 120
cavehouses (*yaodong*): architectural form of, *8fo.2*, 9, *25fo.3*; "Bed and Breakfast" businesses, 81; as cultural attractions, 18; and the grand narrative of Yellow River civilization, 85–86; paper-cuts-decorated cavehouses in, *53f1.8*, 71
Center of Musical Drama (*quyiguan*), 156n5

Central Academy of Fine Arts in Beijing (CAFA): artists associated with (*see* Jiang Feng; Jin Zhilin; Lü Shengzhong); Intangible Cultural Heritage Research Center in, 55, 64; paper-cutting taught by elderly women from rural Yan'an at, 47; survey of paper-cuts in Yanchuan county, 77
Chatterjee, Partha, 11–12
Chau, Adam, 102, 126, 128, 141, 143, 158n8
Chen Shanqiao, 42, 47
Chen Shenglan's *zhuajiwawa* paper-cuts, 44–45, 45f1.6
Chen Yousheng, 34
children: folk art taught to schoolchildren in Xiaocheng primary school, 80; paper-cut designs as wearable baby's vests (*xiaoguagua*), 78; paper-cut designs for protection of, 31; prospect of harsh working conditions as migrants, 23, 79, 101–102; ritual protection of, 94, 96, 99, 103
China model (*zhongguo moshi*) of flexible post-socialism, x, 5
Chinese Central Television Channel: "The New Year Gala" program, 20; "The Spring Festival Gala" program, 116
Chinese New Year. *See* Lunar New Year
chuanghua. *See* "window flowers"
Clifford, James and George Marcus, 26
Cline, Erin M., 139
Comaroff, Jean and John, 6
Csordas, Thomas J., 131–132, 138
cultural reflexivity movement in the 1980s: and the ideas of May Fourth intellectuals, xi, 151n8; and the negative evaluation of rural areas, 9, 15–16; and the reconceptualization of folk culture in Yan'an, 15–16, 33–35, 47–52

dancing deities. *See tiaoshen* (*dancing deity*) ritual
danwei (work units): described, 159; and party-state authority, xi, 27–28; and the production of folk tradition, 28, 92, 105–121, 147–148; storytelling performances sponsored by, 109–113, 112f4.1, 121; structure of SOEs in Yan'an, 22
Dean, Kenneth, 89, 126
deer: "Deer Holding lingzhi" design, 37; tree with face of a deer with branching antlers, 46, 46f1.7
Deng Xiaoping: effect of reforms on rural residents, 16–17, 159; 1980s reforms of, x, 15, 128
Ding, Ling, 149–150n3
Duara, Prasenjit, 12, 34, 67, 89
Dubois, Thomas David, 103, 126, 149n1
Dutton, Michael, 150n4

Efficacious Black Tiger Official (*Heihulingguan*). *See* Black Tiger Official (*Heihulingguan*)
Elder Mo's wife (spirit medium), 135–137, 139
empowerment: of individuals brought by the socialist state, xi, 49, 60–61; of storytellers as propagandists (*xuanchuan yuan*), 89–90, 103, 114–115; of the visually impaired by putting them into a musical drama troupe, 115; of Xiaocheng villagers brought by folk cultural initiatives, 68, 80, 81, 84–87. *See also* gender empowerment

Fang family in Mojiagou village: Aunt Fang, 27, 122–123, 133, 134, 145f5.4; author's visit with, 24, 25–27; farmland of, 122–123, 145ff5.4–5.5, 146; urban apartment of, 144f5.3
Felski, Rita, 11, 32, 61, 150n6
Feuchtwang, Stephan, 126
films: paper-cuts used in, 33; *Yellow Earth* by Chen Kaige, 150–151n7
folk popular religion: and the local economy of rural China, 19, 143; and the production of culture, 5–6. *See also* UNESCO, Chinese cultural practices on intangible cultural heritage list of

folk tradition, as a major site of mediating, contesting, and reflecting on Chinese late socialist modernity, 24–25
Frazer, James, 50
Fu, Peiyuan, 114
fuyun (ritual of elevating luck), 127, 135–137, 159–160

Gao, Hua, 10, 150n4
Gao Fenglian, 31, 56. *See also* Liu Jieqiong
gender: Communist state transformation of views toward, 59–61; Liu Jieqiong's vision of gender equality, 59; new forms of gender inequality, 60–63, 84–86; paper-cutting as a feminized traditional cultural form, 34, 61; role of oriental and feminized Other in the cultural representation of Western modernity, 11, 32–33, 61, 150n6
gender empowerment: of women villagers brought by Han Qixiang's storytelling, 113–114; of women villagers brought by paper-cutting, 60–61, 80
Gluckman, Max, 127
Great Leap Forward, 40–41. See also *Rectification Campaign*
The Great Survey of Paper-Cutting in Yanchuan County, 56, 62; traveling exhibition, 56, 57f1.9, 77, 155n17
Gu Yuan, 36, 37, 38, 39f1.3, 60, 154n9

Han Qixiang: *Fanshenji*, 91–92, 113; popular support for the Communist government's policies due to singing by, 91–92, 113–114; Yanchuan Musical Drama Troupe's performance of works by, 113
Hao Guizhen: and the Ansai Hall of Culture paper-cutting training classes, 52–53; paper-cuts by, 43, 43f1.4–1.5; paper-cuts-decorated cavehouse of, 53f1.8; social and economic instability of, 54
Heihulingguan. *See* Black Tiger Official
Heijiawa village: cavehouse social space of, 156–157n6; demographics, 92–93; Master Xu's performance in, 88–89, 92–95, 101
Hinton, William, 10
Hobsbawm, Eric and Terence Ranger, 21, 66
Hong Kong, 7m1; author's identification with, ix-x, 25, 27, 28; hand-over to China in, x, 2, 25
Huang, Ping, 100
hyper-folk: and Baudrillard's concept of "hyperreality," 20, 152n12 (*see also* theme parks); and cultural practices in post-2000 Yan'an, 1–2, 3fo.1, 20–21, 94, 147–148; and late socialist cultural politics, 21–22, 107; and media. *See* Chinese Central Television Channel; television

Ivy, Marilyn, 6, 138, 143

Jiang, Feng: biographical information, 36, 153–154n3; as director of CAFA, 48–49; objection to interpreting *zhuajiwawa* paper-cuts as symbols of the worship of reproductive power, 154n10; and *Xibei jianzhi ji*. See *Northwest China Paper-Cuts (Xibei Jianzhi Ji)*
Jing, Jun, 89, 126, 149n1
Jin Zhilin: biographical information, 154n9; biographical information, Xiaocheng Folk Art Village, 69–70; cultural development plan for Xiaocheng, 28–29, 62, 69–73; folk-culture-as-fossil valorized by, 62; poem about girl cutting window flowers, 40, 154n7
Jones, Stephen, 89, 91, 92, 94, 96, 99, 100, 102, 156n2, 157n9

*kang*s: and the social space of village cavehouses, 31, 60, 82, 93, 108–109, 156–157n6, 160; spirit medium performance for patient, 128–129, 133; spirit possession by the wife of elder Mo on, 135
Kapferer, Bruce, 127, 133–134
Katz, Paul, 126

kouyuan (spoken wish): defined, 160; "gratitude for a wish fulfilled" (*huankouyuan*) ritual, 93–94, 96, 109

Lewis, I. M., 126–127
Lin Shang, 91, 114
Li Qun, 37, 38
Liu Jieqiong, 56; biographical information, 155n18
Loess Plateau: cavehouse architecture of, 85–86, 160 (*see also* cavehouses [*yaodong*]); and cultural tourism, 65; and the landscape of Yan'an, 8–9, 8*fo*.2, 18, 26, 95, 107; and "Nan Ni Wan" painted by Jin Zhilin, 154n9; paper-cuts affiliated with nonindustrial sphere of, 34–35, 55, 64–65
Long March, 9, 149n2
Long March Foundation, 56, 77
Lu, Jie and David Tung, *The Great Survey of Paper-Cutting in Yanchuan County*, 56, 62
Lu, Xun (Lu Hsun): and Jiang Feng, 36, 153–154n4; story "Hometown," 57–58, 155n19
Lunar New Year: and Chinese Central Television programming, 20; paper-cuts given as "window flowers" (*chuanghua*) during, 33, 38, 54; ritual of elevating luck (*fuyun*), 127, 135–137, 159–160; waist-drum performances, 2, 20–21
Lü Shengzhong, 49–50, 51; biographical notes, 154–155n12
Lu Xun Academy of Literature and Arts (*Luyi*), 36, 153–154n4

MacCannel, Dean, 66
magic, and mimetic presence. *See* mimesis
Mani, Lata, 32–33
Mao Zedong: Great Leap forward, 40–41; outline of CCP's cultural policy (*see* "Talks at the Yan'an Forum on Literature and Art"); *Rectification Campaign*, 10, 13, 150n4, 154n8
Master Xu (performer): author's travels with, 90, 92, 96; *baosuo* ritual performed by, 96, 97*f*3.2; Heijiawa Village performance of, 92–95, 95*f*3.1; localized religious knowledge combined with status as a government sponsored figure (*gongjiaren*), 95–96, 102–103; politically charged preamble of song sung by, 88–89, 93; ritual performed for woman with breast cancer, 97–98; social and business network of, 99, 102–103, 157n9; and the thriving spiritual needs of rural communities today, 101–102; and the Wangjiagou temple festival, 98–99
Master Zhang (performer), Maoist-era storytelling experience of, 115
Mauss, Marcel, 138
May Fourth intellectuals: and the cultural reflexivity movement in the 1980s, xi, 151n8; village literature and art rejected by, 38; and Westernization, 12
media. *See* films; storytelling; television
mimesis: anthropological inquiry into, 50; and fabricated heritage, 66–67; and the folk magic of paper cuts, 50–51; and the presence of divine energy demonstrated by spirit mediums, 133, 137
Mojiagou village: Aunt Gao, 28; bridge project in, 23–24; cavehouse in, 25*fo*.3; cult of Wangmu Niangniang, 139–140, 141; Fang family in (*see* Fang family); lack of farm work in, 123, 124–125, 124*f*5.1, 142–143, 145*ff*5.4–5.5, 146; Mo family visited by author during Chinese Lunar New Year in, 135–137; passivity of villagers to state policy imposition, 23–24; school building on former Fang farmland in, 124–125, 145*f*5.5, 146
Monkey King, 37–38, 40, 93
Moodie, Megan, 102
Mueggler, Eric, 89, 126, 149n1
Museum of the Yellow River Meander Geological Park (*Huanghe Shequ Dizhi Bowuguan*), 82–83
musical dramas: organization of (*see* Yanchuan Musical Drama Troupe); repertoire of musical styles (*diao*) of,

91–92, 156n5; troupes (*see* Yanchuan Musical Drama Troupe)

Niangniang. *See* Wangmu Niangniang (Xi Wang Mu or Queen Mother of the West)

1980s, economic reform during, 152n10

Northwest China Paper-Cuts (*Xibei Jianzhi Ji*), 60; Ai Qing's preface to, 37–38; and Communist urban intellectuals, 36, 60;

nostalgia: for the past, 32, 35, 118–119; and the tourist gaze, 66–67 (*see also* hyper-folk; theme parks); for traditional feminine virtue, 61

Oakes, Tim, 18, 19, 67, 85, 87, 100

oxen: "Picture of Ox Plowing" (*niu geng tu*) by Bai Fenglan, 46, 46f1.7, 47, 53; sympathetic magic of oxen displayed on paper cuts, 50

paper-cuts: "Fish Playing with Lotus" (*yu xi lian*), 50; interpretations of (*see* allegorical and metaphorical interpretations of paper-cut designs); "Passing the Fire" (*chuanhuo*), 50; special place of Shaanxi/Yan'an designs, 33–35; by urban artists featured in *Northwestern Paper-Cuts*, 38 (*see also* Gu Yuan; Li Qun); utilized in state social and political campaigns, 29, 40; as "window flowers" (*chuanghua*), 33, 38, 54, 71

paper-cutting: interpreted by Communist urban intellectuals (*see* Ai, Qing; Jiang, Feng; *Northwest China Paper-Cuts* [*Xibei Jianzhi Ji*]); as a living heritage, 55, 64–66, 70–71, 73, 73, 78–80; as a local art form rather than a living tradition, 82 (*see also* paper-cutting artists); practice distinguished from "paper-cuts," 33; on UNESCO's list of intangible cultural heritage, 55, 64, 70–71, 82

paper-cutting artists, 57f1.9; Chen Shenglan's *zhuajiwawa* paper-cuts, 44–45, 45f1.6; Feng Meizhen's paper-cut vests, 78; individual (*see* Bai Fenglan; Gao Fenglian; Liu Jieqiong); Liu Jieqiong's survey of, 56–59; Li Xiufang's paper-cutting performance in France, 47; modern art elements in Feng Ruimei's work, 78; urban artists featured in *Northwest China Paper-Cuts* (*Xibei Jianzhi Ji*), 38

party-state authority: and the interpretation of local tradition, 147–148 (*see also Northwest China Paper-Cuts* [*Xibei Jianzhi Ji*]); work units (*see danwei*)

peasant mural painting movement, 40–41, 154n8

Perry, Elizabeth, 19

propaganda and propagandists (*xuanchuan* and *xuanchuan yuan*): paper-cut designs utilized in state social and political campaigns, 29, 40, 64; storytellers as, 4, 28, 89–90, 95–96, 103, 114–115, 119–120; waist-drum performance adapted by CCP to promote social-economic programs, 2; and the Yanchuan Musical Drama Troupe, 113–115

Qiao Xiaoguang: on paper-cutting as a living heritage, 55, 73; and UNESCO's intangible cultural heritage list, 70–71, 77

Queen Mother of the West. *See* Wangmu Niangniang

Rabinow, Paul, 26

Ramo, C. Joshua, x

Rectification Campaign, 10, 13, 150n4; and the Fine Arts School Education Reform Movement, 40–41, 154n8

ritual performances: *bausuo*, 96, 97f3.2, 159; "gratitude for a wish fulfilled" (*huankouyuan*) ritual, 93–94, 96, 109, 160. *See also* spirit cult practices; storytelling, geomancy and supernatural healing traditionally associated with

Rofel, Lisa, 60

Rosaldo, Renato, 26

rural-urban divide: and the agrarian crisis, 17, 123, 151n9, 152n11

Index   183

(*see also* state-society relations); and folk cultural productions, 4–8; surrogate rural subjectivity, 127–128, 141, 145–146; and Townization, 17; in Yan'an, xi, 22, 100–101; in Yan'an epitomized by Tugang, 56–57, 59

Said, Edward, 11
Salamone, Frank A., 67
sanxian (three-stringed Chinese lute): defined, 156n1, 160; "sanxian warrior" as a title for Han Qixiang, 92; and storytelling, 88, 93, 99, 106, 116, 118
Schein, Louisa, 6, 18, 21, 32, 55, 87, 100, 115
Selden, Mark, 10
Severe Acute Respiratory Syndrome (SARS), 23, 50
Shaanxi storytelling (*Shaanbei shuoshu*), performers. *See* Master Xu
shoukuren ("people who can bear bitterness"), 123, 142, 160
Silver, Ira, 67
Snow, Edgar, 10
spirit cult practices (*wushen*): dancing deities (see *tiaoshen* [*dancing deity*] ritual); Elder Mo's wife from Mojiagou village, 135–137, 139; and public secrecy, 27, 123–124, 129, 141; and the reinvention of Chinese tradition in Yan'an, 4, 124–125; speech/ "word gifts" of, 137–138
Splendid China, 67
state-owned enterprises (SOEs): and cultural programing focussed on "harmonious society," 119; *danwei* (work units) structure of, 22 (see also *danwei* [work units]); Engineering and Machinery Factory, 106, 110–111, 119; and late socialist political economy, 5; support of the Beijing Olympic Games, 117–120; in Yan'an, 22, 54, 106, 110–111, 119
state-society relations: authority of the party (*see danwei* [work units]); CCP's cultural policy outlined by Mao (*see* "Talks at the Yan'an Forum on Literature and Art" delivered by Mao Zedong); and economic growth, 5 (*see also* rural-urban divide; state-owned enterprises [SOEs]); Lewis's resistance thesis, 126–127; and religious sphere mediation, 89–90, 103–104, 125–128; and the role of rural customs in remaking the public agrarian sphere, 19, 21, 53, 102, 143; and the sphere of folk society (*minjian*), ix, 49, 89–90 (*see also* Xiaocheng Folk Art Village [Xiaocheng *Minjian Yishu Cun*])
storytelling: "Baoliandeng" (Lotus Lantern) performance at Yanchuan County Primary school, 110; as communal occasions for rural villagers, 100–102; Communist-era groups for (*shuoshu zu*), 156n5; at *danwei*-related occasions, 28, 120; ex-propagandist identity combined with current spiritual service of contemporary practitioners, 92, 103–104; geomancy and supernatural healing traditionally associated with, 91, 103, 156n2, 156n2; individual masters of (*see* Cao Boyan; Han Qixiang); Master Xu; new stories (*xinshu*)/ revision of traditional tales (*jiushu*) by urban intellectuals, 91, 113, 156n3; nostalgic representations of, 107; traditional practice of, 90–91
Sun Liping, 152n10
surrogate rural subjectivity, 127–128, 141, 145–146

"Talks at the Yan'an Forum on Literature and Art" delivered by Mao Zedong: CCP's cultural policy outlined in, 13–14, 38; urban intellectuals encouraged to go to the countryside to identify with the lives of commoners, 36
Tapp, Nicholas, 19
Taussig, Michael, 6, 27, 50
television: CCTC (*see* Chinese Central Television Channel); Chinese New Year celebrated via, 20, 55; nationwide broadcast of *River Elegy* (*Hesheng*), 15, 150–151n7; rural entertainment, 109, 134–135

theme parks: and ethnopreneurialism, 6; hyperreality of, 152n12; reconstructed ancient villages viewed as, 66–67 (*see also* Xiaocheng Folk Art Village); Splendid China, 67

tiaoshen (*dancing deity*) ritual, 127, 132, 160; as dramatic spectacle, 132–133; objectification of consciousness, 133–134, 138

Tongdao Zhang, 42

Turner, Victor, 128

UNESCO: Art Masters recognized by (*see* Gao Fenglian); Chinese cultural practices on intangible cultural heritage list of, 29, 55, 64, 70–71, 156n1

urban-rural divide. *See* rural-urban divide

Urry, John, 66

waist-drum performance, 1–2, *3fo.1*, 20–21, 94

Walder, Andrew, xi

Wang, Jing, 18, 53

Wang, Lingyu and Dang Ronghua, 42

Wang, Mingming, 126

Wang, Ning, 67

Wang, Yuhua, 90–91

Wangmu Niangniang (Xi Wang Mu or Queen Mother of the West): about, 137; cult of, 139–140; divination of, 135–138; healing rituals, 141

Wen Tiejun, 17, 152n11

"window flowers" (*chuanghua*), 33, 38, 54, 71

Xiaocheng: folk revival initiatives and grassroots democratic struggles, 81–82, 84; folk revival initiatives and hyper-folk, 64, 147; International Folk Art Festival at, 82–83; Yellow River Meander at, 64, *65f2.1*, 68–69, 81, 82–83

Xiaocheng Folk Art Village (Xiaocheng *Minjian Yishu Cun*): as a democratic grassroots initiative, 81, 84–87; Jin Zhilin's cultural development plan for, 28–29, 62, 69–73; and the listing of paper-cutting as an intangible cultural heritage by UNESCO, 64, 82; popular narrative on the birth of, 69–70; web-of-linkage perspective on, 85

Xibei Jianzhi Ji. See *Northwest China Paper-Cuts*

Xi Wang Mu. *See* Wangmu Niangniang

xuanchuan and *xuanchuan yuan*. *See* propaganda and propagandists

Yan'an, *7m2*; counties and districts of, 152n13 (*see also* Ansai county; Yellow River region); isolated geography of, 15–16; Loess landscape of, 8–9, *8fo.2*, 18, 26, 95, 107 (*see also* Loess Plateau); musical drama society (*see* Yan'an Area Musical Drama Society); rural-urban divide, xi, 100–101; significance as a symbol of the Communist revolution, ix, 8–11, 13–15, 33, 36 (*see also* "Talks at the Yan'an Forum on Literature and Art" delivered by Mao Zedong; waist-drum performance); as a spatial proof of China's backwardness, 9, 15–16, 57–58; state-owned enterprises (SOEs) in, 22, 54, 106, 110–111, 119 (*see also* state-owned enterprises [SOEs])

Yan'an Area Musical Drama Society, 108–113; establishment as a non-profit *danwei*, 92; members of interviewed by author, 90, 117; twelve members of interviewed by the author, 107–108

Yanchuan: Baijiayuan village, 31; and legendary figure *Fuxi*, 64; musical drama troupe of (*see* Yanchuan Musical Drama Troupe); storytelling performance at Yanchuan County Primary school, 110; town center, 108–109

Yanchuan Musical Drama Troupe: establishment of, 113; Hall of Culture affiliation of, 90, 115, *116f4.2*; as the "Musical Drama Propaganda Troupe for Mao Zedong Thoughts," 113, 114–115; "Quality Control System Spreads to Millions" sung by, 105–106

Yang, Fenggang, 129, 157n8
Yang, Shengmin, 27
Yan Hairong, 17
Yan Qingzhao, 107
yaodong. *See* cavehouses
Yellow River region: "Bay of Heaven and Earth" in Xiaocheng, 64, *65f2.1*, 68–69, 81, 82–83; and the founding of Chinese civilization, 34, 46, 64, 83; isolated geography of, 15; tourism, 58, 62

zhuajiwawa paper-cuts, 44–45, *45f1.6*, 154n11, 154–155n12

KA-MING WU is an assistant professor of culture and religious studies at the Chinese University of Hong Kong.

INTERPRETATIONS OF CULTURE
IN THE NEW MILLENNIUM

Peruvian Street Lives: Culture, Power, and Economy among Market
    Women of Cuzco   Linda J. Seligmann
The Napo Runa of Amazonian Ecuador   Michael Uzendoski
Made-from-Bone: Trickster Myths, Music, and History from the
    Amazon   Jonathan D. Hill
Ritual Encounters: Otavalan Modern and Mythic Community
    Michelle Wibbelsman
Finding Cholita   Billie Jean Isbell
East African Hip Hop: Youth Culture and Globalization   Mwenda Ntaragwi
Sarajevo: A Bosnian Kaleidoscope   Fran Markowitz
Becoming Mapuche: Person and Ritual in Indigenous Chile   Magnus Course
Kings for Three Days: The Play of Race and Gender in an
    Afro-Ecuadorian Festival   Jean Muteba Rahier
Maya Market Women: Power and Tradition in San Juan Chamelco,
    Guatemala   S. Ashley Kistler
Victims and Warriors: Violence, History, and Memory in Amazonia   Casey High
Embodied Protests: Emotions and Women's Health in Bolivia   Maria Tapias
Street Life under a Roof: Youth Homelessness in South Africa
    Emily Margaretten
Reinventing Chinese Tradition: The Cultural Politics of Late Socialism
    Ka-ming Wu

The University of Illinois Press
is a founding member of the
Association of American University Presses.

University of Illinois Press
1325 South Oak Street
Champaign, IL 61820-6903
www.press.uillinois.edu